Stories That Knocked On My Door

J Rainsnow

TABLE OF CONTENTS

INTRODUCTION

Stories.

Do we write them, or do we receive them? Do we go there, or do they come here? Does the typewriter, now the computer, hammer them into being at our command, or does something make our fingers move; are we the typewriters, clattering noisily beneath something else's hands?

It's hard to say. Life is a mystery, and we should be grateful for that. How boring it would be to know it all; to inherit nothing but questions already answered, and riddles already solved!

Not knowing, still, somehow, we know, in a way that feels better than being certain. Our heart feels it, but the surprise hasn't been spoiled. The hint of our mother whom we see walking towards us from the shadows, is even more precious to us than the mother who is standing right in front of us. Not taking her for granted, filled with longing because we think she is gone, she is twice the size she is in daylight.

In this spirit, as I sit before my keyboard, I do not consider myself to be a craftsman or an architect. I do not carefully build or enslave myself to a blueprint. I open up the gates inside me and let whatever is there come out. I am just its hands.

If I keep the gates closed for too long, I hear a knocking, and so it is with the stories in this book. They knocked on my door, and I, without seeing their face, opened it, because the world of things unborn is cold for what wants to come to life. Who would leave a lonely traveler, stranded in a snowstorm, on the other side of shelter when one had the warm hearth of a typewriter to offer him? And so, I have let in my guests, one at a time and over a period of many years, giving each one of them a room in this book. For me, writing is not a manifestation of agency, but an act of hospitality, a welcoming into my home of what already exists; and all I have to say to you, now, is: Here They Are!

Of course, it is my hope that some of these stories will be meaningful and interesting to you. But whatever the case, I can tell you that they all came with a purpose. They all formed themselves out of mist, gave themselves the shape of hands beating on my door so that they might say something to us, give something to us. What, exactly? A warning? An exhortation? An idea? A wake-up call? A hug? Maybe all of the above. For sure, they came to the right place. I have a big mouth to lend, a mouth that exhales pages.

In this collection of short stories that have visited me over the years, you will meet a guilt-ridden soldier and the Time Machine he has invented; a tormented composer who has written an aria that is beyond the range of human singing (only an angel could sing it); a furious man in search of the tarot reader who ruined his life; a brilliant dancer with an unforgiving wound; a man who remembers a startling past life (or is he just a fraud?); a Colombian immigrant to the U.S., hunted down by 500 years of history that have been misrepresented; two mysterious visitors to a small town, who possess the ability to fly; a man, discounted, whose crusade to be noticed brings unintended consequences; a man whose life trajectory is set by a woman he knew for only one day; a machine that reveals the power of small actions to change the world; a future city where anger is used to generate electricity; a house haunted by mysterious ghosts who are more than they seem; and that is only half of them!

Please give a listen to these friends of mine, who knocked so insistently on my door: these unexpected guests who showed up without warning in the night with so much to say, and such a huge aversion to the silence.

Though they came to me, they are for you.

J Rainsnow, 2025.

DAPHNE

Who touched you, Daphne? Who touched you?
Who took you away from me?

She was a ballet dancer, from the New York City Ballet. Our point of connection was the Russian novels we both loved, and the flock of geese that I loved to watch gliding in towards the lake. I did not even know she was a dancer when I first met her in the park: a small pensive woman wearing a sweater and leotards, sitting down on a bench underneath the bare trees, the breath of life hovering in the cold autumn air by her warm mouth, hesitating to leave her before it let itself be carried away by the universe towards something she could give but not have. But I could see the wings of the geese in the way she walked.

When I told her that, as the geese flew in, honking in homage to the lake and in gratitude to my eyes, she smiled; but it was as if the smile came from behind a fence. Her grace was made of glass, afraid to be dropped and broken; yet there was courage in her also; the birds do not fly without hearts that know how to fight. You cannot live in the wind without being brave.

"The geese, they are the leaves the trees are missing," she said in that heavy Russian accent that was for me, a kind of auditory make-up: rouge and eye-liner in the air.

"You are a poetess," I said.

"A dancer," she replied. "A poet of the body." She lifted up one agile leg and gestured to her foot simply by moving it. "This is one of my words."

"And can you say more than that?" I asked her.

She moved the other foot; then she raised an arm, not like we humans raise our arms, like bulldozers and cranes, but like a green plant growing; then her wrist moved, and a bud was there, then her fingers, and there was a flower. "I have a very large vocabulary," she said, and she laughed. Her lack of modesty always amused her, but she did not repress it, any more than a bleeding person takes off his bandages.

"And that book in your hands," she said to me. "Is that really a book? Here, in this city, people only read the newspaper. And in the newspaper only the sports."

"Yes, it's a book," I assured her. "*Dead Souls*."

"Russian!" she exclaimed. And she blurted out something to me in Russian that felt like a kiss on the lips of my soul, even though I didn't understand a word of it. But her shining eyes were easily translated by my hope.

We became great friends. In this huge city of artists, with a million chambers of ambition, loneliness abounded; dreams of being taken home by everyone's soul left one in utter solitude, concealed from the living by one's discipline. For me, I was not good enough to dwell among men, I must write my way back to them, I could only cross over to humanity on a bridge of greatness; for her, the wounds that made her eyes deep, and her body display itself like Jesus on the cross, split her off from the rest of mankind; she became like a beautiful splinter that could not be reattached to the world. In the empty space between us and the rest of humanity we met, and loved each other with thoughts and glances that were not consummated. We shared the camaraderie of shooting stars falling side by side from heaven.

Of course, I could not keep her out of my poetry. She crashed into the pages I used as breaths, she set fire to the paper on which I played with tame things, turning my art wild, ripping holes in the craft so that men might spy directly on gods. My pen ceased to wear clothes, I clawed madly like a man trying to dig to the other side of the earth in my effort to reach her with the words that would lift her high enough to see over the wall of my age. She was younger and more beautiful than I, and she danced with men who were savage, animals who could devour me, Rembrandts of motion in the bodies of lions. With words I tried to fight them off, with words: words stolen from dragons, words bled from my veins in the night, words solved by the clues on a blank piece of paper, words given to me by the eloquence of geese.

Her soul was mine, her eyes glowed as I spoke, like a piano under the hands of a master (or just someone who means every note); but her flesh withdrew; it fled like a wild animal in the darkness whenever I shined the light of desire on it. I could not understand how this woman, whose art was her body, could not close the circle of her soul with a touch. I loved her, madly, as no one had ever loved her in the past, and would never love her in the future! I rose to be twice the writer I was like smoke on the draft of her beauty, I worshipped her with my growth, and laid dances of my loneliness at her feet. But she withdrew.

I grew angry. Did not the princess kiss the frog? Did not the beauty love the beast? Did not the romantic heart always seek out a monster to love, just as snow seeks the dirtiest part of the earth on which to fall, to bury it in pure white? Was I so repulsive, even more than the creatures of the fairy tales? No one had ever said I was, though I was no match for the gods she danced with. I knew her soul was strong enough to desire me; was the body that survived the rigors of so many leaps and pirouettes, so much galloping and so much torturous slowness, somehow incapable of love?

One day, after weeks of candlelit dinners that always ended with me alone in my bedroom writing poems, I came to meet her after a practice, through a garage-like tunnel known only to the performers and support staff. Ballerinas still dressed in white and handsome men, bare-chested and in leotards, walked around as though this were another planet, inhabited by different beings. I heard someone raging from behind the closed door of a room: "You are cold! Your dancing is cold! I feel like I am dancing with something cold-blooded, not human, like an iguana! There is no fire inside you, no molten core in your earth! You must lean into me, give yourself to me! You must fall inwards, lose your power, become a part of me! I cannot hold you as though you were poison!"

And suddenly, horrified but somehow expecting it, I heard her voice in return, throwing jagged pieces of English back at him: "You are groping me! You want to steal my life! You want to use the dance to put your dirty hands on me! You are not from the myth, you are ordinary! Why aren't you gay?"

Then a third voice hurled itself into the fray: "Ludi, this is dance! Your body must be open! It is sex, it is kissing turned into air, it is copulation turned into gold! You have a beautiful body, you must throw it into his, you must hurl yourself onto the funeral pyre of your last reservations. Dance has no mercy, no modesty! We are trying to save the world from shame, we must not succumb to it!"

"I am not ashamed!" she raged. "He is dirty! His hands betray the dance!"

"He is a dancer, and this is beautiful!"

"She's crazy! I won't work with her!"

"Go to hell, you son-off bitch!"

I heard a door slamming, and her repeating, "He is a son-off bitch! Son-off bitch," then the more quiet man, obviously a director or choreographer, asking her, at last: "Ludi, what's wrong? Do you have a problem with being touched?"

"He is dirty! No, dancers carry me all the time, but not like that! He is like a pervert who grabs women on the train!"

There was a long silence. I was probably suffering as much as they were, on my side of the door, out among the dancer-ants, scurrying about to change their costumes, to get drinks of coffee or rush in a cigarette.

"Ludi—do you have a problem with being touched?" he asked again. "Your reactions have been very strong. To James and Alexy, both. The other dancers haven't complained."

"Maybe they don't have the high standards I have," she said.

A ballerina with a cup of coffee in her hand, and a long coat draped over her flimsy costume, recognized me, and told me, "Last week she almost scratched Alexy's eyes out when he lifted her. Mr. Nelidov wants to give her good parts, but she's blowing it." The dancer made the shape of a gun with her free hand, pointed it at her foot, and said, "Boom!" Then she told me, "If she's your friend, you better try to talk some sense into her head before she ends up working at Starbucks."

I listened to the director's words from behind the door, unable to prevent myself from feeling invasive, and yet, unable to live without grasping at any straw that might keep me afloat in the water of loving her. "You know, as dancers we can have neuroses," he was saying. "We can have phobias. We can be afraid of riding up elevators, or cry when we see spiders; we can spend hours arranging the angles of the papers on our desk, or vomit when we smell cinnamon. What we cannot do is withhold our bodies. We cannot cringe, we cannot retract, we cannot be unfree. Our bodies cannot break, they cannot wear the chains of anything, of any tyrant or of any crime. Ludi —you are a magnificent dancer—f you have a problem—if anything ever happened to you— something that made you turn your beautiful body into a shell—we can help. There is so much help out there."

But his goodwill was not well enough expressed. Dynamite needs lullabies that only the poet can compose. "I am insulted!" she said. "I have no problem except for dirty men!" and then suddenly, she was barging out of the door, practically crashing into me. Convincingly, I acted as though I had just arrived. She held me by the arms for one minute, burning me with fierce and desperate eyes as though she did not want to let me go, yet simultaneously needed to keep me at a distance. "I am glad to see you!" she exclaimed, at last. "A man who is as wise as a serpent, and as harmless as a dove!" Somehow, I did not feel flattered. In fact, I felt as though she had just kicked me between the legs. Was that the secret of our closeness: that I was a non-man, my testosterone entombed in romantic ideals, the next best thing to a eunuch? A beast firmly on the leash of words? An omnivore able to survive on a diet of fantasies when there was no reality to be had? "I have to change," she told me, grateful for my presence; the sun was always kind to frozen Pluto, generous with its life-giving rays that didn't reach it. "I'll be back! Wait here!"

On the way to the restaurant that took the place of my home, which she would never go to, I gave her an opportunity to talk about her day—her problem—but she merely said, "It is just the Trojan Horse once again. That's all. In everything, the wolf in the sheep's skin. The priest wants little boys, the president wants the movie star while his wife is sleeping, the hero wants a blow job. He saves the world to get a blow job. Everything, the whole world, was just invented to get laid. Jacob's ladder leads to the bedroom. Lord and Master is behind every door." And then she said, "Come on, it's cold out here, colder than I am! Tonight I will order chicken with cashews! Thank God, there are so many Chinese, we will never run out of restaurants!"

Not long afterwards, Ludi was let go by the ballet. It was a devastating blow, though she raved until she was able to make herself proud of the loss, talking to me and to herself at the same time, sometimes in

English, and sometimes in Russian, which slammed me against the wall of my desire to know everything. "Well, that's fine, maybe I go back to Russia and dance for the Bolshoi, real ballet! García Lorca was right, this is a city without art, just pigeons, stupid pigeons fighting for breadcrumbs, taking baths in dirty puddles; they shit on you, and you don't win any money like you are supposed to! Grandmother said! You come like a fairy, they shoot cannons at you; you come like a mermaid, they stab you with a spear; is that how you say, the 'spear' to kill the whales?! Yes, the 'harpoon!' They don't want art, they make a horse stand up on the back legs, and that is ballet! If I were Chinese, I could work in a restaurant!"

I listened to her patiently, like a martyr who would be thrown to the lions before he would renounce his religion. I held up the regal train of her downfall, as though she were a queen, followed her regret and rage everywhere with whispers of my passion, blowing the counsel of angels into her ear; but even collapse would not drive her to me, would not make her body relent. Instead, she kept the fire burning in her head, not allowing it to spread into her body where I could have put it out with love; she translated letters from home that reprimanded her, so that I could hate her family as much as she did. "They think my troubles are because I am undisciplined! How little do they know! My own flesh and blood! They break a branch from the tree and throw it on the ground; this fruit will not bear the family name. Burn it! Listen to this: this is Aunt Paulina, mother's very own commissar. 'You have been possessed by the devil since you were a child! Do you remember how you beat Ivan with a stick, just like he was a dog? Your very own brother! For stealing imaginary apples! For sure, you slapped Mr. Nelidov in the face, or spit in his eye. You loved to spit! Remember when you spit in your father's food?' See this? My own aunt?!"

I tried to get to the bottom of these stories, but could not, there was too much passion; she was beginning to fall out of the sky and demanded solidarity at all costs. If you asked a question that made it seem like you had climbed out of the river of her suffering, she would stab you with a knife. And you had to swim in it, and get wet; she had no patience for those who paddled the boat of the intellect in such personal waters. Neither did she have any tolerance for healing. If you approached her as a doctor, she drove you away as though you were seeking to enslave her. There were times when I felt that my hands were tied, that I could not take a single step closer to her torment. How I wanted to embrace her, to make my soul-love physical, but for her, it seemed, there was nothing between distance and violation, though she teased the planets into orbit with a radiance she refused to bring to its logical conclusion. I could only be her grandfather or a rapist. This delicate land, beyond the terrain of our relationship, was filled with the landmines of terrible secrets, I was sure, but planted by what? By whom?!

One day, I remember her sitting in shock with me in a coffeehouse, telling me about a movie she had stayed up late watching on TV the night before, as I wrote poems in the separate universe of my apartment. We could have been touching each other, loving each other. "The movie was about incest," she said, the look of a city destroyed by war in her eyes: craters and shells of buildings, a kind of awe and terror, and emptiness, as though her soul had fled just before the impact of a bullet. "It made me have goose bumps. Like a spider was crawling over my skin. Terrible! How could a father do that to his own daughter? Smash a hole in the wall of her trust—and then, when she gets older, who else will enter through that hole?" That last part, said with dread.

I looked at her, over a cup of hot coffee, and said, "Maybe no one will enter. Maybe she will close the hole forever. Neither good nor bad will ever get in again."

But she did not bite the hook; she was not a fish; she was a dancer. "Thank God, nothing like that ever happened to me!" she said, with the vigor of a murderer burying a corpse. "Could you imagine? I would be like a crazy veteran from Afghanistan, running from everything, shooting at everything with my heart. Did you know, your heart can be turned into a gun?"

I nodded, over the steaming crater of the coffee cup. I would never know any more about her than she would let me know, or let herself remember. In her eyes there was not any trace of a lie, only a furious effort to have amnesia. And if you tried to reach the answer, your hand would be blown off.

Ludi, Ludi, dear Ludmilla, princess of the closed doors! How many in a row are closed? How many locks are there, and, in the universe, is there any key?

Ludi, Ludi, queen of my ticking clock, ticking away into oblivion, because no woman who could hold me can get near to me, because of you. Why did God make you so mesmerizing? Only to destroy me?

But Ludi, Ludmilla, beautiful damage, eclipser of all that is whole, how could I ever blame you? I see the blood pouring out of you and rush in as though you were my child; and then, I cannot make love to you! Do you know, I can see the disaster, now, written across your forehead as plainly as the mark of the beast? I can see the broken glass that once enclosed the jewel, but now encloses nothing. I can see the question mark that you wear because you don't want to know: that amazing stupidity in the middle of your genius, that 1 + 1 you can't figure out, and the medicine you won't take because that would mean you were sick.

Ludi, Ludmilla, Ludmilla moyego serdtsa, you from the land of snow and invasions, tyrannies, and the bad friend of vodka, the country that ate Napoleon and Hitler and its own people, that beat its children to death with their own toughness, and filled them with the sadness of lonely railroads that don't end.

I write again, I write forever, splatter visions of your soul across my pages, mix them with the flowers of my death. And then the sun comes up, and I'm just a tired man filled with aches.

On that day in the coffeehouse, I finally knew, in my heart, that I would never hold her in my arms. I dreamt on, in spite of it, the same way that people don't ever really think they're going to die. I tried not to know what I knew. But it was inevitable. Time and futility slowly pushed us apart. She became ashamed of living on the edges of the life that God had given her, and also wary of me, for I had lingered too long by her wounds and discovered too much. My eyes suspected things she could not live with, and she had to run from them. The next step in our relationship would have been for her to reveal the dark treasure that made her self-contempt so wealthy. Since she would have had to come out of hiding, there was no next step.

And the nights out became less frequent. Then she changed her telephone number. I mourned, for I felt that something beautiful was melting like snow. I wanted to hear her voice, to see again the face that had fooled me in the beginning, seeming to represent someone almost invincible. I wanted this powerful love to survive. I could not bear to think I had written so many poems that had died like moths flying into the flame, poems that made the sun shake in the sky but did not win her; poems that made the moon weep words to pens that could not sleep, but left the world the same. I could not bear to be alone after having loved like this! But all arguments were in vain. She, like infinity, could not be understood, nor embraced.

The park was once more filled with empty trees, after a season of unrequited love, a season of joyous green, blossoming as it headed towards the auto wreck of the autumn. I had come to see the geese, who were not there, but caught sight of her, instead, practicing her dancing which from now on she must do alone. Her body was still light, graceful, filled with life as long as no one else approached it. She did not see me watching her, but danced for herself. I saw her movements, fast, at first, with elegant bends from the waist as though she were leaning away from some outrage, trying not to be kissed on the cheek by some god or demon. Then, there was flight, she leapt through the air, she bounded like a gazelle, escaping from someone, something; she turned the park into the surface of the moon, and gravity receded to let her movement flourish as though her life had been different. Then the body tired. How expertly she made it heavy, infiltrated lead into her legs, atom by atom, transmuted wind into metal, turned herself into a captive of her beauty, her greatest limitation. She panted, but with the gestures of her body. He came closer. I could see him now, invisible but beside her. At first, she seemed to surrender to him, her body hung drooping, defeated. Then, desperately, she rose up against him, like a storm, but it was hopeless. Now I knew, it was the God Apollo she was fighting against. Again, she fled, like one bird flying from another during the mating season. She proved her intentions with her velocity, but she could not get away, no matter how she tried. Then suddenly she stopped, the frantic dance developed a center, and she began to slowly spin around that center, her body stiffening and becoming erect, her hands stretching upward like the branches of a tree. I could see the god beyond the ring of her rejection, standing back in awe. She slowed down, she took root. The flesh continued to solidify, until it was bark. She finally ceased to move, except for what the breeze could do to her. She was a laurel tree. She was Daphne, and would never again be the prey of man.

TWO IMPERFECT PAINTINGS

When she was just a young child, her father and mother first noticed, to their horror, that she seemed to favor her left hand. They were a strange combination of erudition and conventionality, these two, granted the power to nurture or to destroy the child who they believed was theirs, but who was actually God's, given to them to raise. The father told the mother that the Latin word for "left hand" was "sinister," from which the English word "sinister" was derived. "In the ancient world, the left hand was considered to be the side of evil and misfortune, and those who were left-handed were consequently shunned. They were looked down upon as inferior persons, if not dangerous and untrustworthy."

"Nowadays," the mother said, agreeing that things were not much improved, "they have to follow directions in reverse. To live backwards. The way they cut paper dolls and make puppets, in school... It's terrible for the brain."

"Cars are made for right-handed people. The gears, the clutch... The way doors open, swinging to the side rather than into the body. The way jar lids are designed to open, towards the wrist's strength."

"Aerobics classes on TV. Ballet lessons. How can you keep up when you have to flip everything you see on its head?"

"The stigma of being different."

"Kids notice which hand you're using when you hold your pen."

"It's a right-handed society..."

And so it was agreed. Their daughter would be taught to be a rightie. Every time she tried to use her left hand, she would be scolded, hit if necessary. They would make sure that she held her spoon in her right hand, and the crayons with which she enlivened the outlines of people and animals in her coloring books. They would make sure she opened doors with her right hand, and brushed her doll's hair with her right hand.

In the shadow of benevolent terror, with a mental guard dog planted in her head to snarl every time she reached for something with her left hand, she grew up straight. She was not sinister. But deep inside, a genie raged against the sin of normalcy, it retaliated against the intervention of her parents with a seething, stubborn rebellion which took the form of clumsiness. Her right hand refused to abscond with the birthright of the left; her handwriting became well-known, from the first grade through college, for its nearly athletic illegibility, and no one trusted her to hold a glass or to handle anything that was in any way fragile or of value.

In spite of this deep-seeded but undetected revolt against the imperative to conform, she found her calling in art, a field in which her unbridled imagination and untamed inner eye, in great part overcame the limits of her stunted hand, the hand without talent which she had been forced to adopt. In her mind, she painted unrivaled masterpieces; her visions burned like horses made of fire, in skies that were blossoming like roses of thought, in the summer of her soul. Savage oceans ceased to shout, and whispered at her feet with embers of waves, moons of ours and other planets lowered themselves so that she could look them in the eye, volcanoes erupted into her palette, diamonds tore themselves out of the earth to dance for her. "Too bad," her mentors said, "that there is such a void in her technique, for her ability to conceive is unique." She pursued a modestly successful career, fighting her way into galleries and exhibitions with an unarmed imagination.

His story was different, but not distant. He fought tooth and nail to be an artist from the day he was born. His parents were working-class, and conditioned by the vulnerability of life to be practical. Anything that struck them as a daydream infuriated them, for they protected the things they loved like beasts protect their young, and they despised those who were not willing to break their backs for a loaf of bread. For them, brotherhood meant joining hands to die together. But one must die from labor, not from idleness.

The boy's skill was like a fine-tuning of his father's brilliance with the drill; he drew on canvas instead of making holes in metal. In order to be an artist, he had to go through a terrible night of being mocked and disowned by his father's words, each of which smelled like alcohol: cast like a worthless, selfish thing into a world that was not ready for him, and for which he was not ready. It was not raining as he walked out of the door, but it should have been.

He went hungry; he suffered. His soul ran out of gas. He pushed it like a car along a dark road in the night, hoping to find a light on, somewhere down the way. He clung to the dream, which he alone could see was not a delusion; the skill of his lines, the believability of the faces, urged him to continue. To prolong his capacity to resist, he went back to the factory town, he got a job, he worked by day, standing by a ruthless machine that made artless things, then returned home at night to live by the silence of the canvas, which was like the sky you stare into when you are expecting meteor showers. His precise sketching, inherited from mechanics, was the foundation; then, as time went on, he began to add colors. They did not come easily from his gray world, but he began to learn to dream with boldness. He could feel his ascent, impending from his discipline.

But then, one day, dreaming too much by the fierce machine with which he earned his bread and kept the canvas in his room, the savage blade he had used a million times, made deadly by habit, came crashing down on his hand, and with a scream of pain, he became a painting, a painting of blood with a weeping hand, like a beached fish lying on the work table. It happened in other decades, before the miracle of microsurgery, before the science of reattachment. The excited workmates put the severed hand into a bag with ice and held rags over the spurting geyser of his wrist as they carried him into a car and drove him down the road, past dead lots and electric wires, to the hospital. They saved his life, but the hand was gone. After a while, someone threw it out in the garbage. In despair, once more on his feet but without any reason to be, he buried his brushes in the graveyard in the middle of the night. The policemen who busted him and a sympathetic worker among the tombstones behind the locked gate let him go with words of encouragement, which made him feel twice as useless.

But his forebears had not survived by breaking. They had smashed rocks to bits with hammers, made roads over mountains and through them, united lakes that were not on speaking terms by means of canals, made the world rich under their smokestacks. They had been mistreated, but their souls were as hard as the iron they worked with, as brave as the coal mine is black. Surrender was not in his blood. And so, without a hand, but with art swarming all over his heart like vines that not even reality could cut back, he made up his mind to learn all over again to draw, and to paint, with his left hand, the only hand left to him. And he did. He slipped and fell, he rose; he wept, he wished he were dead, he gave up; he cursed himself for being a coward; he despaired, he loved; he climbed the mountain. Time had been lost, and his left hand was not his right. It was not the same, and the mountain he climbed was half the size of the one whose peak he had almost reached, before industry had triumphed over creativity. But climb it he did: the highest mountain that he could.

One of her paintings, and one of his paintings, met, one day, at an exhibition in New York City. It was not in the heart of the gallery district, where the millionaire buyers and the seasoned culture lovers swarm like bees in a garden, crawling over flowers which they covet; it was in an outlying district, on the other side of the East River, in a place where old factories and warehouses ruled streets that were utterly deserted at night. But it was still a place with a pulse, a place where the will to create, impossible to crush, survived thanks to the charity of lower standards. Everyone has the talent to have a baby, and it is in everyone's soul to love the babies that they have.

Side by side, their paintings stood mounted on the wall, hers exotic and brilliant if you knew what she was trying to do, if you could find it on the other side of the technique that she lacked. His was ravaged but suggestive, like a building whose side has been blown out by a bomb; his skill no longer had skill but if you looked hard enough, you could see that it once had, you could imagine the lines recovering their powerful delicacy, the blur on the canvas becoming detailed and intricate like a Swiss clock. Some people can see ghosts, and some people can see fairies. Those who have failed behind the brush can see the beauty the brush was trying to reach.

He saw her standing back, a little, from the small cluster of people that was looking at her painting, which stopped only briefly before moving on. She saw him, without his hand, looking at her. At once they knew each other. She saw him in his painting, and he saw her in hers. She saw his heart and knew its force from the sound of its falling; he saw her soul and knew its expansiveness from the way it had crashed.

History would remember neither one of them. The history of art is merciless. But we need not be so merciless.

In a mediocre painting, he saw a great woman.

In a mediocre painting, she saw a great man.

After a moment, they approached each other to speak.

THE PLAGIARIST

The professor of literature enjoyed great success for a little more than two years, growing far larger than the small, New England college where he taught. His volume of esoteric poetry based upon the idea of reincarnation, his odes of love to the timeless soul mate he was searching for, his ardent, torturous waiting with giant wings made of words, his overwhelming loyalty remaining by the banks of the waters of time in which she had drowned, trusting that she would surface where his heart was, his faith in the return of laughter, in the immortality of lips that are both wet and burning, his belief that the void is only a deception invented by our minds to test love, had captured the imagination of lovers and mystics everywhere.

In the foreword of his little, intense volume, which some compared to the best of Omar Khayyam and Rumi, he wrote: "This river of poetry which flowed, not from my hand, but of its own will, as if obeying some mysterious law of gravity which dwarfs the known sorrows of my own life, was born side by side with dreams and fragments of memories that I cannot lay claim to."

The professor, in his foreword, bravely exposed strange visions of life in some Middle Eastern land in the distant past, and sketches of himself and his lover in that time, when their skin was dark, nurtured to the most beautiful shade of brown by the tender embrace of the sun, which licked them with fire, like a savage lioness who knows how to be sweet, with claws retracted for her cubs. For months, an artist worked with him to get the faces right: the woman's earth-brown face and eyes like black diamonds, like flames torn from the night; the long waves of soft hair reaching out, with curiosity that could barely be combed, to explore the world; the smile, like legs revealed by a dress that is lifted to cross a stream, quick to undermine the safety of indifference; and his own face, made of fine and chiseled features, a large nose and eagle-like eyes, a thin dust of harshness coating an endless abyss of frightfully articulate vulnerability.

"Did I live these memories or are they only dreams?" the author wrote. "I see that man writing with the pen that is in my hand, I see that life, not this one, as the foundation for the despair that shines like gold; it is his tears that have become the ink that digs into these pages, searching for her grave, searching for her mother's womb. Am I imagining, or am I awakening?"

Looking at the beautiful protagonists of his vision, made even more alluring by their exotic, ancient garb—for modern clothes are so belittling—he only knew that he would never again be happy until they returned to each other's arms. "I believe I am writing these poems, which I wrote before, to find her, to trigger in her a memory of me and our perfectness together. I am fighting against centuries of death to live again." But the threat of the modern world was too much to ignore, and so, even though he was a literature professor and more easily pardoned for forays into the absurd than the engineer who constructs bridges, he still felt pressured into admitting the possibility that he was merely a creative genius. "Or maybe, after all, it is only a fantasy," he reiterated, "although until now my passion has mainly been an appendage of the anguish of others. This is the first time I have ever, deeply, cried for myself, and felt, in my own soul, something that belongs to me."

The professor's admirers, beyond the tolerant, skeptical literary circle which admired the product without believing for a moment in the esoteric processes reputed to have engendered it, had no doubt that he had actually lived before and that the poetry he had written was actually salvaged from the depths of forgotten memories of a previous life. Words the professor had written before, in another time and place—somewhere in the ancient Middle East or India, it seemed, when he had been a poet and a scholar, and fallen madly in love with the life-filled daughter of a practical merchant who did not approve, but who they defied—had erupted from the subterranean prison of memories, which keep our many lives separate by repressing the past, and leaving us stranded in the present with the terrible illusion of mortality. He had rebelled against the silence, broken into the vault where his treasures from another time were stored, seized up in his hands jewels that distraction had hidden, to use again, torn off the veil of One Life and seen his many faces. He had found, in the library of fate, in a corner of his own mind, the map to his heart; no more must he stumble blindly off the road into marshes, plot his course through deserts, or come, unexpectedly, upon uncrossable rivers, barring his path with the raging, indifferent torrents of a fruitless flood. Now he knew. He wanted her, he needed her.

"I think her name was Asha," he wrote. Once again, his life had purpose; the tiny college where he was entombed, living comfortably as a parasite of the great, ceased to confine him. "I wonder what she looks like now?" he asked himself. "Will she be the same sweet secret, hiding in the shadows, made of shadow, but with hands as hot as fever? Will she recognize me, or despise the pale thing I have become? Now that I have smashed the mask that conceals me with the face of my soul, reshaped my body into words, crushed the lie of my appearance with timeless truths? Will she hear me? Will she come?"

He fought against the strangeness of writing the words in English; he felt as though some language he had spoken before had been a more perfect vehicle for releasing the outpourings of his heart, for exposing his bashful depths, hung like laundry out to dry in the breeze of Humanity's love of poetry. There were times when he felt his words were soaring towards a rhyme that did not exist in his current tongue, that somewhere there was a pun he could not reach; at times the legs of his pen felt heavy, he sensed the awkwardness of syllables and cadences which had not troubled him in the past, he had to describe the sun without the words "bright," "shining," or "light," he battled with the place he had ended up, running as fast as an antelope but still feeling he was slow, reshaping, approximating, guessing; he stood in the sea and tried to redirect the waves. But though he remained dissatisfied, the world did not feel his discomfort; it reveled in his brilliance and found the tale of his "writing, uncomfortably, in my second language" forgivably eccentric and endearing.

For the professor, the few months of his fame were both joyful and trying. Lovely coeds showed up in his class, in droves, overwhelmed by the romance, hoping to be her, to be Asha without remembering, though they were now trapped behind white faces, and tarnished by upper-middle-class American backgrounds. Like Cinderella with her delicate foot perfectly matching the glass slipper of the prince, they all hoped to see his eyes light up with recognition when he beheld them in his class, they all hoped to have an essay returned to them with a note written in the margin, with ink as red as blood: "Please come to my office, we must talk." One girl even signed her name "Asha." For the professor, all of this was acutely distressful—he could not bear to have so many hearts to hurt, so many sensitive, poetry-loving souls to disappoint, to hurl back to the earth with superhuman efforts of kindness, to kill with elaborately cushioned *NOs*, which were exhausting to craft—and yet he could not completely barricade himself against the onrush, either, because what if one of them really were Asha?

Naturally, the phenomenon earned him the reputation of being a philanderer and lady's man on campus, although he struggled with great earnestness to resist the temptations of power and to resist the impulse to rest in the oasis of someone else's hope while he was waiting for the caravan of true love to arrive; in this effort, he was greatly aided by the uncompromising ideal of Asha, which sustained him and warded off the hordes of beautiful, deluded impostors, who were enriched by his rejection, because it also contained acceptance. Several times, the Dean spoke to him about the attention of the young women—the "harem" as some called it—but each time, the Dean left satisfied that there had been no impropriety.

However, on the campus there was one colleague, a professor from Egypt who had spent her whole life struggling between her Western upbringing and the limits imposed upon women by fundamentalism, who could not make peace with his presence. She had been driven by the burkas and veils she had never worn and the lashes she had never felt, except on the high-principled back of her solidarity, to abhor every form of the exploitation of woman by man that was possible, and for her, the sight of this suddenly famous and undeniably appealing professor surrounded by scores of fragile, impressionable girls who she could only see as prey aroused her indignation. She had a word or two with the professor, who was surprisingly apologetic, but still, showed no willingness to become aloof. "This is different than Robert Frost with snow-white hair surrounded by young male poets talking about birch trees," she told him.

He replied, "I cannot betray the passion I have discovered in myself by becoming distant."

She said: "You are a predator. They look up to you, they are helpless, like deer in the headlights of your talent; they are like clay in your hands, longing to live. It is up to you to teach them that they can live without you. You are like a father going after his own daughters."

He told her: "You are wrong. I am not using them, I am, in fact, trying to repel them, as gently as I can. I am giving each one of them a parachute, in the form of continued access to me, as a friend."

"You are surrounded by them, you are snorting them like a drug. The literary critics have patted you on the back, but you want more. You need to be praised on a mattress. You are degrading the integrity of this institution."

"You have an axe to grind," the professor replied. "Don't insert me into your private drama, whatever it is. I have done no wrong." From then on, the battle lines were set.

For this intellectual woman from Egypt, the apparent impunity of the professor in the midst of imagined crimes was intolerable, and it drove her to seek means of defeating him. She found a point of attack in the fact that he, himself, had never produced an original work of poetry of any substance in the past; nor had his journal articles on literary analysis been of particular worth, while his thesis on the image and meaning of the nightingale in world literature had really been quite lame. In short, there was no indication in anything he had ever done or said before the mysterious, esoteric production of his masterpiece that he contained even an ounce of greatness in him, that the slightest element of literary potential resided in his sterile, flatfooted psyche. Not believing in the power of epiphanies, she could only come to the conclusion that the work he had produced must be derivative, stolen, and she determined, like a master detective, that she would find the source of the myth he was creating about himself, identify the plant from which he had made his aphrodisiac of words.

As any master detective, she considered where the most likely crime sites might be found, where the most fertile quarries of the deception might be located. Where were the limestone cliffs from which the stone of his lie had been gouged, to build temples for the gullible? She consulted, over the Internet, with professors from Columbia, Yale, Cairo, and New Delhi, in the process discovering that the sketches of his past-life self and Asha contained important errors in costuming: Asha was dressed in an Indian sari, while he was garbed in an Ottoman robe and turban. That, in itself, seemed to disprove the visions that had made his book as much of an occult as a literary classic. In fact, she delighted in informing him of this in an e-mail: "The garments which you and Asha wore during your past-life romance, that is before you flung them off to jump into bed, belong to two widely separated geographic areas, and irrevocably divergent cultures. Your visions are clearly created from a modern foundation, using clothing taken from the West's generic fantasy wardrobe, in which the sari, the turban, the kaftan, the tunic and kimono are all lumped together, with no regard for historical accuracy, into a single exotic category representing the possibility of love and adventure in a land without consequences. These are either inept fantasies, exposing the ignorance of the dreamer, or else improperly researched lies. In no way can they be true memories. I hope this knowledge will deter you from making further use of your 'past-life memories' as a basis for seduction."

Although the professor was, in fact, disturbed by the revelations of his determined antagonist, his mind was able to come up with plausible explanations for the inconsistency, rooted in the possibility of trade between cultures, or more durably, in the imprecision of human memory, which, even in his present life, had played many tricks on him, putting him in jeans when he had really been wearing corduroys, and making the score of the lacrosse game 5-2 instead of 5-3.

The professor from Egypt did not think he would be vanquished by the riposte of the scholars of fashion who she had enlisted in her cause, and so she continued to dig for the secret source of the book she believed him incapable of writing. According to her contacts, the whole reincarnation theme ought to place the original work from somewhere in India, probably a product of Sanskrit and the Hindu sensibility; however, certain references definitely pointed towards Islam and, in fact, a capable linguist determined that many of the professor's lines seemed to mirror Arabic forms of expression and to be struggling towards rhythms more often seen in Arabic poetry. Could the work be based on some sort of historical layering; could it perhaps come from an original Indian text shaped anew by an Arab hand, which tried to batter it into conformity with Arab culture and religion, but finally succumbed to its beauty and surrendered to the power of reincarnation as a literary vehicle for expressing love's transcendence of death?

At this point, another scholar, joining in the hunt, reminded her that the Druse of Lebanon were both Muslim *and* believers in the doctrine of reincarnation, though their version of it was substantially different from the Hindus'; he suggested that a search of literature originating from the Druse areas of Lebanon ought to be launched: "It is there that you are most likely to find the tracks of the charlatan," he said. And it is this concept which shaped the strategy of the professor's Egyptian tormentor, who pursued him with all the vigor of Hatshepsut, the brilliant woman pharaoh whose statues were sculpted with beards so that she might hold her own among men.

The professor was dining out with Shana, a lovely and exotic woman of part-Irish, part-Slavic background, in a dimly lit café off campus, when he received the decisive text message from his nemesis: "You have been busted." A name in Arabic followed. "Your source has been unearthed. Tomorrow, the star of the lady's man will fall from the sky, and the genius will be exposed as a plagiarist. Decency will return to our school."

"What's wrong?" Shana asked him.

"Nothing," the professor said, frowning. "A paper cut, of sorts."

"Ooo, I hate those," said Shana. "They hurt so much!"

Sure enough, next day, the professor was called in to see the Dean at 4 PM, just as his afternoon class on the art of William Blake was letting out. Grimly, without speaking, sitting behind his enormous desk that seemed better suited for the president of a country than for the administrator of a small college in the mountains, shielded from the world it attempted to explain behind ramparts of pine trees, the Dean slid a box of papers over to his star pedagogue. "The original Arabic has been scanned. They found it in a library in Cairo, based on a manuscript written in Baghdad by a poet and scholar whose mother was Druse. Apparently, it was supposed to be destroyed because of certain passages which were problematic from the scriptural point of view, but it was spared by an admirer by being 'misplaced.' It was found a few centuries later and catalogued by bureaucrats who did not appreciate it. Here is a crude English translation, provided by Dr. Sayyid's contacts, which has been scanned and sent along. Take a look."

The professor picked up the pages of the translation, and stunned, read the first lines of his own book: "The wailing with which I tore at her departure has become green, I have awakened in a new land. I know she is here. Scripture cannot keep her from me, love is stronger than what old men have to say about God."

"No!" he exclaimed, amazed, tears welling up in his eyes. "This can't be! Surely, this must be a hoax!"

"I am afraid not," said the Dean. "All of this is notarized by the keepers of the archives, university officials from Cairo, and the Smith-Hasan Translation Services which are so highly regarded as to be utilized by the State Department."

"Amazing!" gasped the professor, the light of absolute joy spilling out of his eyes, like a body gashed open by a sword pouring out blood, if it were possible for such a thing to be wonderful instead of horrible. "I have—I have had such doubts!" he exclaimed to the bewildered Dean. "Such doubts! The Ottoman turban and the sari—but now I see that those are mere trifles! The emerald was scratched, it was damaged by the journey through time, but it is still an emerald! How could you carry a glass full of water for a hundred miles without spilling some of it? And they leap upon every flaw as though it were a horse and attempt to ride the whole thing away. But it is real! I am Abu Fayyad! These words in front of you are proof of immortality! You hold in your hands the fountain of youth, the balm for every heartbroken soul that has ever lived! I, who was dead in this lifetime because I did not have her, have erupted from who I was, because I longed for her, to become the highest peak of myself! And now, merely because I loved like a madman, because I loved so much that I kept on loving after I died, I have inadvertently stumbled upon proof of life after death, my heart has smashed open the sanctuary of eternity for the fleeting and the momentary, all the desperate creatures of the twilight! Or rather, I have been blessed to be the fool who led the earth to water!"

"You don't seem to understand," the Dean stammered out, incredulous at the professor's naiveté. "There is no cause for celebration, here. You have been caught red-handed in the act of plagiarism, and now our school is going to have to spend thousands on damage control. As for you..."

It was only then that the professor understood that he and the world were not on the same page. Whereas, for him, the discovery of the ancient manuscript, which he had remembered and reproduced in modern times, was proof of reincarnation and confirmation of the essence of his past-life visions, for the world represented by the Dean, it was nothing less than a sign of his corruption. Unable to believe in past lives, it could only believe in deception. Unable to believe in miracles, it could only believe in treachery. Unable to give up its prejudice against the impossible, it could only view his vindication as damnation.

"But— but—I never saw this manuscript before," the professor protested. "Not in this lifetime. I remembered the feelings, and from the feelings came words that clung to my soul like stowaways on a ship of longing, weathering the loss of bodies, the violent storms of outer forms collapsing. This manuscript you have found—it is like digging up my body from the grave, proving that I lived! It is like Schliemann finding the gold of Agamemnon!"

"You have it backwards, I am afraid," replied the Dean, with a coldness the professor noticed for the first time, like the winter winds that swept down from the mountainside, making one wish for a lover underneath the blankets. "Don't dare to deny what you have done! The manuscript is not proof that you lived before, but proof that you have lied! It is not your baby, it is your mother! You did not give birth to your book; it gave birth to you! You have not remembered, you have copied! You have not soared with inspiration in the sky of poetry; you have crawled with deceit in the mud of self-interest! You have not created a work of beauty, you have stolen another man's heart, scavenged his magnificence, you have committed the high crime of artists and academics, you have plagiarized!"

The professor was stunned, shaken by the sudden hostility of a man he thought had been his friend, but he tried to reassure himself, after he staggered out of his office, feeling completely naked like a concentration camp prisoner underneath his clothes, that things would be set right. How could he have plagiarized the text of an obscure volume of poetry hidden away for centuries in the back chambers of a labyrinthine library which he had never visited; a text written in Arabic, a language which he did not understand, which had never previously been translated into English? No, the world would realize its mistake in a matter of days, after the hysteria and fear of disgrace died down. Logic would reassert itself. If the ancient manuscript which he had rewritten in the present, from memory, had finally been unearthed, the only possible conclusion was that the essence of his memory was true, in spite of the superficial mistakes of the sari and the turban.

The essence of the memory was true, meaning that Asha, whether that was her name or not, was real, and that past lives and future lives were also real. A great tree of hope had been planted in the middle of mankind's despair. This did not lead to the humiliation of a professor, but to the liberation of a world which lived as though nothing but today mattered, but which might now commit itself to broader visions and to deeper truths.

However, much to the dismay of the professor, the Dean proved to be absolutely correct. He, the professor —Abu Fayyad in another time— *had* got it backwards. The concept of reincarnation was so esoteric and at odds with the tangible, and so dangerous in terms of what it might do to the world, that it seemed much easier to believe in the dishonesty of a man. "But how could I have seen the manuscript in this lifetime?!" the professor protested. Critics replied: "It is easier to believe in the ingenuity of a man than to reorder the cosmos." Somehow, another copy must have existed, one of which fell into his hands. Was it not easier to believe this than to learn how to desire and to cry a different way?

From being a hero, a sensitive and valiant prodigy, the professor was turned overnight into a cynical bandit, despised by all. He was forced to leave the college, and blacklisted from obtaining comparable posts. The sales of his book plummeted, the tours to colleges and bookstores dried up. The girls who had flocked to his lectures and dazzled him with their fresh, womanly light, limped away from the wreck, feeling wounded and betrayed; they let deep truths become mere fads and put them away into boxes alongside their childhood dolls. They erased the timeless arms of the love he had taught them to seek to find men their own age on the edge of dances and drinks. There, they found lives that were tangible and doomed, and they built altars of not looking too far in the center of their new homes.

"I am sorry," Dr. Sayyid wrote to the disgraced professor in an e-mail with which she tried to assuage her conscience, "but I had to stand by the young women of our school. Every teacher must recognize the power of his position and strive to insulate himself from the seductive effects of his status."

The professor shook his head like a man whose house has been blown away by a tornado; this woman had successfully used him to gain revenge against someone else, perhaps a shadow. He wondered, in fact, if perhaps he had known her in the past: perhaps, he thought, she was Asha's angry father, hating him without knowing why, driven by a subconscious compulsion too powerful to resist; Asha's father, determined to get his daughter back and to destroy the man who had run off with her. Wherever Asha was in this time, she must be kept away from him, and what better way to separate the lovers than to beat the poet to his knees and poison the words with which he sought to woo her? The songbird is a liar. Do not wake up, it does not mean the sun is coming. Whether true or not, Dr. Sayyid had won, but only on the shallow field on which she was playing.

For the professor, there was ecstasy in the downfall. The tears came out as drops of gold. For though he had fallen in this time and place, though he was utterly disgraced—by means of the instrument of his destruction, he had wandered through the gates of Eden, and now stood triumphant in the garden mankind has longed for since the dawn of time. The doubt that had lurked around the edges of his experience, his angelic moment of digging through the desert sand to yesterday's water, had been vanquished. The absurdity of withholding conviction because of the turban and the sari, mere wrinkles in the cloth of a great revelation, had become obvious. "The sun flashed on the wing of an eagle. I thought its wing was the color of gold, I did not perceive it perfectly. But though I was wrong about the color, I perceived an eagle, nonetheless." The ancient manuscript discovered in a library as far away from his knowledge as the surface of the moon had proved this, had become embedded like veins and arteries in his vision, given it life and strength, like the arm of a giant. Though Asha still eluded him, and though he had lost his platform for finding her—his voice and his position in the limelight—he now knew that she was as real as the hand that had written about her, and covered reams of paper with her aura, filled pages of unbearable silence with the ink of her footsteps, and the rustling of her dress turned into words cascading like a waterfall from the heart she had changed. He knew she was an immortal part of the universe, just like him, and that there would be time to find her, in this life or on the other side of this life's empty hands.

What troubled him most as he struggled to survive in the world of shame and obscurity into which he had been cast was the terrible fate of the truth that had been uncovered in his wake and then abandoned. What of all the suffering, desperate people, the greedy mad impulses without perspective, the blunt grasping as if the world was about to run away, the callus of mourning grown thick over life, entombing soft things that could no longer stretch their hands to the God of Joy, the paralyzing fear of death, the invulnerability of appetites which only had to answer to one life; what of all the people who could be healed if they only knew what he knew, believed what he had discovered to be true, believed in the light shining through the window of his life into their room, believed he was God's proof given to them to free them, and not a plagiarist? It was heartbreaking to see the sunrise alone; to hear the desperate cries of children whose mothers were already holding them.

"How is it possible?!" he cried out in frustration, "That I who have loved proof of life-beyond-life into the world, and rung the bell of the universe's greatest secret by following a woman's trail through the valley of death, have been dismissed as a mere plagiarist, and cut off from Humanity like a leg with gangrene? Is it possible that only I can be saved by my salvation?!" It was unbearable, at first, this thought: this thought of being the only man in the world who was happy without being distracted. But finally, painfully, he got used to it. He had no choice. Around each human being's revelation, around each human being's miracle and awakening, around each human being's proof that holiness is a fact and not just an ideal, there is a wall that separates him from the rest of the world. His revelation, his miracle and awakening, and his proof are for him and no one else. Discovery is personal and cannot be shared. Nothing is sacred until it is experienced; truths are recited but not believed, until they crash like a meteor into the middle of a life. What a devastating insight for the compassionate, but the wall around the moment of being convinced, which shuts the world out from a man's epiphany, is too high for his altruism to leap over; it is as high as the peak God has given each of us to climb.

One night, after a hard day's work on a different rung of the social ladder, as he left his job and came out onto the street, he chanced to meet Dr. Sayyid, who was visiting the city into which he had disappeared— his battleground, and her field of leisure. "Lies have a long reach," she said, "and their repercussions have great stamina. They are like wolves who never tire, hunting down those who sought to profit by them."

The professor, now merely a "worker," looked at her; he saw, in her eyes, her pride, her elaborate ignorance bristling with the weapons of the intellect, the thin layer of the earth she fought for and the pain of the crusades that did not reach the place where she was bleeding. He was open to feeling rage for what she had done to him, but he did not. Tranquility was not his intention; it just happened. There was quiet in his soul, and sorrow, not for him, but for her: like the time, when he was a child who could not swim, that he saw a cat drowning in a river, and just watched the waters carry it away, meowing to the shore. He wished he could have done something for Dr. Sayyid, helped her in some way, but for her, he was only a plagiarist. She was too tenacious in the defense of her desolation to take his hand.

EARTH REFOUND

"What is going on?" we asked the wise man.

We gathered around him by the ancient tree. The weather was warm, the world was in full bloom, rebelling against shame. We did not wear clothes, for it seemed the whole earth wanted to touch us and see us, and we did not want to deny it. Among the blazing petals and fantastic shapes of flowers championing life, we stood, flowers in human form, joining in the celebration of things not dead.

"What do the lights mean?" my best friend, Eurydice, asked the man of many years, who had never once lied to us, nor demeaned us with unripe thoughts. "Last night I saw three balls of fire fall onto the mountain." Beyond the forest and the gardens, there was the mountain that meditated upon us all, never blinking, yet never keeping us at a distance.

"My people," said the white-haired man, the last snow in the world on top of his head. "Do you remember the day when we made the trek, from the swampland to the forest?"

"We do," we said.

"Do you remember the scarred place?"

"The place with the giant circles burned in stone, where you said the others left in ships of fire, because they had destroyed the world and could not live here?"

Said the old man: "They melted the ice and raised the seas. They turned the sky gray and gasped for breath, as birds ceased to fly and fish died on the beach. They looted the ages stored underneath the earth: vaults of treasures filled by geology and cosmology. Billions of years of labor they squandered in a single flash of greed. They ate themselves into oblivion, razed the world with their towers, pillaged it with joy that could not run faster than what haunted them. Like a swarm of wild ants, they devoured what they needed to live, until, at last, they had no choice but to flee from the generosity that could not satisfy them, and to lift themselves on top of mighty fires into the blackness beyond us, in search of another world, green and unspoiled as ours once was."

"And is it not true," Eurydice asked him, "that we were the ones they left behind?"

The old man nodded; he had the memory of the rocks. "Not us, but those we come from. They were the ones of no account, the ones who would not fit in the great ships that bore the others to safety, out of the reach of a world that success destroyed."

"We were abandoned!"

"Left behind by the beasts who knew no limits, we clung to the surface of a world left for dead, we clung to its faint heartbeats of green persisting in the desert, to its last mountains desperately leaping out of the clutches of the sea. We breathed its fallen air, lived off of its sputtering fruits and wheezing harvests, clawed and dug for its accidental gifts. We were buried together—our world and the worthless ones—left drifting in the void without a pulse. But somehow, somehow, this mighty planet did not surrender. The power of green was too great for the tracks of dead machines. For the empty mineshafts and the craters ripped into its sides, for the poison poured into its water and air. The muscles of its will to live bulged with things that continued to grow, its breath fogged the mirror of Creation, held up to its silent mouth. From under the ruins, insects crawled, as precious as gold, even the cockroach seemed like a swan; then, one morning, we heard the chirping of birds. The people who were left to die awoke in a healing world, over cuts that had become forests. The earth was recovered by those who had always loved it. Those who merely used it were gone."

"You told us, long ago, of an ancient book," Eurydice reminded him. "It was as it was said."

"'The meek shall inherit the earth.' The proud and uncaring owned it to the point of losing it. It fell back to us."

"In no other way could we have got the earth back," surmised Eurydice. "Only by losing so badly that there was no one left strong enough to stop them from destroying themselves!"

But then, my dear friend's face grew strangely dark, afraid of a cloud passing over her mind. I held her hand, which was the way I first approached her body long ago, when I wanted her but was not sure what she wanted. "The three balls of fire?" she asked the old man again.

"For centuries, now, we have lived well," the old man said. "Left by those who thought themselves better than us, left by those who thought the earth was only dirt, we learned to flourish. We recovered hand-in-hand with our world, we reinvented ways of living that were dignified and beautiful. Before, they trod down the green places with hearts of lead; after they left, our hearts danced with all things rising from the dead. Our people gathered in deep and worthwhile ways to partake of the miracle of existence. A thousand diseases of the soul were overcome. But there were those of us, in spite of it, who sometimes slept unquietly, with thoughts of those who had spurned us with their fleeing ships."

My love's deep-feeling, far-seeing face grew darker yet, and it made me frightened.

"We wondered," continued the old man, "what had become of them. Those who fled from their incompetence. Those who left our ruined world to seek another. How can you start from scratch when your mistakes are your religion? How can you escape from a disaster when it comes from who you are? What hope is there for one whose answer is to change one world for another, rather than to change himself? We thought, what virgin green world will these ravenous, unvanquished ships of fire reach; and what will prevent the men who destroyed the earth from doing the same to their new home? And once it, too, is destroyed, after its own cynical cycle of history, to what new world will the hungry, unrepentant ships turn? What new garden will appear in the crosshairs of their lust? What new planet will they discover blossoming in the dark, to be plucked by their insatiable hand?"

"No!" Eurydice suddenly protested, trembling, her words barely comprehensible. "And if they know no other world, but remember the one from which they came? If they have not erased it from their map? If they tell themselves that if it was once green, it might be so again? If nothing else is left to them in the void, but the starting point on their great map of evasion?"

"Fallow earth!" I gasped. "Leave the field bare, that the soil might regenerate!"

"No such foresight, only desperation," said Eurydice, before rebelling against her intellect and her intuition, which were partners in her soul, always on top of each other like lovers. "Tell us, wise man, that it is not so! Please tell us!"

"I wish I could," he said. "But the evidence is overwhelming. The balls of fire are their ships. They have not ceased their habit of laying waste to beautiful things. They have wrecked the worlds they fled to after destroying ours, and now they have returned to the only one that is left, the one they started from! Paradise is at an end."

THE FRENCH TIME MACHINE

My friends, I have something to tell you, and I'll keep it brief.

Time is like a broken mind, but it has made me whole. What I saw in Algeria, what I did, trying to retain the glory of beloved France, the illusion that I still love, snapped my consciousness, fragmented my soul beyond repair. I saw my heart beating and my lungs contracting and expanding like mere balloons, and my absurd testes wielding the hammer of Michelangelo. But the stone he used to sculpt his greatness never screamed. You'd be crazy, too, if you built the minefield that killed so many patriots, but it was beautiful for its day—with spotlights and electrified fences and sensors tied in to the command station that dispatched the helicopters. As for the mines themselves, they were a new generation. It was art underneath the ground, and the supply lines from Tunisia were taking a beating. We were choking the life out of the rebels, before De Gaulle, of all people, lost his nerve and handed the country to Ben Bella on a platter of guilt. But that was my misused teenage joy, the thought that Professor De Riviere's star pupil, the one who invented the electrical review imager, could somehow become such a prolific inventor of widows. May Allah have mercy on my Christian soul, may the colonized never cease to rattle the chains that are like diamonds for us who do not wear them.

But as I was saying, before the complexity of the world distracted me, I have something to tell you. Wonderful things that can come out of a devastated mind; a soul that has ingenuously served evil is relentless in its efforts to atone.

The war was over; we had lost Indochina and Algeria, and my technological masterpiece was now as outdated as the Maginot Line, or the rusted cannons that guarded the beaches of Martinique from pirates whose ships were at the bottom of the sea. I was coveted by all the engineering firms and scientific research teams; the dismemberment of the colonies must be compensated by new avenues of virility. My mind never lagged, its great weakness was always its inability to wait for my heart. My intellect was an Olympic athlete, my morals smoked cigars and sat all day in a chair. When the dam of everything I had done finally broke one day that I saw a boy with an artificial leg hobbling about a hospital in Marseilles, I nearly destroyed myself like Oedipus, after he found out who he was.

But the lust of invention refused to let me go. Justice was thwarted by the prayers of unknown things. The feats of psychics, who publicly humiliated me merely by handling my car keys, convinced me of the constant occurrence of time, and the time-nature of space: a small price to pay for thirty people in a nightclub finding out about my vices. The past, the present, and the future depend upon each other and yet, they exist simultaneously, and access is lateral rather than vertical. You need not age to see your future, only step into your parallel form, which already inhabits the future, which is nothing but the trajectory of the present. I call this form the "personal vehicle." The question which consumed me was not this, but whether one depended upon one's personal vehicle in order to travel through time, in which case, barring the possibility of reincarnation, one's range of exploration must be considerably restricted; or whether one could travel, without one's personal vehicle, into a time in which one, oneself, did not exist.

Various thought experiments, so generously vindicated to us by Einstein, convinced me of the possibility of traveling without a personal vehicle, both forward and backward, as a displaced phenomenon, which could be balanced out by a corresponding depletion of energy in the system intruded upon. The energy loss to the system would be so slight and need not cause any grievous damage to any sentient being located within that time, that the impact seemed minimal and wholly worth risking in light of the potential reward.

But what of the impact of one's *actions*, which might dwarf the negligible effects of one's *presence*? That was harder to calculate.

But once again, thank God, a variety of thought experiments convinced me that none of the more frightening scenarios most often attributed to time travel applied. I could not alter the past, or if I could, it did not matter, for it was as it was, and if I could alter it, I already had. Therefore, I could not, by some colossal mistake, thwart the meeting of my mother and father, negate my own birth, and vanish into nothingness. Nor could I deliver a crate of machine guns to Hannibal at Zama and change the course of history. Or better stated, if I could, I didn't. And I never would. Furthermore, I need not fear being killed by Caligula or Robespierre during my adventure, and equally important, I need not fear jolting the consciousness of mankind off its known path by introducing into its perceptions the legend of a man who disappeared into thin air just as a lion was about to rip him to shreds in the arena. On the downside

, I could not stop the Holocaust; I could not abort Hitler or rescue Joan of Arc from the stake. On the day I finally understood that, I walked out of my house and stood for three hours in the rain, saluting the fallen who would never rise, except through us, as we rose because of them. Some souls lift us all by falling.

As for the future: I determined through a simple application of the commutative principle (5 x 6 = 30, 6 x 5 = 30), that I could not rescue the present from the platform of things to come, nor alter the future in any way inconsistent with its projection from the present. However, I could experience it, as well as the past, with full sensory awareness. I could suffer in other times and enjoy them. Like the number 0 in addition and subtraction, I could be a part of them without affecting them, except as they had already been affected ("would be" and "had been" were moot distinctions at this level of reality). Existence is elastic and stretches with human transgressions to accommodate the violations our brilliance is capable of producing, but remains intact. Bellerephon, by the time he reaches the peak of Olympus, is as tiny as an ant.

This theoretical knowledge, arrived at through a combination of mathematics and the wild imagination I used to flee from the tears that my toys had inflicted on mankind, was backed up by the laboratory results of my "psychometric scanner," an absurd but grand device funded by the police department of Paris and LaSalle Technologies to attempt to recreate crimes from the time-multiplicities of the crime scenes. The police wanted visual imagery, something akin to the movies or TV, but that was not what I gave them. Instead, they received a device that "destabilized" the time fixation of a scene assessor, who began to receive leaked images, similar to hallucinations, from the multiplicity, until he could re-fix on the time-strand in question. The interface between man and machine was extremely difficult, and effective only in the case of highly sensitive individuals, the kind who rarely go into police work.

However disappointing the results were, there *were* results, and now I knew, beyond all shadow of a doubt, that time travel was, indeed, possible, it was only a matter of developing an appropriate energy source which could rupture the time-borders and deposit the brave explorer or forlorn refugee, as it might be, into another epoch.

For me, the joy in the world I lived in was meager, and I longed for an escape. Since I knew where the past led—to this dismal world I inhabited and wished, with all my heart, to leave—I knew it was to the future that my effort must be directed.

In these days, the Americans had taken over our role in Indochina and were floundering badly. I watched them die, each night, on the TV, while our own reckless students threw up barricades and made absurd gestures of changing the world. American companies bound to the military-industrial complex contacted me; they wanted me to help them mine the Ho Chi Minh Trail, and to help them fortify vulnerable outposts around some important Vietnamese cities, such as Hue, Da Nang, and Quang Ngai. They were especially interested in my work on CCMs— code-controlled mines—which I had proposed to build around Fort Bonalie before De Gaulle's cave-in—damn my obsolescence, for I truly believe he was a visionary, whereas I was an evolutionary dead-end! May God forgive me by using me for the good of man! The Americans were also intrigued by the potential of my psychometric scanner, especially for "forward viewing," which could, if developed to capacity, unveil the guerrillas whose elusiveness depends upon their use of time. By proper scanning of the terrain, the speed and the stealth of the guerrillas' movements would be lost, they would be exposed as if they were camped out in broad daylight for weeks at a time.

Huge sums were offered for these projects and promises made to finance my construction of a genuine time machine, which was more of a bribe than an act of support since no one really believed it could work.

However, I knew my soul was already dangling by a thread for what I had done in Algeria; I could not take the knife to my slim chances for salvation by reliving the sin of North Africa in America's valiant Asian folly.

At the time, my good but sterile and rather simple wife, Matilde, was killing me slowly with her lack of curiosity and indignation; it was like living with a cow chewing grass, God forgive me to speak of a human being like that. But she was the wife of a soldier who didn't need a companion, because war absorbed him totally. When peace delivered him back home, and awoke in him the desire for a friend, he found he had nothing more than a pillow of flesh to lie on and hurl his fruitless liquids at. The way she seemed to melt like wax in the summer, and to sit in her chair reading magazines that were no better than staring at the wall, sickened me. I think I was more lonely than I was arrogant.

What restrained me in these days from destroying myself, was Khadija , the little Arab girl we adopted, my way of pleading to the universe for forgiveness for the brilliant crimes against humanity I had buried under her earth, the belt of land mines that made a thousand cripples for a lost cause. How many legless men and women, now, were free? Those are the ones De Gaulle could not save.

Khadija was to be my salvation, my heart restored, but every time I saw her, I remembered why she was in my home—to hide all the others who had died. When she smiled at me for something so simple as giving her a piece of candy, I thought of myself: Disgraceful pretender, do you think this smile you win with chocolate can change who you are? Do you think this laughter you coax from her with toys can pay her for the mother she lost? The mother who you may well have killed? Should I go ahead and tell her who I am? Khadija, I am the one who buried ten thousand cobras beneath the sand. I am the one who stalked the bare feet of your nation with all of my sinister cleverness. I blew up the ones bringing guns, and I blew up the ones coming for water. I blew up guerrillas, and I blew up children dancing in the wind. I replaced joyous feet, flying like birds across the ground, with scar-covered stubs, and eyes chained to sorrow, like animals that can't leave a post.

When Matilde began to take Khadija to the Church, I said, "Maybe we shouldn't, Matilde. Maybe we should wait. She can make up her own mind when she's older."

"We'll have ourselves a good little Catholic," Matilde told me. "God forbid our girl should ever become a Muslim—to wear one of those scarves. You know, they whip them if they read a book!"

When I saw Khadija with her rosary beads, praying to Jesus and Mary, I thought, "So now, my sin is complete." You cannot cover over a coffin with good deeds; the earth of compensations is too thin to bury what is irreversible.

My depression was enormous, my self-hate, my despair. I saw myself already dead, a walking corpse, I saw my civilization, my empire, tarnished and fallen, I saw my world slowly killing itself with repetitions of tragedies not believed in, I saw the clear warnings of only yesterday discounted like stories of mermaids of the deep. I saw folly not even scratched by thousands of years of history, I saw compassion not elevated by the lives of a thousand saints, I saw madness high in the sky and wisdom on the bottom of a soldier's boot, I saw hope faltering like an aged body whose heart is failing, I saw proud and beautiful heroes falling like flags to the ground, words of justice treated like spit in the eye, utopian visions betrayed by factories bearing litters of guns and by children floating like balloons away from the hunger of the world. I saw unfettered apocalypses resisted by blind Edens.

I am not sure if I wanted to escape or simply to see if the future was worth the suffering. If there was something for Humanity to look forward to, a light at the end of the tunnel of history, or if all this fighting, dying, and dreaming was only to reach a black cloud, to crawl into a coffin of tyranny, injustice, and mayhem.

In these days I worked harder than ever to build my time machine. I must break out of this darkness, I must rip away the veil from the face of what lay ahead, I must see the beauty or the wretchedness, otherwise, I could no longer motivate myself to be a member of the human race. The suspense, however, was ruined by the pervasiveness of barbarism, which seemed to spoil the ending. *How else could the story end?*

But still—hope—less than 1% probability of hope—kept me digging for evidence. Digging with mathematics, physics, and mechanics. Digging for something that could redeem my species. Only something extraordinary like that could redeem me! In the end, with nothing more and nothing less than the massive particle accelerator they built in the south of France in the late 1970s—dear heroic, pathetic France, still trying to keep pace—I was able to design a potentially viable time machine. I built an energy spur off the accelerator and, within a geometrically perfected vortex generator, constructed a sheltered time-mobile with which I intended to pierce the time border and enter the future as a displaced phenomenon.

By this time, I was aging; we were already in the 1990s, and I felt myself terribly frail to be a pioneer, a Columbus made of glass. Khadija, my light and joy, was a mature woman now with a family of four, a Moroccan husband, and a scarf on her head. She had found her way back to her rightful folly, or perhaps to the truth, who am I to say? Time has not led me to God, or taken him away from me. I have chosen to be obsessed rather than spiritual. And yet, now I understand that even one in love with machines cannot help but see a beauty that is beyond his hands, some angel in the metal with which he transcends the starkness of matter.

Khadija, my beautiful orphan daughter, stolen from your home by the beasts of land mines I scattered like seeds into your native soil. Thank God, my guilty arms could not hold you back from who you are! She was, in the end, a strange, disturbed, and serious girl who could, nonetheless, smile like a rainstorm ending, like leaves still dripping water beneath a bright and healing sky. She cared for me because her heart was twice the size of mine.

"Please, father," she told me, hurting me terribly by using that word I deserved so little. "Do nothing foolish! Your machine—shouldn't you test it with a chimpanzee, like they did with the space capsules?"

"First I must try it to make sure it's safe for a monkey," I jested.

"Please!" she told me. "Don't joke at a time like this. I am concerned."

Her husband, cryptic and ever skeptical of me, with eyes that seemed to be in a constant struggle against anger because of the damaged state in which he had received his wife from us— from me and poor Matilde, may she rest in peace—walked away. He couldn't stand anything resembling affection between his wife and Christian father-in-law.

But though Khadija protested, I knew she was unhappy, too. Lately, anti-Muslim sentiment had been growing in her neighborhood; her kids had been teased and bullied in school, and on the street someone had thrown a bottle of soda at her. Although I, myself, had used bullets and explosives against Muslims in their own land, the thought of someone here, in France, throwing a coke bottle at her was unbearable to me. A disgrace!

"Listen, my dear," I told her. "The world has worn me out with its cruelty and unfairness. With what is outside of me and what is in me. I need to see what is beyond this. I need to drive around the curve on this highway of pain, to see if something better lies around the bend. Without that knowledge, I can't go on. How can any of us go on? Khadija—if I find the world is worse than it is now, I won't tell you. God forbid you should be disheartened even more than you must be now. But if I find, by some miraculous chance, Khadija, that the world is better than it is now—that it has finally pulled itself up by the bootstraps, finally looked into its tormented soul and recognized the beautiful possibility of what it could be and chosen that over what is easier to be, then I shall, by all means, tell you, and if it is possible, open for you the door to that world. Do not deny me this first true act of fatherhood, my dear Khadija—the chance to find for you a golden world and bring you to it. To discover a refuge for you and your family, beyond the hatred and contempt of those who I once served with a rifle."

In tears, Khadija forbade me to make the effort, knowing that I was as stubborn as a hundred mules, and that, in all events, her love could never deter me, because I felt I did not deserve it.

Though I told her I might find a paradise, I dreaded what I might find instead. Observing the ups and downs of history, one found the ups to be brief and not so high as the longer nights were low. Who could believe that a world which had seen the Inquisition and the Nazis could ever be saved? Who could believe that a world which saw Dien Bien Phu, only a few years later could stumble into the Tet Offensive? Savagery stretched from the beginning of time to modernity, while the lessons of history were forgotten in a decade. What hope was there?

Fearfully—because even though I was old and now knew that death would not overlook me, I hoped to die imagining a dawn rather than a ceaseless night—I set the controls of the machine three hundred years ahead. I must give Humanity a little more time to find its way!

Dear God, I thought, *if you exist, please: blow me and my machine up if the world to come is dark. I would rather that my time-mobile erupt into flames, or that I perish from the force of acceleration through the time barrier, than that I awaken in the rubble of Paris, in a charred and uninhabited wasteland, or in a city of slaves or gluttons standing upon the dead.*

And with that said, challenging the visions that make us persist, I threw the red switch inside my time-mobile, as the engineers at the accelerator hurled all the power at their disposal into my audacious energy spur.

What they saw beyond me, I am not sure, but I saw a blinding light and felt my body violently shaken. Everything was vibrating, humming, shaking as though Pythagoras had just been hit with a tire iron, and the musical pitch of stars making light was thundering by, deafening me, biting me like that mad prostitute from Lyon. *Good God!* I thought *the universe is ending, it's melting, its insides are spiraling out like a tornado!* My head was struck by something— again!—I felt a cap pop out of my tooth, and my lip was bleeding, and I started crying, even though I tried not to. And suddenly there was a jolt, it was like that time I was driving drunk, well, the wine bottle was kinder to me than any friend, and I crashed into the sign post, and suddenly there was no more Laplace Street, just a road with no name and pieces of glass from a headlight.

My God, I wondered, *is my neck broken?* But it wasn't, and gradually, I became aware of my time-mobile sitting in a field of luxuriant grass, greener than any green I knew, and suddenly throngs of beautiful, healthy-looking people were swarming all around my machine, and a tall and handsome one, who was what the human race has been striving to achieve ever since our stooping ancestors first came down from the trees, came up to me, and said through the window I rolled down: "We've been expecting you."

And I wept tears of joy, because merely looking at them, I knew the world had been saved.

In the days that followed, I learned I was not wrong. These splendid creatures who called themselves men, but were radiant like we never let ourselves be, with the broken chains of ancient fears and resentments lying discarded to the side of their world, welcomed me as if I were a brother.

"You knew I was coming?" I asked them.

"Of course," they said. "We never doubted you."

"You know what I have done?" I demanded, determined, for once in my life, not to be admired because I was not known.

"That is what makes your coming so special," they replied.

"The land mines," I said, not sure if they understood.

"That is what makes your coming so special," they repeated.

They showed me the world they had made, a mere three hundred years after the nightmare I had come from: a world technologically advanced, in which technology did not seek to invent a way around justice. A world socially inclusive, that did not demote technology, because it knew how to control it. A world not divided, yet not leveled, in which greatness did not excite envy, nor demand servitude; a world kind, yet vigorous; a world peaceful, yet passionate; a world pleasing to the eye, yet deep; a world generous without manipulation, wise without pretense, and reflective without lethargy. A world utterly fascinating, not like a redundant battery-operated toy which you quickly tire of, or a card trick that amazes you just once, but a richly-souled woman who can think, feel, write, dance, sing, listen, speak, play a thousand different instruments, and make love each night like she was the one you might leave her for.

It was a world whose human development astounded me, whose institutions arose from foundations of philosophy and spiritual attunement; whose laws were fair and far-sighted, whose customs were dignified and life-filled, whose streets overflowed with constant gestures of understanding, touches, laughter, and galloping thoughts, joyful to stretch their legs and run.

Three hundred years! I gasped, bewildered by the difference. Though Paradise is what all men dream of, one notch below Paradise in the real world is surely better; and this is what I had stumbled upon in my great gamble to see what lay beyond the darkness of my times.

For a moment more, I lamented, exclaiming: "I am not worthy of this!"

But my gracious hosts told me, "But it comes from you."

And that is when I knew that, in spite of all the aches and pains of my aging body which they could assuage and my old world could not, in spite of the resplendent abode they offered me to dwell in for a hundred years more of life, in spite of the noble exciting world they gave me to live in, I must go back to the world from which I came. I must spread the word to the disheartened. I must tell the pessimistic and the depressed, the hopeless and the vanquished. I must tell

Khadija that she was as beautiful as the morning light, that those who hated her were a dying breed, that after the dark wave pounding our own times had finally finished with its bluff of doom, we would arise to be what was intended for us.

I must tarry no longer in the land of my dreams where but one day was enough to heal the damned.

I must come back to tell the world I knew about this world to come, and to help build it. I must accept my responsibility to carry it into being upon my shoulders.

When I offered, nonetheless, to take my dear daughter back there, so she could finally live as she deserved, her view was the same as mine; she chose the struggle over the refuge.

Truly, there is joy in living in a beautiful world. But there is even more joy in making the world beautiful.

DANCING SALSA

He came back when she wasn't expecting him. There had been a mix-up at work, someone else was covering the shift, and he wasn't due in till tomorrow.

She must not have heard the key opening the door.

Maybe it was the music.

Curious, leaving his coat draped over the sofa, he peered into the other room, through the open doorway, which seemed to frame her, like a painting, except that she was moving.

It was the sensual rhythm of salsa, which seemed to hold her body captive, strangely upright and rigid, except for the hips that had a kind of magic in them, which could not be overcome.

It was one of those well-structured Puerto Rican songs—romantic salsa—not the wild Afro-Cuban rhythms with the horns screaming like a lover about to climax, or the drums like the heartbeats of someone running away from a plantation.

It was not without brakes, this song, but somehow, something in its self-control was painful, as though there was an emotion, here, that you could not dance into oblivion. Something you had to face, just like Death, when the last day is at hand.

The song was dripping with nostalgia, like secret nights you cannot tell anyone else about, without revealing their own inadequacy or irrelevance.

At first, he wanted to tell her he was home. Then he thought, why should he? She was bound to turn around in a minute and see him. Then he thought, if she did, she might be startled by his presence, even frightened for a moment. He thought he should quietly exit the apartment, and call her from the street, to tell her he was on his way back. But then, he simply fell into the trance of watching her dance.

Of course, he knew some Spanish. It was the natural product of an intercultural marriage, between a gringo and a latina. Now he could understand bits and pieces of her Grupo Niche and Jerry Rivera records, and she could say: "Dana, you wanna go play?" Dana was the child of a doctor and a lawyer who she took care of. She looked beautiful standing with the child (he sometimes watched them playing together in the park). She was so warm and caring with the kid, that sometimes people thought Dana was her daughter. But she wasn't. And sometimes he hated that sparkling little kid for receiving all the beauty and energy of Socorro's sweet mothering, while her own womb remained silent and closed, like a bud killed by the frost of the world; while her own body's clock ticked away, and poverty slowly killed the child they had always had in the back of their minds.

"I never promised to take you to Eden," the singer was saying, or something like that. "Only... [something about] ... feeling good. But I said if I came back, it would be true love..."

He recognized the singer: Eddie Santiago.

And then, suddenly, something about the song ripped into him, like a slug from a .38. Right into his corazón. "Tú me haces falta—(I miss you) ..." Over and over again, a voice smooth, yet somehow able to carry the pain, to feel it and bring it right out of the tape deck into the room. And her body was responding to the touch of his voice, like a woman responding when a man is loving her body, only it was in his embrace of pain that she was writhing. It was subtle, her dancing seemed outwardly the same; maybe it was by the way she moved her head for a moment, like a horse protesting against the reins, as it is being ridden to a place it does not want to go; or the way her body (except for the hips) stiffened, like it had just been given an electric shock. He thought of her cooking, and the way her hands, with the slightest motion, would break open bean pods to let the beans fall out. It was just like that, something almost invisible in her dance seemed to have broken open the place where her heart was hiding, and let it fall out, right in front of his eyes.

"Without you the nights are like a ghost, a punishment… I miss you. I miss you."

Who? he asked himself. *What?*

Was there some long-lost *novio*, some long-lost lover or suitor, someone like Michael Furey in Joyce's story "The Dead"? The boy who died in the pouring rain outside Gretta's window, before she became entombed in her life with Gabriel?

Or was it her country, her people? Or the dream everyone has of being more than a beast of burden, more than a slave used to build someone else's pyramid, and then left to die nameless in the sand?

Of course, she'd come to America to help them—her family. To the land of milk and honey. To the streets paved with gold. Planning to get a job, or find somebody, then send back everything she could.

Said one poet, who was criticized when his green card failed to dull the sharpness of his tongue: "No vine porque allá no sabíamos vivir. Vine siguiendo las dulces entrañas de mi país…" More or less, that meant, "I didn't come because we (Latins) didn't know how to live in our own land. I came, following the sweet guts of my country."

What did the poet mean?

He didn't know for sure, but he had once heard that jeans that sold for $130 up here were produced by workers who made as little as 50 cents an hour down there. And he'd heard similar stories regarding bananas, sugar, coffee, and those beautiful blankets the indigenous women sometimes made. Maybe it had something to do with that?

Bewildered, he watched Socorro dancing, he saw the body he had first fallen in love with, when he had been Prince Charming, and given her her green card, which, he didn't know then, was just like killing her.

"Estoy muy feliz, I'm so happy," she'd said on their wedding day, so long ago, still fresh from her country, before the years of grinding work, the bitter cold winters, the eyes of rejection every day telling her she was nothing, the pain of the neighborhoods that, trying to recreate home, only increased the loneliness, especially when the Christmas lights went up.

Once, he remembered them stopping by the window of an appliance store, where a TV was turned on. The late afternoon already seemed like night, and his hands were in his coat pockets, and her hands were in hers. It was a replay of a boxing match between Roberto Duran and some gringo, and a bunch of Latinos were gathered around the window, cheering him on, even though the fight had already taken place months before. "Knock him out! Knock him out!" they were yelling, in Spanish. "Túmbalo! Así—Manos de Piedra es el rey!"

And he remembered her jumping up and down and cheering with the rest of them, all lit up like it was her birthday. The redemption, the triumph, none of them would ever have.

Once again, Eddie Santiago's voice broke in with, "I miss you! I miss you!" And it pierced him, now, destroyed him.

"I've failed," he thought. "I became a part of this beautiful woman's illusion. Once she lost the streets paved with gold, there was only me. And I was no more real than them."

Of course, he'd tried. But what good is trying without succeeding? It was his country, and he was the one who should have done something. Or was it his country? Maybe finding her was his way of trying to run away from it. But if that was so, he should have told her from the very beginning. He should never have deceived her, by wanting her so much.

"Without you—the nights are like a ghost, a punishment..."

Quietly, tears streaming down his face, he backed away from the room. Silently, he slipped back into his coat, and headed for the door. It was too painful to be here. Or perhaps just overcrowded. He would give her an hour, then call from the street.

As he began to quietly slip out the door, he heard the song stop for a moment, and paused, thinking maybe he had been discovered. But it was only her pushing the rewind button. In a moment, the song was on again, and the dance was resumed.

The dance he could not answer, or look in the face.

ROMAN BRITAIN COMES TO EARTH

It was a good class, thought Professor Reginald Hartford. A very good class. Those naive students, spoon-fed on politically correct, liberal bullcrap; shaped like clay by the overeducated refugees from the real world who were his colleagues. Oh, how well they knew to love the victimized and defeated of history, whose only recourse was to fight back with guilt, to rewrite the chronicle of mankind from the bottom, from the point of view of the losers; to snipe at the triumphant world with impossible moral standards; to poison the great achievements with slave ships and dead Indians. Well, he had taught them a thing or two today, hadn't he? Especially when Alexy, that Russian immigrant lady's man in the back row, had dared to call his lecture "retrogressive." As Professor Hartford had then explained, " 'Retro' means 'backward' in Latin; 'gradi' means 'to step.' 'Retrogressus' is the past participle of 'retrogradi.' If England had not been conquered by the Romans, you would not have that word to throw in my direction." Anna, the girl who Alexy seemed to be trying to impress with his audacity, let out a sigh of admiration at the professor's comeback, as if he had just performed a spectacular magic trick; as Professor Hartford went on to explain: "Were it not for the Roman conquest of Britain, begun by Caesar, and perfected by Claudius and his successors, the language of Shakespeare and Dickens would not exist; the wealth of Latin would never have entered our vocabulary, we would be speaking an ancient tongue as flat as paper, our imaginations shackled. Without the roads and aqueducts of Rome, we would be centuries behind, not ahead; stragglers in the race to civilize. We would have been the Africa of Europe. Without the input of Roman laws, we would never have developed the legal consciousness that has become the basis of our modern political system, nor the ingrained commitment to human rights without which we might well have gone the way of the Nazis whenever danger knocked upon our door, or else become merely a more muscular form of banana republic. Likewise, Roman concepts of organization, military and civil, laid the foundations for the creation of the complicated administrative systems which insured our national success; just as Roman concepts of Citizenship and Empire have laid the foundations for the construction of our own rapidly growing European Union, as well as the most idealistic visions of international cooperation and human brotherhood." Reginald Hartford's eternally recurring point was that it made no sense to kidnap historical realities to use against the world one lived in; no sense to demand that progress dance lightly like a ballerina across the world map, or that the past join hands with Gandhi and banish its kings and generals, hurl its makers and shakers into the abyss. Why whip the back of time with liberal fantasies? "As bees help to cross-pollinate the fields and enrich the flowers which delight our eyes and the crops which give us life, so strife and conquest fertilize the fields of history. Alexander did not only conquer Persia and India. He impregnated them with Greek culture, and in turn, they expanded the Greek mind. Rome did not merely subdue Britain; it raised Britain out of a pit of darkness and gave it new means and a new horizon. Britain, in turn, rescued Africa from primitiveness and utter obsolescence. Oh, certainly, slavery got mixed up with it: a terrible injustice which was ultimately paved with gold. And then colonialism. Hard to see how it could become such a dirty word in a continent which practiced cannibalism."

Professor Hartford no longer had any fear to speak his mind, he had recently published two books which were well-reviewed by the "Conservative Culture Review": *Tools of Envy: Liliput's Unending War To Conquer History's Winners Through Guilt*; and *The Procreative Power of Conquest: Cultural Progress as a Product of Strife*. Powerful figures now backed Professor Hartford's right to enjoy the same level of intellectual freedom as those liberal pseudo-scholars who got away with all kinds of outrages against the truth: like Professor Jenkins who insisted that the ancient Egyptians were actually black rather than Hamitic, and talked about the Songhai Empire as though it were the equal of ancient Greece or Rome; or that crazy feminist teacher, Ms. Cousins, who called God "Goddess" and believed that everything wrong with the world could be explained in terms of patriarchy, her own particular form of the devil. Privately, Professor Hartford referred to her as an "intellectual Lorena Bobbitt."

Of course, the sanctuary which Professor Hartford now enjoyed was not unchallenged. Every once in a while, an irate colleague would give him a piece of his or her mind, or an overconfident student would attempt to pit his strident ignorance against the professor's seasoned and overwhelmingly erudite replies. Edna, an Irish girl who was nearly as irritating as Alexy, had come back with some Celtic-glorification response to Professor Hartford's lecture on the benefits of the Roman conquest of Europe. There were actually some concrete facts in there; she must have read some books on the Druids to match the prominent Celtic cross, which she always wore hanging down by that most distracting cleavage of hers. How titillating, to be able to utterly refute the arguments of a woman who had such provocative breasts. Poor Edna, after he had gotten through with her, she just stammered a few angry words which did nothing more than to prove her helplessness, and began doodling furiously in her notebook. Art school material, nothing more. By the time the bell had rung, Professor Hartford was the complete master of the terrain, presiding over a room of the converted or the silenced. He did not mind that divide, nor the smoldering residues of bitterness which would be confirmed in the low exam grades, which habitually reflect the disengagement of the proud. He was influencing the modern generation, winning some over to his side and driving others into shells of pure emotion. From now on, they would do nothing more than rant impotently without facts.

The drive home, after class, was always pleasant, so long as he had been in control; and he had been. Smiling, cheerful in spite of the violence which filled his subject, Professor Hartford slipped a cassette of his lecture into the tape deck and listened to himself once more. He was amused by Alexy's coughing in the background, too much vodka last night, he imagined. Or was he merely choking on his own words? Suddenly, in the midst of Professor Hartford's self-congratulatory thoughts, a car came out of nowhere, it seemed, hurtling around him from behind and roaring past his, nearly flying off the road as it continued onwards in the same direction he was going. "Speaking of vodka," the professor chuckled, trying to relax his nerves with humor. But then, suddenly, he heard a skid and a crash. The car in front of him had been driven off the road by two more coming in the opposite direction, driven just as impetuously.

The professor, stunned, pulled his car over to the side of the road to come to the aid of the wounded motorist. For Hartford was, of course, a civilized man whose only irremediable vice was that he did not like to feel guilty about the past; and civilized men come to one another's aid. "Say there, are you all right?" he asked the motorist, who staggered bloody and confused from his badly dented car. The professor kept his distance at first, you never know who you are dealing with: England is such a different country these days. "Mister, are you all right? Do you need an ambulance?"

"Need a f**king miracle," the man gasped, wrenching at his hair. "That's what I need. A bloody, f**ng miracle." And he fell to his knees and began praying to God, and crying at the same time.

"He must have a concussion," concluded the professor, edging closer to determine whether he ought to try to help. From the injured man's car, he heard a radio report trickling out from behind a shattered window. *There is currently no clear information concerning the source of the attack, but it is massive and appears to be directed from the air. We are receiving conflicting reports of cruise missiles, ICBMs, space-based lasers, and aircraft. The Soviet Union has denied any involvement. London, Manchester, Liverpool, and Glasgow have already received substantial damage, there are fires everywhere, and continuing explosions. The firepower involved is said to utterly dwarf what the old-timers remember during the Battle of Britain.*

"We're being invaded!" the injured motorist wept. "My God, Ruthie! She's not answering the cell phone!"

"This is impossible!" Professor Hartford exclaimed. "No one would dare. This is a big leap from some half-brained suicide bomber!"

Large numbers of wingless craft have been sighted the radio announcer continued; *reports describe them as being saucer-shaped, the classic image of the UFO. This latest report is now being compared to earlier reports which described aircraft consistent with the profile of stealth bombers, which admittedly have an otherworldly appearance. The Defense Ministry has thus far issued no clarifying statements.*

"Oh Jesus!" cried the injured driver, "it's a f**ng invasion from outer space!"

"It's a hoax!" Professor Hartford cried out, in relief. "It must be! Mister, don't worry—"

"Don't touch me!"

"Sorry! But I have to tell you, it's a hoax. It's obvious. Don't you remember the story from Halloween —1930-something? Orson Welles putting on a radio version of HG Wells' *War of the Worlds*? In a realistic format, complete with 'interrupted programming'? Thousands of Americans fell for it, thought it was something real, were scared out of their wits, and all it was was a radio drama, by God! Come on, mister, an invasion from outer space? Get real!"

But just then, the radio connection fizzled out.

"They've been burned alive there, in the studio!" the kneeling motorist exclaimed. "Burned by some kind of laser!"

"How do you know?" demanded Professor Hartford. "The connection was lost, that's all."

"I could hear the crackle of the heat. I could almost feel it! The building was melted by some kind of laser! They're all dead! "

"You're imagining it!" protested the professor.

Suddenly, the motorist's eyes filled with the awe of a pilgrim beholding an apparition. Who was it? Mary? Jesus?

Professor Hartford looked away from the motorist to what he was looking at. "My— my God!" he gasped. There, in the distance, was a formation of seven spinning wheels, flying on their sides, it seemed, with their rims pointed towards the ground.

"Flying saucers!" the man screamed.

"Experimental aircraft," Hartford blurted out, hopeful.

Three more cars hurtled past them, fleeing from the stretch of road which Hartford and the disabled motorist had been approaching. In the direction the cars had come from, over the tops of some trees, they saw a sudden pillar of flame rise up. They heard frightening roars and saw billows of smoke begin to pour into the sky, as though the whole world were bleeding upwards. There was a town over there. The professor would sometimes stop there on the way home to buy presents for his wife, a kindly woman who had no quarrel with patriarchy and avoided her husband's infatuation with controversy by knitting constantly. Suddenly, two more disks appeared from the direction of the flames, flying rapidly to join the formation, which had now come to a standstill, hovering some two hundred meters away.

Shaking, Professor Hartford extracted a cell phone from his pocket, and dialed home. There was no answer. "Please, Jane, answer! Please, answer!" He got the voicemail. "Jane, please, you must call me as soon as you are able! I am on my way home!"

"God, no! They're headed our way!" screamed the motorist. He wrenched himself up from his knees to try to run, then, seeing that it was impossible, he fell once more to the ground to pray, hoping God would not notice his momentary lapse of faith.

"Christ! It's the end!" gasped Professor Hartford.

But the formation suddenly changed gears and flew past them in a split second.

"They may have coated us with radiation!" the motorist wept, tears streaming down his face. "We'll die like those poor suckers from Hiroshima, in two or three weeks, or maybe a year."

"There's no reason to believe that," snapped Hartford.

Without warning, one of the disks stopped on the horizon, and in a single second bolted back to them and was directly overhead. The motorist collapsed to the ground, sobbing, unable to utter a single intelligible word. Professor Hartford, for his part, stood paralyzed, looking up at it. For a moment, the disk seemed to be studying him, staring at him, judging him. He imagined some terrible weapon aimed at his heart, a giant laser on the verge of burning him to a crisp or evaporating him without a trace. He wished he could look inside the window of the disk to see who it was who was aiming the weapon at him, to see the eyes that were about to watch him die. But he saw nothing. And suddenly, the disk was gone, and he was still alive, staggering towards his vehicle. To hell with the other man, he had to try to get home, to find Jane!

As he struggled to crawl back inside his car, Professor Hartford noted that the cassette inside his tape deck was still playing. The last thing he remembered hearing, just before he gunned on the engines to try to reach home, was: "The best thing that ever happened to Britain was to be conquered by the Romans."

HANDCUFFS

Handcuffs. Handcuffs. She just wanted what everybody else had. Why does Fate hand life to some people and make others have to fight for it? Why do some people receive joy and hope and love just by sitting on their sofas, while others have to climb Mt. Everest to find a toilet? Why does manna fall out of heaven for some people, while others have to dig into the vaults of the earth through uncaring stone to find a meal, a meal locked in some worthless speck of geological vomit they call a jewel? Why is the treasure of flesh and blood thrown under the wheels of the diamond, and the emerald, green as the trees that hide the snake? One half of the world materializes gold by pushing a button on its TV remote, while one half carries the threat of bombs falling from the sky on its back, and spreads its legs of flowers for sleepwalking pillagers to pluck; or else, it says no, the password to oblivion.

Handcuffs. All she wanted was what everybody else had. Some people who want to receive towers, palaces rising up like smoke from a burning earth, mansions in the clouds that seem to float above the pigsty, disembodied stomachs of the earth. Inside their doors are carpets fit for kings, and delicate paintings of flames. Pet cats slink like little tigers amidst magazines and figurines; they, too, sailed into the sky aboard Noah's Ark, the ship of the few. They are loved more than the hands that lit the sun. Some people want, and they hear the sound of rain clawing at the roof, they hear the sound of angry landlords waiting in the mailbox, the sound of children's eyes searching for presents on Christmas morning, the sound of jobs landing like a single coin in a tin cup, the sound of aching hands and aging faces condemning them from the mirror, condemning them for cowardice, the cowardice of being good, of playing by the rules, of obeying the law, of lying down with their family in a coffin.

Who wrote the book? a vengeful angel asks, charging from Heaven with the sword of a free thought. The book of law is but a tomb! The strong lifted their leg and urinated on the world as it was, they marked their territory with a law and a jail, ejaculated a priest into the vagina of what they stole to impregnate the crime with a broken will.

See it in the faces of the former slaves, they never recovered from their chains, the whip marks remain inside, on the backs of their souls!

See it in the faces of the proud *indígenas*, they fought like jaguars, like pumas, until their blood turned into stone; then they remained silent like birds who vowed never more to fly. 'We will carry our intestines to you, you shall have your silver and your gold, but never more will you hear the jungle the way it used to be. The trees deny you! The mountain peaks look down on you, our frozen tears forever loom above you. Our snow-peaked defeat.'

Handcuffs. When wars are over, crime begins. They call it crime, but it is only the reaction of history, the instinct of the patriot who has been dragged into another world.

Invaded by the windows of your stores, his mind sees freedom like you see freedom; he wants his heart back from behind the glass. He wants to learn to speak the language of the dollar bill, and the plastic card that the altar eats and then obeys with gifts of green paper, the paper words the world speaks, which end hunger and loneliness, which resurrect the impotent man and restore the petals of his withering family to the stalk of his pride. Without this Eucharist, men are ghosts.

They wander through every desire without substance, cannot touch a face, cannot lift a glass of water to their lips.

Handcuffs. Her ancestors, long ago, were Paez Indians, they fought and lost, they were pressed into cages deceived by the open sky, helping hands came to lift them up without their land, farms awoke on the other side of a piece of paper; cities and haciendas beckoned with breakfasts of sugar water, and lives of crawling. Babies of the damned cry like arrows aimed at the hearts of the ones who love them. Good men don't listen. Bad ones pick up their children, and blow out the candles of deaf saints.

Handcuffs. Miranda, wasn't she a princess in the middle of a storm? The money was in the side of a carry-on, nice Colombian leather. It was going back, back from the noses of America, back to a little outfit of perverse, angry men with insatiable d**ks, protective stags of the wounded herd that wanted the revenge of living. They were bandits, all right, these pint-sized capos, like crumbs of broken glass left behind by the shattering of the chandeliers of the great cartels. The giants were dead, shot and displayed like the animals hunted by Hemingway, or carted off to gringo prisons in their pajamas. But the laws of physics remained. Matter can neither be created nor destroyed. You will not pay us with the green land God gave us, pay us for the mere fact of being human beings by leaving us masters in our own country? We will pay ourselves with the harvest of the white genie, we will serve the despair of paradise with our carnivorous leaf, our sacrament turned into a bomb. History is like water; it will flow into any form you give it. Conquest and self-defense will pursue each other forever, like butterflies that change into birds, then into wolves, then into rivers roaring with the voice of native warriors who have become water.

Handcuffs. Miranda's mother and three sisters lived in Popayán, divided between deaths; and a new generation was clamoring beside their skirts, from within their bellies, and in the eyes of irresistible boys who would not stay. One brother who had not come in from the land had been sliced open like a fish by the paramilitaries; they filled his body with stones to sink him in the river, under the shadow of helicopters that did not care. The other brother was maybe with the guerrillas, maybe with a wild girl who used to sing in bars. They had vanished around the same time. Miranda imagined them fleeing like Adam and Eve from Eden, as God hurled the lightning bolt of her brother's death at their frail farm, a last drop of Paez history. Meanwhile, two more sisters lived in the Big Apple, as did Miranda.

Miranda remembered when Ofelia first came to New York, when Ofelia was new and not broken in. It was in the middle of the winter, and the wind was spitting out the people of the tropics, lashing their brown and black faces with ice and sleet, brutal rebuffs from a gray racist sky. Then the snow came, mountains of it pouring down from helpless heaven. Miranda was working near home, cleaning offices, washing away her dreams from the floor with a mop. Ofelia, in high heels, completely unprepared for the weather, was due to be returning from a job interview at that very moment. Excusing herself, Miranda struggled back through the snow to retrieve an extra pair of boots from home, because Ofelia had left when the skies only seemed to be bluffing. Tortured by the thought of her sister's frozen feet, the overly idealistic heels trying to navigate their way through incursions of snow already up past the ankles, Miranda stumbled back out into the storm, heading towards the street her blinded, ice-pelted sister must be trying to follow back. "Aiay!, it's like we're being stoned!" Miranda said. "Like we were adulteresses!" She wondered why the Bible, with its abundant stories of calamity, had no blizzards to add to the torments of sinners, then remembered that the Holy Land was a desert; sandstorms were as close as it could come. Above her, the elevated train track lay silent like a prehistoric beast beaten into submission by the ice age; icicles hung like fossils from its impotence; the periodic roar had not been heard for over twenty minutes. "Aiay!" A huge cascade of falling ice shattered by her feet, while another collapse merely disappeared into the snow with a heavy thud, like a falling body, like some poor soul finally giving in to what they all felt and choosing a day of white to leave the impurity of the world. With her head down, pushing against the wind, she passed by men with shovels, standing still like statues as they tried to smell the time left to the storm, to decide whether they should resist it yet or just wait.

Painfully, the extra boots in a bag in her hand, she blinked her snow-crusted eyelids. A taxi glided in and out of view, seemingly free of the laws of gravity—a ghost car driven by a ghost, somebody's shortcut home that was going to take hours. "Dios mío, where the hell is Ofelia?" Miranda asked herself. "Her poor, poor feet!" And she began to cry.

But not long afterwards, she finally saw her sister, she recognized the "Inca cap" that Ofelia didn't wear before the interview, so as not to disorder her hair. But now the interview was over, and the hat was on her head as tight as could be. Seeing the cap—it was like Columbus seeing land! (Columbus, that *hijo de puta*. But the land was beautiful.)

"Ofelia! Ofelia!" cried Miranda, joyfully.

As though destined to alarm Miranda even more than her high heels had already been able to accomplish, Ofelia chose that very moment to lose her balance in the middle of an intersection, suddenly spinning wildly about and hurling her arms out to the sides in a melodramatic effort to keep herself from falling. She was an utter novice walking on ice; this was her first time; she was like a virgin who, for the first time, hurts.

"Ai, no!" gasped Miranda, rushing towards her falling sister. But somehow, heels and all, Ofelia persisted, against her will she skated in the street like Oksana Baiul, she imitated the tragic acrobatics of their race which lost its footing but not its life, which lost its grace, but not its spirit, even when that spirit had to hide, and fire had to assume the form of stone.

"Ofelia! Ofelia!" cried Miranda, embracing her in the middle of the street.

A car, unsure of its brakes, honked, Miranda dragged Ofelia to the corner as the car *did* stop, bowing down to the love of the two sisters.

"Ofelia! Ofelia! Are you all right?" demanded Miranda. "Look—I brought you boots! Here, you have to get out of those heels right away! Can you feel your feet?"

But Ofelia just laughed, it was like being a child in a world of magic; she stuck out her tongue and tasted a snowflake, then remembering that she had heard that no two snowflakes are alike, she said: "There goes the last of its kind! Melted on my tongue!" Stoically, she stood still as Miranda struggled to get the boots onto her feet.

"Are you all right?" Miranda asked again.

Ofelia hugged and kissed her and said: "My first day of snow! A sister who loves me! My feet can fall off, for all I care!" And leaning on each other with love, they fought their way back through the storm to the little apartment, the *cuchitril* they had decorated with their tastes and souls until it had become a mansion, a little mansion in the cold.

Handcuffs. But life does not linger on the peaks of its unsustainable highs. It flows downwards into the *masa* of every day, the flour of the ordinary with which you make the food you eat to live. Cleaning. Watching kids: rich kids with the innocent hands of utterly different lives, which cling to you in the middle of the night, as old dreams sit heavily upon your chest. Buried alive like a Vestal Virgin by equal aspirations in an unequal world, by a bored soul that wants spice. Days, grueling without a rose. Ofelia has a boyfriend, now, a swollen belly, Miranda's boyfriend has left, she's alone with the songs they danced to, and now, this guy Pedro, a cousin of Ángel, who's Ofelia's *muchacho*, drops in with his Leon Trotsky glasses and starts talking shit about the gringo brainwash. "They've turned us all into colonies. We dig up the ground underneath our feet and put it in a ship bound for America. Do you know the international division of labor? Bananas and coffee don't stack up against machines. We sell cheap crap, they sell shit that costs. We need a product that can command a high price, not this shit that keep us in the Third World."

"Well?" she asked him.

He pointed to his nose and sniffed. Since she didn't get it, he did it again.

Pedro was an intellectual; he wouldn't put his preaching into practice. he had chosen criticism, not risk. He would whitewash the controversial, bless it, but not carry it.

She didn't think too much of what he said at that time, but somewhere in her mind, which loved books, but mainly novels and metaphysics, not politics, he had made an impression. Where others saw a devil, she now saw an act of self-defense. Where others saw a sin, she saw only a gamble.

Handcuffs. Geraldino was the New York boss of Lilliput. The cartel fragment's great recruiter. At first, over drinks in a club that was a whirlpool for the lonely, who flaunted their depression with low-cut blouses and tight-fitting jeans, he just joked about it. "The Great White Way—Broadway, or is it powder? Nice guys, these Americans, they help us out a lot!" He took her to have a *bareto*, a good deep smoke of pot in the parking lot, then drove her around in his car, which was like a God's chariot. "You know, this girl Alicia made $10,000 last month," he told her.

"Oh yeah, how?" she asked him, becoming nervous.

He motioned with his finger to his mouth. "One airplane trip and some Ex-lax."

She looked out the window stoically.

"That was *manteca*. Heroin. Coca gets less, but hey, it beats mopping floors. Say, you know—your sister is pregnant, and your family is rolling the giant boulder up the mountain like that guy from the myths. It's something to think about."

But the idea of going down there first and coming back with bags of drugs in her intestines was too much. "I'm afraid of the dogs," she said. Ever since she was a child, the big dogs. Neighbors had had one who mauled a boy sneaking onto their property to get a fruit; he was covered with scars for life. Another one had chased little Betina on a horse, and she had fallen off into the river. The thought of the dogs.

"They won't smell a thing, you chew gum and use deodorant. You just don't want to sweat a lot."

"What if they x-ray me?"

"They don't do that unless you're shaking in your boots. All you need is a little nerve. You've got nice tan skin, you won't turn red."

But it was too much. Miranda said no. He didn't ruin the nice time out by insisting.

Handcuffs. Funny how some ideas live inside you like an animal, like a tapeworm in your gut, they wear you out, they get their way. Miranda's world had cracks in it. Ofelia and Ángel had been fighting, Ofelia had to rush to the ER with some terrible pains in her stomach. "My God, the baby's dying!" she cried out.

"Maybe you're giving birth!" shouted Miranda.

"No, it's only seven months!"

"Maybe it's premature!"

"It's like someone stabbed my baby with a knife! I'm feeling it! That damned Ángel, he'll be the death of us yet!"

It was a false alarm, but things were shaky. Then, there was the giant toy tank in the store window that their cousin Linda's boy wanted. It had a rotating turret with a little guy you could put in or take out, flashing lights and a barrel that fired plastic pellets. You could steer it with a radio signal by remote control, and it could climb up a ramp.

"Oh please, mama, buy it, buy it for me!" he begged Linda, over and over again, like a vine climbing up a tree with tears.

"No, baby, not now," she said. "Damn!" she told Miranda. "Why do they make such expensive toys these days? Remember when we were kids, we used to play with a stick? A stick and a hoop? No!" Linda said as the boy persisted.

"But it lights up in the dark!"

"So, what good is that? The bad guys will see it and blow it up."

"No they won't, it's too strong, their bullets will bounce off!"

"Our country is already violent enough," Linda retorted, "we don't need any more violence. This time for your birthday, I'm going to buy you a Barbie—no, just kidding!" she said, as he began to wail.

Miranda thought, Why do we always have to be counting pennies in this cornucopia? Why, when paradise is filled with fruit trees, do you have to cut off your arm for a coconut, and cut off your leg for a mango? The child's disappointment outraged her, it was like they whipped you with other people's joy, flagellated you with thirst you could not quench, shoved your face into gold coins you would never own; in the eyes of your kids they turned you into parents who didn't care, or weaklings who could not provide. They branded you with the burning hot poker-iron of loser.

Geraldino came back.

Handcuffs. This time he told her there was another end to the business. "There's there and there's here. Here's where the money's made There's people down there to be paid. They smuggle the drugs in, we smuggle the money back."

"Don't you launder the bucks?" she asked him, enjoying the church of the car where all was forgiven by the god of reality, all that could be hidden.

"It's not that easy to work with banks these days," he said. "You need a real in, and we don't have it. For a while, we had this Belgian Jew in the jewelry shop, till he lost his nerve, and quit on Yom Kippur. So now we move it down in money belts, bags, suitcases. Dogs don't smell money," he added.

Miranda couldn't stand the idea of having bags of dope inside her that could break open and hammer her to death from the inside; and having to pass the gauntlet of dogs, that was like going into Hell. But moving the money in the opposite direction?

"No," she said. "I'm not cut out for this. I don't have the guts. They'd hear my heartbeat from a mile away, I'd bite my fingers off along with my fingernails."

But Geraldino only smiled. "They say one of your brothers became a guerrilla."

"Nobody knows that," she retorted. "Maybe he just went to a safe place to be with his girl, to love her and have kids like people are supposed to do."

"Or maybe he's a real man with balls," said Geraldino. "If a guerrilla kills your brother, you become a paramilitary; if a paramilitary kills your brother, you become a guerrilla. The politics doesn't matter, in the end, it's only about being a man."

"Those ideas are bringing our country to ruin," Miranda protested.

"Maybe you've got it in your blood," he suggested. She didn't acknowledge his idea. "Paez?" He saw a flash leap into her eyes, a spark. "Your ancestors knew how to fight."

She said, "I'll think about it."

Handcuffs. She was dressed up that day in a stylish white suit with white slacks, a pair of sunglasses fit for a movie star, who was always one step ahead of the glare. Glasses of a chameleon, changing color equal to the tricks of the light. The bag smelled fresh, recently crafted, singing praises to the artisans of Colombia with every step; cosmetics, a comb, two magazines, and a water bottle protected it. The money was sewn into layers inside the fabric, undetectable. Five others were part of the mission, three women and two boys; they would swim together to their country like a school of porpoises, swim through the sky in an airplane, which was as magnificent and fragile as their plan.

As Miranda took back her ticket and stepped into the waiting room, a security woman made up like an Avon representative passed by, spreading leaflets into every hand she encountered. On the leaflet, in Spanish and English, it warned that any money brought back to Colombia over the personal amount allowed to travelers must be declared.

Miranda began to sweat. Why this warning? This was not a standard feature of travel, as far as she knew. Did federal agents have a tip? Were they setting up a crystal-clear legal environment in which to prosecute Geraldino's money-bearers? She wanted to call him, but maybe the undercover cops wanted to see who went for a phone. She must wait to call. But the flight was ready to board.

Out of the corners of her eyes, she could see one of her co-conspirators on her cell phone. The woman nodded with a tight face, submitting to an invisible pep talk, and proceeded to board the plane. Miranda, who was pretending to perfect her eyeliner, the sunglasses raised like a lookout on top of her head, packed up and followed.

They were all sitting down in their seats, clearly intending to leave the country, when five men in FBI jackets and six or seven security personnel, including two women, suddenly barged onto the plane like terrorists. A man with a New York Yankees jacket, corduroy pants, and shades as dark as the night came on board with them. He had a Latin face, but wouldn't show it. "Ladies and gentlemen, we need to ask a few passengers some questions," an FBI operative said. "Please remain seated and cooperate fully with our agents."

The New York Yankee then proceeded to walk down the aisle, pointing out members of Geraldino's team to the cops. He found four of them, but passed by Miranda, who felt her heart was about to jump out of her chest like a frog.

They took them out into the connectible tunnel that joined the plane to the terminal and began to question them.

Horrified, yet also hopeful, like someone who has found a good hiding place during a massacre, as the people all around her begin to fall, Miranda waited in her seat.

"No, no!" she heard one of the women screaming, "the people will see! Don't take my clothes!"

In wretched Spanish, seemingly spoken with a mutilated tongue, but then, this was their country and what did they owe the Spanish language?, a female agent was saying, "Nobody's going to see you." And in English, she was saying to someone else, "Nobody wears underwear like that anymore. Looks like she's wearing an inflatable life jacket, gonna float all the way to Colombia! Here, mamma, gonna make you skinny, come on, we'll make you more shapely now, let the padding come off! See, she's not chunky anymore, just became J-Lo."

"No, no! I'm naked! I'm naked!" the woman was screaming hysterically. Miranda imagined her make-up coming off, washed away by tears, while the agent was saying, "This don't count as naked in nobody's book. Maybe the pope's. Lotta money here, huh? And look, here's the leaflet we gave you, right along with your ticket. Do you know what the word 'jail' means?"

"*Carcel.*"

"You got it. Car-sul on the way."

Miranda became aware that she hadn't moved for ten minutes; she was frozen as though impaled on a stake in the Tower of London. Her Indian face was as pale as a Spaniard's, her mouth was dry like a country where it had not rained for months, and all the corn has wilted. "Come on, airplane," she thought. "Rev up those engines. Get us the hell out of here. Deliver me to the sky. Carry me above this crazy world, ruled by thieves, where people who loved are turned upside down into criminals!"

Handcuffs. But just then, like a priest to deliver the last rites, one of the captured women came back into the plane with an FBI agent. "That one," she said, pointing at Miranda with a finger that seemed like a gun. Miranda could see the flash, hear the explosion, smell the gunpowder, feel the bullet flying into her heart, look down and see the blood. She should have maintained the impassive face for which her race was known, the mystery that enraged and terrified the Spaniards. But she could not prevent herself from exclaiming, *"Hijo de puta sapo!" You son-of-a bitch snitch!*

"Miss, we need to talk to you," the agent said, indicating that she rise and follow him.

Miranda's head was spinning, she was dizzy, falling in her own mind, though she stood up with surprising command of her body. "This way— *with* your bag," the agent said.

"Too bad, such a nice, well-dressed girl," somebody was saying in English.

"Don't cut my bag," said Miranda, in a voice that was more the twitch of a corpse than an act of life, though it came out clear and bold. But she had no hope; she had heard from friends how Customs slashed through bags of coffee, ripped heels off of shoes, and dismantled radios in such a way that they could never be put back together again. It wouldn't be any different here, in this direction. A nearly invisible blade was out, in someone's hand, the black inner lining of the bag was cut, green blood oozed out, blood of paper, the reward of thieves, and the lifeline of good hearts living behind glass walls, on the other side of the world. Who wouldn't smash the wall? Who wouldn't? Who wouldn't lift the hammer of a crime to live?!

Like a surgeon performing an operation, removing a tumor, the hand extracted a giant wad of hundred-dollar bills from the bag—then more. "A lot of our boys blowing their life out of their nose," one of the security ladies said, staring at Miranda disapprovingly.

Maybe, thought Miranda, *they want something more in life than walking around with a walkie-talkie like you.* And she said, "Nuestros muchachos faltan mucho para vivir." *Our kids are missing a lot that they need to live.*

The woman told her, "This isn't the way to right the world."

"This is war," Miranda said. "The war to be happy. —Once upon a time, we were happy in the green forest, if the trees had fruit and the streams had fish. You took that happiness away from us. You changed happiness and took it back to your own land. You put it on a high shelf, out of our reach."

"Tell it to the judge," the woman said. "Add some years to your time."

"*Sapo!*" Miranda spat at the traitor.

"No use to hate me now," the woman said. "Why should my life be ruined, and not yours?"

"You're already licking their shoes to get less time," Miranda told her.

"And what of it? We're going to prison now, compatriot bitch. We'll be doing a lot of licking, might as well start now! *Puta!*" And she broke down, crying.

"Put your hands up against the wall," someone was telling Miranda. As she stood there, exposed and vulnerable, she felt someone's hands patting her down; already her flesh belonged to someone else.

"Put your hands behind your back."

She didn't want to obey merely because following orders seemed so cowardly, a confession of inferiority, and yet, she did exactly as she was told, like a machine, a machine of submission; her body was enchanted by their power which began to caress her muscles from the inside, to quiet her, like land sung to sleep by a corral.

She felt the embrace of the first cuff about her wrist, and then the other; her hands were chained together like twins, devoured by circles of steel that were passionate in their devotion to her helplessness.

She felt conquered, like a woman naked underneath a man who rides horses in the day; a terrible sexual electricity she did not understand flowed through her body, her knees felt weak, she felt like collapsing, her captivity reached her most intimate parts. Weren't there pictures of hangmen having erections? It was like an act of sex, this being eaten alive, this being prey, this being kissed by the jaws of the lion, a form of sexual intercourse between police and criminal, winner and loser, this was the shameful core of human beings and the secret of history. This eroticism of destroying others, and of being destroyed.

"You're going to be doing a long time," the security lady told her, now that the cuffs were on, a hard, iron face that looked like a lot of men had done her wrong when her badge was on the table. "I hope you like orange jump suits. This nice white suit's gonna have to come off, till sooner or later, you'll be just another naked bitch standing in the shower."

For a long time, Miranda had held out, but this last little bit, this last unmistakable proof of where the power lay, proved too much, the gates finally blew open, she burst into tears and wailed like a baby. "Oh no! Oh no, God, no! No! No!"

"Should've thought of that before," the tough lady told her.

A strong hand grasped Miranda's incapacitated arm, she heard a voice tell her, "Come on," and followed the rest of them, well-dressed young Colombians who had just ruined their lives, led out of the terminal to a waiting police van, like captives in a Roman triumph, while mobs of travelers headed to happy reunions and exotic vacations pressed their faces against the vast windows of the lobby to observe the spectacle.

And at that moment she wept for Ofelia's feet, and Ofelia's unborn child, and for the tank dreamt of by Linda's boy, and for her large and creaking family and for her dead brother and her missing brother, and her country torn by war and broken by poverty and for her Paez ancestors and five hundred years of being lost.

As she stepped into the police van, far weaker than she had believed, but also far more beautiful, she thought, "Handcuffs do not lie! For five hundred years this has been our history, and this is our history, now. Thank you, handcuffs. Thank you for not pretending!"

THE TAROT READER

It was closing time, but I barged in anyway, past the jingling bells in the doorway that warned her, past the pink and white candles, the bundles of sage hanging from the wall, the poster of the Virgin, and the golden angel staring dreamily towards the things we all want, which were inside of its head.

She had just rolled up the wads of bills and put them into her bag. When she saw me coming, she started, and you could tell her heart froze.

"Doña Ada," I raged. "Explain yourself!"

You could see the faces of hundreds of clients spinning around frantically in her eyes, her memory sliding over the ice of everything she had ever done wrong in life. There was a look of horror and desperation, and a vacuum in her soul, as she tried to place me, to pull me out of the silent masses she carried with her. Her expression had no quarrel with the guilt. She completely believed it, you could tell. She just wanted to remember what she had done to *me*.

Shaking with fury, yet also triumphant, because I had found her, I threw the photo of Elizabeth down onto the table.

"Please," she said. "This is a sacred table."

"You were wrong!" I exclaimed. "Wrong! You told me that she was not the one for me! I stopped trying. I let her go. I moved on to other things. For a while, those things covered over the emptiness; they hid the mistake from me. I was too busy to realize what I had done. But now, too late, I realize she was the one for me: she was my soulmate. The emptiness! The pain!" I smashed my fist down upon the table. I picked the photograph up, brandishing it like a weapon with which I meant to kill her; I shook it in her face, then threw it down in front of her again. "Remember? I showed you the photo then! Remember?"

Doña Ada seemed to relax. The tension was released. She did not want to be strangled in the back of her store because of her sins; but she had no fear of dying if she was right. "This is a sacred table," she told me, once again.

It was still covered with the plain black tablecloth onto which she cast the cards from her Tarot deck.

"Sacred enough to count your money on?" I demanded.

She carefully tied the money bag shut, and placed it behind her, on a shelf.

"You wanted her?" she asked me, casually.

"I loved her! I wanted her! I needed her! But you told me she wasn't the one for me!"

"Is that what I told you?" she asked me, softly.

I trembled with fury, I was honestly thinking of killing her. What did I have to lose?

"Sit," she told me, quietly. She sat down in her chair at the table, and, from a drawer underneath the tablecloth, took out her deck of cards. "Sit," she said again.

I don't know why, but I did as she said. I sat down in the chair opposite her and picked up the photo of Elizabeth I had carried with me for all these years. How tender, how sweet, how intelligent, how vivacious was the woman I had frozen in time, immersed in the preservative of a photograph, like an embryo in a pickle jar! In those days, I had imagined that such women must grow on trees, like fruits in an orchard. Now I understood how rare they were—like sightings of a bird verging on extinction. All over the world, I had searched for another Elizabeth, without ever finding one. She was happy now with someone else. She was the mother of three children.

"Look!" I demanded, shoving the photograph of Elizabeth over to Doña Ada's side of the table. "Look!"

She put down the cards in her hands and picked up the photo. "I did this the last time," she said, after a while. She was beginning to remember. "You wanted me to look at her photo before I drew the cards."

"You said she was beautiful," I said.

"It was the truth."

"You said her face was beautiful like the surface of the ocean, and that in her eyes, you could see what was in her depths, leaping above the surface like a breaching whale. Her face was like a sculpture, her soul like a habitable planet in the void. I was so moved by what you said that I decided to place my complete trust in your reading."

Doña Ada returned the photograph to me.

"I *can't* move on," I said, answering the implicit challenge. When you are with a psychic, you, too, begin to lose your dependence on words.

Ada looked at me, then closed her eyes, summoning herself.

"Don't do me with the routine," I told her, determined not to fall for her tricks again. "Why did you tell me that shit? Why did you destroy my life?"

Ada opened her eyes, which were shining now, with a look of defiance and indifference. If I meant to kill her, it did not matter to her. She turned the cards towards her and began to flip through them.

"You're not supposed to look when you throw the cards down," I told her.

"Who says I'm throwing the cards down?" she answered. She began to carefully pull out cards, one by one, and to lay them down on the table in front of us. "I can't remember the whole spread," she said, at last, "but I remember these cards: The Lovers, The Hermit, The Page of Pentacles, The Magician, The Queen of Cups, The World, and The Five of Wands."

I regarded her with controlled savagery. "Your reading was entirely wrong. I talked with one of my friends since then, who is an expert in the Tarot, and he told me, while I could still remember some of the cards, that you should have predicted a life of bliss for us. Why did you tell me it wouldn't work? You irresponsible and incompetent fraud! Or are you only a witch who wants to torture human souls, to derail our rightful destinies and stand back and watch the train wrecks which you have created?!" I stood up violently, again, as though I might overturn her table and trash the place, delivering it to utter chaos.

She only smiled, faintly, so as not to set me off; but she could not help herself.

"Sit down," she said again.

Looking at me for a while, watching my body shake and resist, then finally sink down again into the chair across from her, she said, at last: "Your friend was not here. There is more to this than the cards that are drawn. Did you tell him their position? More than that, do you know how much space there is inside each card? Do you know that each one is a universe unto itself?" She shook her head at my ignorance and went on to demand: "Do you think the cards are castle gates meant to lock the reader out? I go in through the door whenever I wish." And again, she shook her head. Slowly, she worked with the cards. You could tell there was still some nervousness left in her hands, which trembled slightly in my presence, but it was only a remnant of what she had first felt when I burst into her little storefront property, with the thought of smashing her to bits. The flame of fear had burned down to a few embers, inevitable traces of human nature which none of us can fully master. She spread the cards out in the form of a cross, with the Queen of Cups in the center, the Page of Pentacles laid on top of it, the Lovers above it, the Five of Wands below it, the Hermit to the right of it, and the Magician to the left of it. Off to the side, she laid The World.

"That card!" I exclaimed, pounding my fist, again, on the table. "It is the card of bliss, union, the attainment of all dreams, fulfillment! On that day, the card meant that Elizabeth and I would have been perfect together! And look—is that not the end position, the final result? You lied to me, Doña Ada! You unredeemable bitch!"

"I remember the reading well," she told me in a barely audible voice, her eyes showing that she had already drifted away into some impervious trance state which was like a sturdy house that keeps all who dwell within it dry, as the rain pours down mercilessly on those who remain outside. I was furious to be so close to this woman, only one or two steps away from her throat, with the power to kill her throbbing in my hands, and yet to feel that I was on the other side of a wall behind which she felt perfectly safe. "It wasn't conventional: my reading. But why should it have been? You do not have to walk in a straight line unless you are trying to prove you are not drunk." She nodded, which was a way of washing her hands. Like Pontius Pilate, or merely someone working in a hospital who had just changed the sheets of a sick patient? "I told you exactly what I felt."

"What you felt ruined my life," I told her.

She shook her head again, as though the possibility of there being people like me in the world utterly amazed her. And then she began to explain: "Elizabeth was the Queen of Cups. The Goddess of Love. The Beautiful One with the Giant Heart. The one who was the center of the reading. You wanted her. You wanted to be with her. Over here, was The World, your union with Elizabeth, your euphoric and inseparable connection, the end result of one possible trajectory of your life. The end of one road you could have traveled. But, before that, there was a fork in the road. To get to The World, you had to take the right turn; to choose the correct path."

"You told me not to take it!"

"Here," Doña Ada told me, warding off my objection, "is The Lovers."

"We were the Lovers. We *should* have been the Lovers." I looked at that card, with a naked woman and a naked man standing near each other beneath an angel with spreading wings who seemed to rest upon a cloud. It was as if we were pieces on a chessboard who he was on the verge of placing together.

"It is not just about lovers," she explained. "It is about choices, about dilemmas in love, *who* to love, *whether* to love, whether to love only skin deep or to reach down into the soul. Of course, a beautiful and romantic love is its highest possibility."

"You didn't say that then."

"I am sure I did," she objected. "Below it in the spread is the Five of Wands," she continued, forging ahead. She was flowing now, like a hissing, frothing river, racing amidst sharp rocks, like angry waters plunging off the side of a mountain that weren't going to stop for anything, least of all for me. My rage was being reflected, like sunlight from a mirror, directly back into my eyes. It meant she was no longer afraid. In that card, there was a band of men who seemed boisterous, to be shouting and fighting each other with giant poles.

"So what?" I demanded. "Strife. It's everywhere. Conflict. Struggle. Every couple has to face that. We could have overcome it."

"Competition," she said, sweeping my interpretation aside. "If you want something, you have to fight for it. Do you know all that Jason went through to get the Golden Fleece? Did you ever read the Arabian Nights? Don't you remember all the trials that the suitors had to go through to win the hand of the princess? And the more beautiful she was, the harder they had to struggle."

I felt a sudden wave of nausea in my stomach, a lump in my throat. I couldn't speak.

Doña Ada pointed to the other cards in the spread. "The Page of Pentacles. That's you." What a blow; I felt that I was shrinking by the minute. "Elizabeth needed the Knight of Wands, or even the Hanged Man. A woman such as her deserved nothing less than that audacity, that sacrifice. But here you are, the Page of Pentacles, with your industrious, hard work, your incipient economic success, your mastery of trivia and small victories. Do you see a hero here? A hero worthy of her hand? And here you are again, this time, in the incarnation of the Hermit. Transfixed by a solitary nature, that in your case, has nothing to do with deep reflection; it is all about egotism. You do not physically withdraw from others, which might make you wise, but deny them your heart even as you dwell under the same roof; you live among others without ever giving yourself, without ever sharing yourself."

"How can you say that?" I protested, mad with pain. She might as well have shot me with a gun.

"You are in front of me. Am I wrong?"

"You have no right to judge me in that way, to rule my possibilities, like a dictator!"

"I am a psychic."

"You are a monster!"

"I am a mirror."

"You are a liar!"

"I am a Magician," she said, pointing to the final card. Everything was still, I could hear the ticking of the antique clock on the wall, which was like a heartbeat coming from Heaven. It seemed that we, ourselves, were not alive. I could not even hear us breathing. "I am the Trickster," she said, at last. "I am the Alchemist, the one who can transmute lead into gold, the one who can put the dragon that guards the treasure that is yours to sleep, the one who can quiet the unforgiving storm, calm the vindictive sea, and deceive the wind that would tear you to pieces. I can show you the way to everything you have ever desired, or trick you into walking off a cliff, by making it seem to lead to paradise."

I stood up, now, my rage as fierce as when I had first walked in the store.

But she merely looked at me with pity, and my fury hung its head in shame.

This time, it was she who pounded her fist on the table. I was taken completely by surprise. "Look at her!" she demanded, indicating the Queen of Cups. I saw the Queen peering intensely at the mysterious lamp in her hands, as though her own exotic power had been externalized and she was looking at herself; and I saw the tiny angel hidden underneath her throne, which might have been our child if only I had had the courage to court her. Ada did not need to say more, and yet, she went on, in spite of it. For men such as me, who cling so madly to the past, must be definitively led full circle. We must have others tie up the loose ends of our lives for us. "Look at her," she said again, this time in a tone of reverence. "She is the Queen of Cups." And pointing back to the Five of Wands, to the men battling each other with giant logs, she said: "She deserved a man who was willing to fight for her. A hero. Look at these men. Battling each other so ardently, with entire tree trunks, it seems, which they are wielding as weapons. And all I asked of you, to win her, was to love her enough to go to her in spite of what my cards said!"

Again, she shook her head. She was sure she was right and did not care if I killed her over it. I was sure she was right, now, too.

Tears in my eyes, I removed the photograph of Elizabeth from the table and placed it back into my wallet. I didn't know what to say. She didn't either.

In days of old, men had crossed the sea for the woman they loved, braved oceans of towering dark waves in fragile wooden ships, because they could not stand to be separated from the one who they knew was God's gift to their soul. They had battled dragons, searched for treasures on the other side of the world, fought off lions and serpents, pitted themselves against mighty warriors in single combat; Orpheus had descended, with his aching heart and songs of love, into the frightening depths of the Underworld—the terrible, tortured land of the dead, from which no living man had ever returned—to reclaim the woman whose embraces he could not forget. These men in love, these heroes of love, had climbed great mountains because their hearts would not succumb to prudence; they had pulled themselves up rocky ledges until their hands bled, and leapt over chasms thousands of feet deep that stood between them and the women who waited for them on the other side; no slip, no fall, no plunge to the bottom of the earth seemed more dangerous to them than a life lived without her in their arms. These great men, dragged behind uncompromising, valiant, generous hearts, had overcome a thousand deadly obstacles for love. I had failed to fight my way past a deck of Tarot cards. Was this the man that Elizabeth deserved? This woman who, had she lived in other times, would have been burned forever into human memory like Penelope, like Helen, like Eurydice?

Fate, you are no match for true love! The fault was all mine. I had proved myself unworthy by not making war on Destiny.

"I am sorry," I said at last, as I forced the wallet back into my pocket. Always, before this, I had felt that the photograph of Elizabeth belonged with me. Now, I felt sordid, corrupt, contemptible for having it; as if, somehow, I had kidnapped Elizabeth at gunpoint and was keeping her chained up in my dirty basement, which had taken the form of a photograph. "I am sorry, Doña Ada," I said, again, as I prepared to leave. "I failed the test. I have no one but myself to blame."

Whatever craft this clever woman used to survive in a world that she sometimes had to con to get by in, it now gave way to sympathy. And I could tell that it was genuine. You could see that she wanted to wipe my tears away, but that would have been too intimate. So, she spontaneously drew a card from her deck and laid it down on the table.

It was the Eight of Cups. She and I just looked at it, without saying a thing. There was a man in a cloak or coat, leaning on a staff, weary and defeated-looking as he walked away from a stack of eight cups symbolizing love, which he must leave behind. Above him, the moon watched his departure with a face that was simultaneously cold, impassive, and satisfied with the sentence that had been passed on him: the sentence of losing what he thought he could not live without. And yet, at the same time, one did not feel that the moon was crushing him as he left; she did not weigh a thousand pounds, nor did she have sharp edges; she dismissed him gently. One could detect her allegiance to the laws of love, and a trace of hope in her serene face that he would finally understand those laws and find happiness by obeying them.

"You can't change what has already happened," Ada told me.

I stood there for a moment, so filled with emotions that I was still not fully conscious of the tears running down my face, which would have embarrassed me and caused me to flee back into the dusk had I been aware of them. "The future is for me to make, not your cards," I said, at last.

She bowed slightly. I was taking power from her yet also freeing her.

"You must let go," she said.

I agreed. "Let go of what I lost, but not of what is still within my reach. Let go of Elizabeth, but not of my will."

"You must never let anyone or anything take away what is inside of you. No one can live well who is not brave enough to live from the inside."

"You were arrogant to play the part of God."

"You were foolish to let me play that part."

"I loved her."

"But not enough to push me aside to reach her."

"You protected her. Thank you," I said, at last.

"Let go," she said. "You still have years of life ahead of you. The world is waiting for you to return." And she drew one final card before I left, which happened to be the Ace of Cups. "It's starting again," she said. "Once your heart is open… It's in the air. It's in every bud that's opening, in every flower that's blooming. You can't get away from it. This time get it right."

As my hand wiped the tears from my eyes, I finally realized that I had been crying, and saying, "Thank you," I quickly left. The bells on Doña Ada's door jingled supportively as I staggered out into the street, returning, at last, to the world I had not been a part of for many years.

THE WATER PITCHER

He was gifted, but no one believed him. He had power, but they said he was only dreaming. He was the least of men, because he could not ride a horse or camel, he could not shoot an arrow straight to hit the mark, and no one feared him.

He lived, as though with a giant scar across his face, not one to be proud of as the mark of a warrior, but something to cringe from, as a child born defective.

As a young man, the beautiful, practical women who were the hips of his people strode lazily past him as though he were not there. He watched them tighten up and hold their heads up high, whenever other young men passed them by, but to them he was as familiar and as harmless as a dog.

They did not know his power.

One day, it became too much for him to bear.

It was a harsh day of sun and thirst, a day of being lost, far from the trails and the wells. A terrible sandstorm had rewritten the geography of the earth, erased hills, and made hills where there were none, swallowed up the dry *wadi* which was the line they had been following towards water, towards life. For seven days, they saw nothing but dust. Even in the night, the stars hung their heads in shame, the world let the wind command it, and do with it what it pleased, while they crouched low to the ground. At last, they had to move to find water, even though the world was still in turmoil, and that is when they became lost. No one can survive in a world that is utterly new, without the friendship of a mountain or a river that they know.

By now, there were only a few of them; the others had already gone in different directions, scattering like birds when they hear a shout. Every band had taken its own course. That is the havoc that storms wreak on the human soul.

The water was all gone, now, except for what remained in a large glass pitcher, which rested on the table by the rocks where the elder sat, outside the tent, with his two beautiful daughters, across from the young man who blushed, and whose heart pounded whenever he was near them. But they did not raise a finger to make themselves look more beautiful.

"Let us drink just a little," the elder said, after a while, as the storm began to die, "for who knows how far we are from the nearest well, or how long it will take us to reach it."

It may seem strange to you that these stalwart masters of the desert chose to hold the last of their water in a pitcher made of glass, but if you think a little, you will realize how most of us guard things that matter little with all the power at our disposal, while neglecting the things that truly count. We covet what distracts us and pay no mind to that which saves us or damns us. We cherish what is superfluous and forget that there is such a thing as essence. We stay up all night to stand watch over trinkets and fall asleep beside treasures.

The water in the glass pitcher was no different.

Each took a small sip of water, the young man the smallest of all, but no one noticed. Such gestures are like the paths made by an ant, for those who judge a man by how he rides a horse.

The young man could finally endure no more. Perhaps it was the hot sun beating down on his head. Perhaps it was the pity of seeing such lost people; or only the pain of beautiful women who did not look at him.

"I have power," the young man told them once again, as he had told them many times before.

"Please, not again," the elder implored.

"I have power," the young man insisted.

The girls yawned.

"I am not who you think I am. I am a great man."

"Words mean nothing," the elder said, at last. "You have been going on and on like this for years. You have not stood out on the raids, you have not distinguished yourself in battle, you do not ride a horse convincingly, nor are you graceful on a camel's back. We love words, but only from poets. None of us have power, now, only the wind."

But the young man, today, would not be deterred. "I will show you, at last," he told them, "that all power does not come from a sword, nor a bow, nor from charging horses. I will show you the power that is in a soul, in a thought. I will you show you how a heart can overcome an army."

Now, even the daughters were looking at him, so intense and strange was his outburst, so unexpected his passion. Though a beautiful, strong man makes the heart of a desert woman crumble, like dust, to see a fool humiliate himself is not uninteresting.

"The pitcher," the young man said. "I will move it without a hand, without touching it at all. I will move it with my mind, alone, I will show you the power of the mind."

By now, all eyes were upon him, the silence grew; even the troubled noises of the earth, the last of its howling winds and the laments of its sorrowful beasts, ceased, that he might finally have the moment that the boldness of others had denied him all his life.

"Well," said the elder. "Go on, then, show us this power you have been telling us of since you were born."

Furrowing his brow and leaning slightly forward, while all eyes clung to him, the young man stared silently at the pitcher. After a time, the girls were about to laugh, when, all at once, they thought they saw the pitcher quiver. They looked like they were about to cry. Then, suddenly, as all let out a gasp, it began to move, trembling slightly as it slid across the table, picking up speed until suddenly it was flying, and before any of them could think to stop it, had leapt off of the table, and crashed against the rocks, shattering into a thousand pieces and spilling the last of their precious water into the thirsting, immortal mouth of the desert sand. Those who needed water would have none; that which drank without need used all.

For a moment, no one spoke.

"You have power," the elder agreed at last.

The girls lowered their eyes and became radiant.

No longer was the young man marginal.

He had power, he had proved it, but now there was no water.

THE POWER OF ANGER

Not many understood, that night, why we were all standing in the plaza by the giant bonfire, with stacks of holy books in our arms. The writings of GSM—the Great Spiritual Master, who centuries ago wrote beautiful poems on behalf of brotherhood and peace—came packaged in a thousand different ways: in simple, unpretentious paperback books easy to carry around; in sturdy hardbound editions, heirlooms as complete as altars, which were best left at home; in surprisingly thin folios which transmitted the essentials to an impatient age, and eased the busy mind with soothing tracts of white space in the place of words; in a wide assortment of data chips, CDs, DVDs, and diskettes designed for modern times. Tonight, all the differences of these diverse media had been put aside; they had come together to the edge of the leaping flames so that we might save the world by destroying them.

Not many understood. But I did. Those others simply listened to the government, I reasoned. What chance did the GSM stand against the NT—the Necessary Technology which had resurrected our human prospect on the earth? What chance did the True Understanding stand against the Great Discovery? The rest of them had come to the fire merely because the government asked them to. I came to the bonfire, whose ravenous flames climbed high into the night, because I understood.

Before our time, civilization as we know it had reached the verge of collapse. Fossil fuels were running out, our entire system of transport, supply, and manufacture was breaking down. Solar, wind, and geothermal technologies which sought to pick up the slack, along with nuclear power plants, had not covered the ground we thought they would, and some alarming accidents had occurred which dimmed our enthusiasm for them: the Breeder Reactor explosion in Tennessee, and meltdown in Louisiana; the malfunction of the computers which directed the giant energy beam from the orbital solar-collection stations to the power-dissemination plants on the ground. The ancient myth of Phaethon's runaway sun-chariot came to life in one prolonged scream of hope gone wrong; Carl Sandburg's paean to the great, wind-swept city of iron and human muscle lost its frame of reference. A charred and lonely place was all that remained on the shores of Lake Michigan, whose puzzled waters searched in vain for laughter and ambition. Besides this, terrorists succeeded in dipping their hands into the proliferating network of uranium and plutonium shipments, which were streaming, uninhibited, over the rail lines and highways between our mines, ports, and enrichment centers, and between our power plants and waste sites. Two suitcase bombs and three dirty bombs were fed by our lack of caution, and the suddenly empty spots on our map did not endear us to our new choices, our reluctant reply to the faithlessness of oil, gas and coal. Neither did the wars we fought to control the last sputtering oilfields of the world, which left thousands of families grieving beneath electric lights that only succeeded in illuminating their weary, heartbroken faces.

In these turbulent, anxious times, dangerous radicals emerged, eager to convince us that the only remedy was to change the nature of civilization itself. These unwanted critics told us that there was no new energy source that we could "simply plug into the gap left by the collapse of fossil fuels"; they told us that a complete re-envisioning of society was in order, that our material expectations must be drastically reduced, that the car must be abolished, that industry must be lightened and what was left of it returned to the city, and that the city must be expanded to incorporate agriculture. Government planning must replace the freewheeling dynamics of business. We must surrender our wealth.

The air was fierce in those days, filled with revolutionary ideas: wild, untested premises pitted against archaic dinosaurs that could barely take a step but which embodied everything we cherished and believed in. Strident, grating militants clashed with beloved, senile clingers-to-yesterday; raucous, irritating prophets who stuck out like a sore thumb, did battle with elders who were dear to us, but who we could see had nothing left to say. We listened to their arguments on our behalf, and knew we were alone. We were desperate, confused, attached to the ship that was sinking, but afraid of the water. What could we do?

That is when, thank God, the Great Discovery was made. How history loves to lead us to the edge, before it lifts us with gentle or angry arms, as it may be, out of one age and into the next. The foundations of the Great Discovery (GD) were laid by research done at MIT, brilliant place of minds that it is, where a machine capable of detecting and enhancing human brainwaves, and transforming them into "industrial-grade electric current," was devised. In this research, it was found that in the "spectrum" of human emotion, the band of mental energy corresponding to anger was the most intense and the most easily converted into electric power. A group of grad students was exposed to infuriating circumstances, and ten of them together were able to light a 100-watt light bulb. It was a modest beginning, but within a year, thanks to an improved energy-collector, anger-isolator and overlapping circuit loop, these same ten subjects were able to simultaneously power a television and an air conditioner. With the incorporation of advanced superconductor technology by the device (once it was adopted by corporate R & D departments and properly funded), and with further improvements in design, the anger-to-electricity conversion ability was vastly amplified, and for the first time in human history, the feasibility of using anger to create power was convincingly demonstrated.

The Great Discovery was at once followed by the Great Implementation (GI), which occurred within the context of the free market, which only a decade before had seemed to be gasping with emphysema, but which now rose robustly and with rosy cheeks from its deathbed to do what it did best. Enormous receptor antennae were placed throughout the major cities, capable of picking out the energy of anger from all the diverse brainwaves radiating from our human abode. Less effective energies were tuned out, while the energy of anger was collected, reinforced, converted in underground power stations to electricity, and then transmitted by wire to all the hungry homes of the nation, starving for the lifestyle we had almost lost. Like blood through the arteries, the beautiful, life-giving currents of electrons raced through power lines to TV screens, to stereo systems, to computers, to heating units and air conditioners, to lights and appliances, to factories and machines, to rail lines and to the electric tracks which guided the latest generation of automobiles. Civilization was saved! We who had stood on the precipice of a new Dark Age, such as ancient Rome had faced as it plunged into the abyss of barbarism and feudalism, were rescued from the very brink of catastrophe by the genius of the human mind with its back to the wall. Foresight was rendered unnecessary by desperation, austerity was dismissed by the cleverness of our will to prosper. We humans are magnificent in procrastination, our seemingly fatal delays always have a last card up their sleeve. We did not give in to the radicals who would have demeaned us by forcing us to live as our ancestors lived, we did not yield to the timid ones who would have turned the world upside down. We were saved by a brilliant panic. Realism did not cheat us.

As time went on, the amazing new system was improved still further. The government, quite intelligently, I think, became involved at the request of the utility companies, which is perfectly legitimate for a mixed economy. Deliberate provocations were engineered and worked into the fabric of society to keep the anger levels, which were the key to the success of our civilization, as high as possible. Construction projects which knotted up our highways and created maddening traffic jams were used to elevate the rage which our infrastructure depended on; housing shortages were manipulated into being, in order to force large numbers of people to live together in cramped quarters, which laboratory studies had already proven drives rats to new heights of aggressiveness; a new professional organization, the League of Responsible Business Owners (AKA the League of Unfair Bosses) was formed to promote and support workplace abuse, which sociologists had determined was a major potential source of anger; while psychologists conferred with politicians on the usefulness of having foreign enemies, whose atrocious images could be cultivated to produce indignation for the benefit of the economy. As one notable philosopher wrote: "The incredible potential of the human heart for generating electricity seems nearly inexhaustible." What an astonishing change from only a few years before, when civilization seemed to have reached its limits and to have no choice but to grind to a halt and consider some other option: something self-deprecating and utterly beneath us. How blessed we were, in our moment of need, to have come upon a new source of energy which was endless and renewable!

But then, the teachings of the Great Spiritual Master got in the way. Persistent ancient writings: perniciously humane, tenacious in their impracticality, centuries-old, yet refusing to die! Once before, they had been tolerated for their ability to keep the masses in line; the masses who were reared with the ideal of gentleness in order to deter the dangers of pride. But now, instead of preserving civilization, the teachings of the GSM threatened to destroy it. As often happens in times of tumult and confusion, there was a great revival and resurgence of the archaic morals, a desperate search for meaning, a grasping at spiritual straws in the midst of the material freefall. As the GD and GI struggled to lift us out of the pit of the earth's ungenerous resistance to our invulnerability with the brilliant new gift of anger-technology, the teachings of the GSM countered the recovery, dampening the output of rage which was needed to keep the gears of civilization turning. Millions of people were kept outside of the energy-generating system by their rekindled commitment to the wisdom of the GSM, by their philosophical nature, by their calmness in the face of aggravation, by their disengagement from the boisterous ego, which is the champion of strife, by their focus on beauty rather than frustration. Experts in the energy industry, working together with corporate sociologists, estimated that the nation was losing up to 1500 billion kilowatt hours per year on account of the GSM revival, and as the recovery of civilization seemed threatened by the obsolescence of their mindless faith, which suited pastoral times centuries removed from the present, but which was as arsenic to the present, pressure mounted to do something. Widespread brownouts were the final straw. At last the government, which was always wary of doing too much, had no choice but to intervene, lest the goodwill of fools who did not understand that we were no longer a simple tribal people running after sheep in the hills, derail a highly advanced and complex society which now required anger to maintain its standard of living. "Our lifestyle does not grow on a tree," one economist said, for the benefit of the ignorant. "It is a great economic achievement, a feat of social athleticism whose lifeblood is energy. Our most important duty as citizens and as patriots is to stand by our way of life, and to generate the energy which will preserve that way of life, the way of life for which our forefathers died;

and to keep our nation strong." And thus, the government had, at last, reluctantly declared war upon the teachings of the GSM—*reluctantly,* for interference with the constructive anarchy of history is always the last option. As patriots of our country, we had no choice but to come to the edge of the fire with the holy books in our arms.

The people who stood beside me on the momentous night of the book-burning did not know why they were here except that the government had called upon them to come, and that everywhere there were flags waving. But I knew what was at stake: the future of civilization itself, which depended on the power of anger. For men at liberty to express their rage, for men who are free to hate and despise others, there are cities. Men of peace would take us back to the days of the caves. We would live in forests like animals. When the bonfire organizer cried out to us over the PA system, urging us to hurl our sacred books into the blaze, I did not hesitate. I loved my country and I believed in the promise of civilization.

As the giant yellow flames hissed and struck at the air like snakes, I watched the ashes of the sacred books climbing upwards from the inferno, like snow falling backwards: snow that was black and gray instead of white. Some fools cheered without knowing why; other fools wept. I said nothing, I merely complied, without misgivings or nostalgia; I, alone of all who stood there, understood the power of anger.

THE ANGEL'S ARIA

It is a little known fact of opera history, but in the same year that Verdi's first staging of *La Traviata* was an utter disaster, Salvatore R., a composer who was less known for his music than for his disgraceful lifestyle, which was suspected but not definitively proven, lost his mind. Today Salvatore R. is not known at all, so that the little bit of notoriety he enjoyed in his own age was, perhaps, something he should have been grateful for, even though, were he to live in our own times, he would not be notorious at all. Call it progress, that the degeneracy of one era has become the normalcy of the next.

Certainly, it is a shame that Salvatore R. did not go to witness that atrocious premiere, which embarrassed his great rival no end. Jealousy was Salvatore's fiercest demon, and it would surely have been assuaged had he been a personal witness to Verdi's calamity. There, at the opera's debut in Venice, a leading tenor with a hoarse voice, and an obese leading lady improbably cast in the role of the romantic heroine wasting away from consumption, was too much for the audience, which, at first, booed furiously, then later, roared with laughter, in the best Italian style, at the plight of the giantess who was supposedly fading into nothing from her disease. Salvatore R., who was, at that very moment, wasting away himself, not from consumption but from the neglect of the Italian public, which was distracted by superior talents from his sincere competence and oversized longing to be loved, would surely have felt great relief to behold the audience all around him marring Verdi's masterpiece with cat-calls, guffaws, jeers and whistles. He would surely have felt less superfluous and less lonely in his rejection. The thought of killing himself would probably never even have entered his mind.

But as it was, at the very moment that Verdi's great act of genius was being brutalized, still one year away from the redemption it would finally receive thanks to a new cast, new costuming, and some judicious editing, Salvatore R. was sitting at his piano, staring out the window at the rain, which seemed to make the houses across the street weep. He lived in a handsome neighborhood but knew he had done nothing to deserve it; he had, in fact, inherited the money of landholders who had accumulated their wealth through the unjust exploitation of others. By means of music, Salvatore hoped to purify himself of the sin of his good fortune. He wrote several unnoticed concertos, a symphony which was performed by one of the most mediocre orchestras in Europe for an uncultured audience, with the logical results, and an opera which he thought was great, *Scipio Africanus*, which received scathing reviews, however, from wine-filled critics who seemed to hate him, as if unconsciously possessed by the spirits of the peasants his forebears had worked to death. The opera had some wonderful arias, and some wonderful lines. At least Salvatore thought so. Scipio sang, to the ghost of his great enemy Hannibal, the Carthaginian: "I spent my life trying to defeat you, now I miss you. When I finally vanquished you on the plain of Zama, I lost my reason for living. I cannot enjoy life without being threatened. Now that I am safe, I am in peril." The great Roman commander, portrayed by a completely credible tenor, went on to sing: "You, great invincible genius, love of my life, who I never thought I could destroy. When I saw your army break and run, I knew that human beings had limitations. I proved that we are only men, and we are not enough for the things we dream. Now, with victory, the world is empty. Better to have an idol than a home. Better to have an enemy than to have nothing. I don't know what to do with my life, now that I have won. Only victory could show me how small I am." Critics, missing its profundity and the implicit exhortation to redefine the purpose of human life, called the opus "depressing" and chastised it for lacking the "vitality of a sympathetic female protagonist. Whoever heard of a great opera textured only with the voices of baritones and tenors, and the fleeting presence of a diminutive mezzo-soprano?" They went on to add: "Salvatore R. may not suffer from the absence of the gentler sex in his opera, but for the rest of us, the lack is unforgivable."

How ruthless they were, with their career-crushing innuendos! They did not know how madly he loved a soprano, Antonia Maria C., who did not take him seriously as a man, however. She had her own unattainable cravings, worshipping men she could never walk arm-in-arm with in the open but only sneak away with into dark and unnoticed places that simultaneously satisfied and demeaned her. She needed the attention of the powerful and could never feel aroused in the presence of the irrelevant. And yet, she was tender, and you might say, fraternal— for the woman in her withdrew behind a moat whenever she was with the eccentric and the brilliantly marginal who did not correspond to her ideal of manhood. She was dear, kind, witty, and she laughed freely and honestly, favoring bohemians with her personality; she simply had no passion to offer to them, except through her vocal cords. Thanks to her, Salvatore had to turn to dark places, as well (almost as if he were her shadow), in order to find the momentarily exhilarating, but ultimately destructive semblances of what she would not share with him. Together, they would have glowed in the world like the sun. Without each other, they turned into animals, running like deserted dogs through filthy streets, obeying hunger instead of shame. Vanity killed the one; a fanatical dedication to beauty killed the other, who must preserve the emptiness of his universe for the sake of his imagination, which needed an enormous open canvas on which to paint her over and over again. Degradation was preferable to compromise. But what a cross to bear; he had not the strength to reach Golgotha.

As Salvatore R. watched the rain falling on the lovely houses outside his window, that morning, houses which seemed like temples from which the gods had been stolen, a sudden, amazing thought occurred to him, which was simultaneously brilliant and pathological. He would play a high-stakes game with the mediocrity which was afflicting him like a terrible disease from which he could not bear to perish; wager his life on the outcome of what happened between him and the empty sheets of paper which lay before him, propped up on the piano rack, waiting to be filled with notes. He would find the meaning of life, with his piano, and his pen, or else hurl himself from the world before the absence of God could. He had the gun to do it with, his father's old dueling pistol, which had killed a man once. How ferocious men are to avenge an insult; how indifferent to correcting the world's ills!

Salvatore, like most raised in such a Christian country, knew the passage from the Bible in which Jesus refuses to leap off the roof of the temple in spite of the Devil's urging. "Why not?" the Devil asks him. "If you are dear to God, surely all the angels of Heaven shall come to catch you as you fall and set you down lightly upon the earth." And Jesus tells him: "Thou shalt not tempt the lord."

But Salvatore was a rebel, and Italy's attention to his nonconformity was making him even more so. The upright loved scandal and needed profligates to prevent their source of outrage from drying up, like an old well. They therefore made it impossible for Salvatore to escape from his image, by barricading him from everything that was acceptable in life, and by manipulating his pride, so that he could only return to normalcy by crawling back to them on his knees. His spirit would not allow him to step down from the pedestal of the outcast. Thought Salvatore: "*I* shall tempt the lord. *I shall leap off the roof of the temple, and demand that he proves He exists, and that human life is worthwhile, by catching me as I fall. I, who have always thought my music came from Him, and that my purpose in life was to bring divine insight and feeling into the world through music, have been abandoned. I am not respected; I am, in fact, despised as a man, and what is worse, ignored as an artist. God: I am tired of this abuse! I demand that You show Yourself to me! My father's pistol is in the other room!"*

And then, Salvatore began to write. By this time, it is fair to say that the sound mind he had been blessed with at birth was gone; life is not always kind to the gifts we receive from God, and finds ways of sweeping them away, like a storm which incites the sea to carry off huge tracts of land, and changes the shape of the shore. Sometimes, there is little of the prodigious child left by the time the world has done its work on him.

Salvatore immediately recognized the alteration of his consciousness, but did not care; in fact, he relished it, for his good mind had got him nowhere in the world. He felt the need for something more, another level of awareness, another level of energy, something more powerful than the senses which had failed him till now: something which he could detect in madness. Laughing, as he began to experiment with his piano, he thought: "Till now, all the composers of opera have been hamstrung by the limitations of the human voice. They write only what the human vocal cords can deliver, and the range of our art is constrained by the power of the throat, which is so much less than the power of the mind. Thus, our music suffers and is small, and the sensibilities which music gives birth to remain withered and incomplete; as human beings, we can rise no higher than our music. We are a stunted, broken race, obeying not the mighty light of intangible thoughts but only the pitiful handful of notes which we can produce with our fragile voice. We are trapped by our physical vessel—

or are we? No, that is only the curse of the sane!" he assured himself. "Madness—dear madness—welcome, I invite you between my ears! As the Sibyl did before Aeneas, I open the door that others fear to open, the door inside the mind through which the terrible winds blow, that lead to thoughts too powerful to bear! Today, I shall write another kind of opera: an opera which shall surpass the limitations which keep us small; an opera not meant for humans; an opera written for the voice of an angel!" And Salvatore began to compose. Feverish and sick, more alive than he had ever been except for those delusory nights when he had imagined Antonia might actually give herself to him, he wrote and wrote, attacking the virgin paper with an unsparing pen, which was the utter slave of his ear, and which ruled the universe as surely as Rome had once ruled the earth, if only for a handful of majestic, unseen hours. "Diorio and Costa!" he raged, crying out the names of two of his unkindest critics; "you may kneel before me and bathe my feet! I will allow it!" And he laughed again, then once more, disappeared from the gutter where they lived into the cathedral of sound inside his mind, where the holy Eucharist was being given out.

What other composer would ever have thought of writing an aria that could not be sung, an aria whose notes climbed too high and fell too low for any living man or woman to reproduce? The piece, for one character only, who he appropriately named "Angela," began with several bars in baritone, next climbed the stairway of sound to a point far above soprano, then crashed recklessly down, again, below baritone; then, in a final act of rebellion and defiance against human limitations, leapt upwards, one last time, above soprano. Salvatore, inspired by his sudden discovery of the pointlessness of sanity, charged furiously at the universe, to smash out of it, with the hammer of his desperate soul and his underestimated talent, its most impossible notes: notes that were useless, but incomparable. "What I am writing," he thought, congratulating himself with tears, "it has never occurred to anybody before me to write!" He laughed, proud of himself, to be at the forefront of musical history. "All stuck in the trap of their little formulas, held back by the trifle of plausibility! Do we believe in God in this country, or not? Are all the churches for nothing?! Are we all hypocrites, living in a forest of crosses we have no faith in? It is time to resurrect God in our lives, or else to follow Him to His grave! My life is nothing; I have finally reached the point where I need Him. Fame has eluded me, love has avoided me, comfort has laughed behind my back. I am tired of this earth, unless it can be shown to me that it is more than what it seems!"

Wildly, he pounded away at the keys of the piano; he wrote more. He had to add new lines to his music pad which did not have room to incorporate his vision, he had to imagine notes that neither his piano, nor the violin which he also knew how to play, could reproduce (he even burst the E string on his violin, attempting to tighten it beyond its intended degree of tension in order to expand its range). And he laughed, and continued to laugh, for there is something delightful in losing one's mind. A prisoner no more! Today we would call it "thinking outside the box." But in those simpler times, insanity was the term most frequently used.

"Beautiful! Beautiful!" he told himself, substituting his own approval for that of the audiences which had never appreciated him as they should have. "Bravo! Bravo, Salvatore R., Salvatore the Disgrace, Salvatore the Black Sheep of the World, take your rightful place beside Mozart the genius, and that competent workman Verdi!" He clapped his hands together. "Finally, someone recognizes your talent!"

And, at last, the masterpiece was finished; the mad piece of music which was utterly beyond the range of the human vocal cords.

"Done!" he said, at perfect liberty to talk to himself since he had decided to discard his mind; "now then, to find an angel to sing it!"

Of course, the one who must play the part of the angel was none other than Antonia Maria C.: who else? The splendid, treasured, distant one, who had glowed throughout his wretched life with kindness that refused to grow into love, the one whose beautiful portrait hung in his artist's mind, tormenting him and caressing him; she, the soprano of the darkness, who gave herself, in secret, to those who held her in contempt, yet would not redeem the one who worshipped her by loving him. How painful to him were the countless thoughtless kisses she gave him on the cheek, which were demanded by the warmth of Italian culture but had no more content in them than a handshake between businessmen! For years, he had wanted Antonia Maria to be his angel. Now, for one moment, she would have no choice but to be his angel. Either that, or the witness of his bloody demise.

Antonia did not know what was in store for her that stormy night, with the candles flickering in the room, and breezes such as those that accompany the presence of spirits, but as soon as she entered Salvatore's salon, she could sense that something extraordinary or dreadful must occur before she would have the chance to leave. She was frightened by the wild light in his eyes. He was much stranger than she remembered, and she had never once thought of him as normal.

"Welcome, Antonia," he told her. "Welcome Toni, most graceful of the nobodies, you have always said that the best roles are dominated by the lovers of the producers, the owners, the composers, the business elites of the opera world; and that your failure to become one of the great performers of our times is the result of not being properly connected, or provided with a top-notch original libretto. You do try so hard to be connected, but what can mere bankers and shipbuilders do for you? Especially since they cannot be explicit regarding their affairs. Don't you see, *how can they fund a lover who they do not have?*" And he shook his head with pity. "Such a miscalculation." And he added: "The manna from Heaven fell not upon the starving Hebrews in the desert, but upon the troops of Pharaoh, in their golden chariots."

"Are you passing judgment on me?" she asked, ready for a terrible fight. That part of being a great diva, at least, she possessed.

"No," Salvatore assured her.

"Apologize to me!" she demanded. "You sent a messenger to drag me out of my house, on such an awful day. I thought you must be dying. When you did not greet me at the door, I was sure of it. But then your servant led me, not to your deathbed, but to your piano, and here you are sitting utterly oblivious to my arrival, and with that unpardonable tone of voice! I won't be despised, no matter how far from the rigid ideal in which you seek to imprison me I choose to live! Who are you to look down at me? I won't stoop so low as to say another word; but if you live in a glass house, don't throw stones!"

"I am sorry. I am truly sorry, dearest Antonia," Salvatore apologized.

"What—and still no hug?" she asked him, offended.

Salvatore smiled bitterly. "Each hug, a denial," he whispered.

"What?" she demanded, unable to hear exactly what he had said, but certain that it was intended as a barb.

"Look at where all the meaningless flirtation that is a part of our warm, eternally enthusiastic culture has brought us," he said cynically. "You are a frustrated opera singer, and I am a frustrated composer; both of us trample over our pride to appease the flesh, and both of us are alone. Antonia, I would rather be whipped than kissed one more time on the cheek by you; I would rather be nailed to the cross than to be hugged and feel the impossibility of you so close to me."

"Salvatore, are you ill? Should I call a doctor? Or are you merely being inconsiderate? I could catch a cold coming out in this weather: even bronchitis or pneumonia. You are my friend. We talked about this once before, and you swore you would never talk about it again. It was so painful! Are you a man of your word or not?"

"Who can merely be a friend of the sun?"

"Salvatore, you must be drunk. I am going to go."

"No, please!" cried Salvatore, leaping up from the piano, waving the aria he had just written in his hand. "You mustn't go, you must forgive me! I am an artist, I am meant to be awkward and unsociable! From my inability to live with others comes my light! You have always tolerated my kind!"

"Some mistake tolerance for more than it is," she reminded him. "You feed a hungry cat, because you feel sorry for it, and suddenly it follows you all around and wants you to take it into your house. You can't get rid of it, no matter what you do." She looked at the roll of paper in Salvatore's hand and finally took it from him. "You've written something. For me? If you truly cared for me, like you said you did, you would have put a soprano into *Scipio Africanus*. You would have given me my big break. It was such a promising opera, if only its main goal hadn't been to punish me for refusing to love you! You could have made me, then, Salvatore, and I could have made you. Instead, you left the woman out just to spite me. But you shot yourself in the foot, Salvatore, because all the critics hated *Scipio*. Whoever heard of a major opera without a girl? And you fanned the flames of the rumors. They're true, Salvatore, aren't they?"

"I didn't leave out a female protagonist to spite you. You are so egocentric!" Salvatore exclaimed.

"Oh, why then?"

"Because I am a loyalist to history. What woman of note was there, back then? I won't invent history just to satisfy the erotic callings of the masses. If that is what compels them, let them go to a whorehouse instead of the opera house."

"No women of note? At times, you are such a prehistoric man," Antonia protested.

"No. Not me. If I were, you would be my wife. Because I have not dragged you behind me by the hair, into a cave, you hold me in contempt."

Antonia would have responded, but by now she had unfurled the rolled-up sheets of music which he had placed into her hands, and begun to go over them, in utter amazement. She read, from a cover page: "THE ANGEL'S ARIA, the culminating scene in a standard five-act opera, still to be completed. A despised composer who has lost his interest in life and faith in God decides to put an end to his miserable existence. But first, he will give God one final chance to save him. The disillusioned composer calls, into his chamber, the beautiful opera singer who, throughout his life, has been both his greatest source of torment and his greatest source of joy, and places in her hands the music for an aria, which is beyond the ability of the human voice to sing. Only an angel could sing it. The composer shows the singer, who is a friend of his, though he wished that she had been far more, the pistol in his hands, and informs her that with it, he intends to blow his brains out before her eyes unless she is able to sing the aria which she has before her. If God loves him and wants him to remain on the earth, God will give her the voice to sing the aria; He will send angels to her throat to sing what no human being could ever sing on her own, thereby providing the distraught composer with irrefutable proof that there is a divine realm beyond this mortal existence which means nothing to him; and that, though the world cares but little for him, God *does* care for him: enough to break the rules that have condemned mankind to doubt for hundreds of years, and to send to him an angel from Beyond. Will we hear, for the first time in human history, the beautiful impossible notes which we have waited centuries to hear, or only the silence of a throat that cannot answer our longing or redeem our vision, followed by the clear, familiar ringing of a gunshot, which is the music of reality, which we know so well? The music of human cruelty, of husband beating wife and battering child, of mobs persecuting free-thinkers and strangers, and of hoarders haunting the stomachs of the weak; of nation blowing out the brains of nation? How will the opera end—the life of the writer, and the world? Will the angel come? *Or are there no angels to come?*"

Antonia, by now, was highly agitated, her hands had even begun to shake. When she passed from the synopsis to the musical notes, themselves, she gasped in disbelief. No one could sing something like that! She lifted her eyes, in anger, to reprimand Salvatore, but instead, cried out: "No, Salvatore, don't do it!"

She saw him sitting there on the stool in front of the piano, the pistol in his hand, raised, now, to his head and pressed against his temple.

"No, Salvatore!" she exclaimed again. She took a bold, unconsciously compassionate step towards him.

"Don't take another step," he warned, "or I'll pull the trigger!"

She stopped in her tracks, assessing him, desperately trying to gauge whether he was only bluffing and she could barge past his warning to take the gun from his hand and slap him in the face for being such a fool, or whether he really meant it, and had decided to leave the world in the most dramatic and creative way of an opera personality. After a moment, she discovered that he was serious. That little trace of a smile at the corners of his lips which gave away his jokes, the quivering by the eyebrows attempting to deceive, were lacking; his face was shining and resolved, his eyes hiding nothing. This was not a prank. He was mad. As mad, and as pure in his madness, as Caligula, but too moral to destroy anyone but himself. Yet, even so, this was not moral. She told him so.

"Salvatore, this is monstrous, this is unfair!" she chided him. "To blow your brains out in front of someone who cares for you! To place the responsibility for your life and death on my shoulders! No one can sing this aria, it is impossible. Not ten Farinellis standing in a line, each one's voice beginning where the other's left off. How cruel, to bring me here to witness this irresponsible bloodbath!"

"Impossible?" he asked her. "Not if God exists, not if God is real. I need to find out. Today. Right now. I don't want to live another minute if God is nothing but a hoax, if the universe is empty."

"It is not empty," she pleaded. "We are in it. And of course, God exists! Of course He does! He parted the Red Sea for Moses, He made manna fall from Heaven, he saved the life of Daniel in the lion's den; through Jesus He turned water into wine, He multiplied the loaves, He brought fish into the nets of the fishermen in the Sea of Galilee, He healed lepers."

"So the Bible says. But what is the Bible? Who says that what is in it is true? Only men who are fallible. My father, who betrayed it with every breath he took. My poor mother, who, were it not for my father, would have lost our fortune in a year. The time she bought a horse one day before it died! Maybe, *The Magic Flute* is more real."

"Blasphemy! The Pope says! The Pope says it's real!"

"The Pope! You, such a little rebel and convention-breaker, entrusting your soul to such an absurd caricature of faith! With that ridiculous hat he wears on his head!"

"Blasphemy! Salvatore, watch what you say! God will punish you!"

At that Salvatore only laughed. He moved the pistol slightly, to remind Antonia that it was loaded and still in his hand. "Perhaps He is about to punish me. Don't you think this pistol is far more practical than lightning?" Antonia wanted to say something, but her temperament was so volatile that words couldn't escape from her mouth before they seemed to be inadequate in the shadow of her burning passion. She tried so hard to speak, that nothing would come out.

Salvatore, taking advantage of her predicament, continued: "The testimony of past generations is as cold as the hand of a corpse. I need to see for myself. Or, since I am a musician, to hear. I need to hear that God exists. Your voice will let me know, Antonia. *Your voice.*"

"No, Salvatore," she whispered. She waved the papers of impossible notes in her hands, in front of him. "No one can sing this. My voice is only human. You can't ask me to do what only an angel could do."

"Do you remember the part in *The Aeneid?*" he asked her, "when the Sibyl was possessed by the ancient God?"

"Of course," she replied. Antonia was proud, always proud, even in the midst of desperation.

Salvatore recited: "*She seemed to grow in height, her breast heaved, she spoke in no mortal tones!*"

"They were pagans," Antonia protested.

"If the gods of the pagans could speak through the voice of a human priestess, how could the voices of the angels of our own great God, the True God, the One God above all others, not do the same? There is no difference from the stories you have just reminded me of, the Red Sea, the loaves... This shall be merely one miracle more piled on top of the others. Only this time, the Manna that falls from Heaven shall be golden notes, falling from your throat over the desert of my cynicism. My hungry spirit shall be kept alive in the wilderness. Or else I shall depart from it, with a last shred of honor intact, my uncompromised ideals, gone from a world that is not worthy of kissing my dream's feet."

"Thou shalt not tempt the lord!" Antonia exclaimed, amazed by her friend's audacity.

"I *shall* tempt the lord," he replied, unruffled by her indignation; astonishingly unruffled.

"And what makes *you* worthy to trouble God in such a way?" she demanded, unrelenting in the offense which she took at his revolt.

"As the least of your brethren, I am fit to be treated as a king," he retorted.

She stood back, mouth agape, once again at an utter loss. He knew the scriptures, he knew them well, inside out, in fact; he simply did not believe in them: life had beaten their meaning out of him. In his house there was a great treasure chest, but in it, there was nothing.

At last, Antonia told him: "Salvatore. Put the gun down. Please. I am a good singer, for sure, but not this good. You need to write to Marta Angela Rossi or Gabriela Gotti, they surpass me. They would have a better chance than me to sing this aria. I am good, but much as I hate to say it, they are better. At least for now. If Giovanni Campanella will take me on as a student, who knows, but for now..."

Salvatore, of course, recognized that she was only trying to buy time, to defuse the situation, and to manipulate him. He smiled. "Dearest Toni, you mustn't try to outwit the mad. We see everything!" She trembled as he said that, from the intensity of his gaze. "I have chosen you," he continued, "because you are really quite fine, if you will allow yourself to accept the praises of an unheralded composer, whose motives might be more romantic than professional; you are close enough to the top of this game for me to attempt to extract the great miracle from *you*; more than that, you care for me, you want me to die a little less than the others."

"Salvatore, I don't want you to die, no one does! What are you talking about?"

"For all these reasons, I have decided that you are the most likely vehicle for the manifestation of the miracle which I am requesting God provide me with, in exchange for the honor of my continued residence on the earth."

Tears began to drip out of Antonia's eyes. "Salvatore," she pleaded again. "I can't." Then her eyes lit up momentarily; her mind was as fast as a child's hands reaching for a ball. "You must give me time to practice!" she insisted. But, just as quickly, she shivered as he shattered her cleverness with his perception, which took the form of a merciless laugh. She was quick on her feet, but no match for his resolve. The barrel of the gun seemed to grow an inch, it seemed to become darker by the second and she imagined she could see the bullet inside of it; at least, she was sure, she could hear it breathing from inside the barrel, giving itself away, like a criminal hiding behind a door.

"Sing it," Salvatore told her gently. "The aria. Sing it. Give it a try. See if the angel will come."

"Thou shalt not tempt the lord," she begged him.

"We are past that point," he said.

"I can't," she insisted, carefully at first, her words tip-toeing as if not to awaken a sleeping monster. "I won't. I won't disappoint you. I won't be the one." Then, suddenly furious in spite of her terror and confusion, and unable as ever to impede the eruptions that came from her unpredictable changes, which left one to wonder if there was actually one Antonia in the midst of the several that one knew, she said: "My voice belongs to me! You can't tell it what to do! It's my voice, mine! It obeys me, not your sickness! Your sickness disguised as beauty! I don't want to sing your aria, I have the right to choose my own material! I'm a free spirit!" She regarded him, one half a lioness, one half a doe paralyzed with fear.

He smiled gently, nodding, attempting to reassure her. "It's all right, Antonia. It's all right. You can go," he agreed. "You don't need to sing the aria. I see your pain, I see my own domineering and self-centered nature. I thought I had wanted to find God, but now I see that perhaps all I want to do is tear up the world before I go. I see a callous man whose spirituality is nothing more than a weapon used to hurt others. I thought I was a seeker, now I see I am merely a beast. Thank you, Antonia, for showing me to myself; you can go. I am sure, now, as I was not before, that I must die. I don't deserve to live another day, another minute. Someone else ought to eat the bread that my mouth squanders. Do you know, in my Will I have left this piano to you? I'll try not to get blood on it. Go, quickly, so that you don't have to see!"

"No, stop!" she screamed, observing the look of resolve in his eyes, the sudden ripping away of his gaze from her, its turning inwards to the self-hatred that thrived between his ears, the rigid, terrible impulse that seemed to jump through his arm like a current of electricity into the hand, the trigger finger. He was a split second from carrying out his threat. "No, stop, for God's sakes, Salvatore, stop! Stop! Please!"

He regarded her, his spirit disheveled after only one instant of being prepared to die, like a man who has lived for a year in the forest without a bath.

"Salvatore!" she pleaded, trying to come to him.

"Not another step!" he warned. He knew if she got close that she would try to take the pistol away from him.

"Salvatore! Salvatore! You are a beautiful man! Don't do it! You mustn't misunderstand my rejection! I am a prisoner of my own vices, my own excesses! You are too serene, too noble to be stained by my need to explore, to be practical, to demolish myself, whatever Devil it is that possesses me! I don't know, but you are not a part of the sin! You are a romantic, an artist—I adore you, which is why I could never be close to you, never allow myself to prove you were not the man I thought you were. I, too, have my ideals, I need you far away if I am to survive the mire I have fallen into, I need you to be outside of the mess! I need a lifeboat in the sea of my lust, shameful woman, disgrace to God that I am, but I'm an artist, too! I can't help it that I like brutal men, men who break my body in two and throw me away! Do not misread what I am saying! I don't want you, do you understand, not as a man! I don't want to see your member, hanging down between your legs! I want to see you fully dressed in those romantic, billowing shirts, and black pants, sitting with an ecstatic look above the piano; sometimes with a patient look, the look of a fisherman with his line cast into an ocean of sound, waiting, waiting for something big to bite. I don't want your piano, Salvatore, I'll burn it, or have it thrown off a cliff into the sea if you kill yourself, I swear I will! Don't misunderstand me, this isn't going to end with a kiss, I have the bravery to say that even though you have a gun to your head!"

"I am that hideous?"

"No, you're beautiful, and that's why I don't want you! Do you understand? Your madness and mine were born to walk side by side in the world, to hold hands, but never kiss! You are my dearest friend, Salvatore, and I love you, but I will not betray my nature or cause you to betray yours by giving in to desire! Not with you! I am Pasiphae, hidden inside the wooden cow, with my dress lifted, praying for the white bull of Poseidon to mount me! Disgraceful, how dare I show my face in Church! How carefully I comb my hair to hide my horns! But I will not change, Salvatore, though I boil like water, I am as unchanging as a rock; hammers will break on my spirit before they make a dent! This having been said," she continued, and that little phrase— *this having been said*—seemed so charming and utterly out-of-place in the midst of the chaos: "I think you are the most beautiful man who I have ever known, and there is no one who deserves to live more than you do, with your creativity and you kindness, and I know you hate to hear me diminish your manhood by saying that you are kind, but there are enough beasts in the world, Salvatore! In the name of Jesus, in the name of Mary, spare yourself, Salvatore, my dear friend, give yourself a chance!" She looked at him, but saw that her words had not soothed his determination to die, only thrown rose petals beneath his feet, which were marching resolutely towards his doom.

"I thank you, Antonia," Salvatore said. "From the bottom of my heart. You know what you mean to me, I will not deter myself by reminding myself of it. But this is—and everything I understand seems to come as a result of your dramas, which have taught me all that I know—this is about God. About God, Antonia, not you, and not me. He has not come. He has not sent an angel. And so, I must die." How peaceful with his choice and utterly convinced was his tone of voice, how impervious to restraint! "*I must die.* I vowed to myself I would pull the trigger unless I heard the voice of an angel singing, and I must carry through my threat. My threat to the Universe."

"Salvatore!" Antonia begged. The same words, like a battering ram, "Please! No!" She reached her hand out towards him, but he was far away on his stool with the pistol, beyond her reach.

"Thank you for everything," he said, again, but also troubled, now, by the delay, the repetition, this teary-eyed running around in circles, even if each circle was a masterpiece. "Now, please go! You don't have to see it. I will pull the trigger; in ten seconds I will pull the trigger. GO! Go, quickly, do not let me poison your future with the sight of my bloody demise! You have not failed me, God has failed me. You have given me everything you could, while staying true to yourself, and I would never permit you to be who you are not! Not now, even if I would have before! Go! God has failed me, not you! Never you! Go, Toni, go quickly before you see!" And he began to count.

Antonia trembled, her mouth opened and said nothing, she shook wildly, she nearly fainted, and as he counted aloud to seven, she finally screamed, which was nearly a miracle in itself, since she was frozen like a hare in the jaws of a hunting dog: "No, Salvatore, I'll do it! Let me try! By God, I'll do it!" And she fell upon her knees, praying to God to somehow change her throat, to make it ten times greater than it was, to stretch her vocal cords beyond the mortal limits of human beings, even if it destroyed her voice forever and she could never sing again. She took out the rosary beads she had brought when she first came, imagining Salvatore to be sick in his bed rather than sitting on a piano stool with a gun pointed to his head, and she prayed and prayed, sounding, he thought, like his befuddled, persistent mother in the Church; till finally, as he began to grow agitated, thinking that once more she was attempting to outwit him and dampen his enthusiasm for self-destruction, she rose from her knees with a look of desperate courage in her eyes—the look of the children standing before the Mediterranean in 1212, hoping that its waves would part to let them walk across the sea bed to the Holy Land - and holding the sheets of impossible music before her, she began to sing.

The effort was poignant and pathetic. She tried her best, but at once, she began to butcher the notes, to miss them entirely, to sing out of key, to leap up and grasp at them and slide off of them as quickly as she reached for them, as though they were made of slippery ice; and to dig for them, octaves beneath the earth, notes far below baritone which were barred from her by miles of solid rock on which the shovel of her intentions was broken. In spite of her great talent, she was like the most awful of vocal students, the kind who makes one's music teacher cringe and finally tear up the money he has been offered by rich parents, and walk away, choosing sanity over wealth. But in her eyes, there was fury and love, an unbroken sincerity that gripped her, even as she floundered. And Salvatore, in his turn, began to shake. He saw this beautiful woman trying to do the impossible to save him. He saw the tears pouring down from her eyes in uninhibited, desperate streams, heard the badly cracking voice, battering itself against limits it could not break. He saw her trembling, fighting with the ocean, *because of him!* And suddenly, every note she could not reach seemed beautiful, because in its absence, there was a person who loved him. How dare we try to define what love is; it is defined by those who love us! Let them love us as they can! And Salvatore, too, began to weep. He wept because no angel could have moved him as Antonia moved him, failing to be an angel.

For others, it might not have been enough. But far from the realms of the intellect, Salvatore understood. Antonia, standing there on that day, trying to be an angel, proved to him that God exists.

Slowly, Salvatore put down his father's cruel gun, stood up, and went over to embrace Antonia: the embrace of a friend, which would never stain the immaculate wall that separated their bodies but let their hearts and minds commune as one. "Thank you," he told her. "I have heard something greater than the voice of an angel. Behind the shattered notes, which you could not bring into the world, I have heard the music of your intentions and your soul. A concert such as this would not be possible without a God."

For over an hour, they stood together without speaking, holding one another, crying in proud and tender silence.

Now, over a century has gone by since these two great friends passed from the earth, and you may wonder what became of them, and why their names are not enshrined in the history books (though those who are addicted to the lore of the opera may recognize them as one of many radiant footnotes, which taken together, enliven all that has been forgotten). With regard to this, there is nothing much to say, only that: Life needs to leave no record behind it in order to be worth living. Below the heights of success, great empires of feeling reign and rule the earth, and forever will. Most of the earth's gold is invisible. What we read in our history books barely scratches the surface. And what matters most are the unseen histories which we write with those we love.

Somewhere, within the gigantic realm of the unknown, Salvatore R. and Antonia Maria C. spent the rest of their lives dreaming, and rising to the height of angels by failing to be angels.

———————————

Postscript:

In a handful of obscure libraries throughout the world, but mainly in Europe, copies of the "Angel's Aria" remain. To this day, no one has succeeded in singing it. But, perhaps, because a few brave souls from every generation try to, Humanity is not yet a lost cause. DEO GRATIAS! Thank you, Salvatore, thank you, Antonia! And thanks to the rest of you! DEO GRATIAS!

THE WIND-UP WOMAN

No one knows how it got there, but it did not take long for us to notice that there was a giant metal gear protruding from her back, such as are used to wind up children's toys. I had had a marching soldier when I was a boy who had precisely that same kind of gear emerging from his back, which I would dutifully wind to the maximum level of tension (you could feel when it was time to stop), before setting him down again on the floor to watch him shuffle obediently forward towards whatever destination it was I had pointed him. My friend, Billy, had had a toy robot that worked on almost exactly the same principle, except that Billy's robot made a delightful buzzing sound as it slid, step by step, across the floor. As for Andrea, our mutual playmate and first girlfriend, before we met the WIND-UP WOMAN, she had had a toy monkey whose arms moved back and forth as soon as she wound it up. Since the monkey didn't walk, but only gesticulated, and since it hardly made a noise (Andrea, herself, had to supply its chattering with her own vocal cords), Billy and I thought our toys superior to hers, which made her cry. Fortunately, we had reasonable mothers who sorted things out.

Thanks to our common childhood experiences, we were not stupefied by the gear which we noted in the WIND-UP WOMAN'S back, although it did surprise us. We had the knowledge necessary to assimilate it, to take it in stride and continue viewing her as a human being.

All of us loved her, this new friend of ours. She was witty, charming, highly intelligent, and sometimes seemed almost wise, although she had a way of letting down our expectations whenever we allowed ourselves to have them. She was like the baker of the most perfect cake that would have all the master pastry chefs of the world green with envy; but every time the hour of triumph arrived, just as she was about to serve her spectacular creation and be proclaimed the queen of the world, she somehow found a way of dropping it on the floor. We forgave her, always, not because we were magnanimous, but because her charisma was irresistible.

However, much as we loved her—and we discovered we were not the only ones, which made us simultaneously jealous and proud—we began to be troubled by her relentless and apparently uncontrollable path in life.

She could not stop moving forward, even though we wished to detain her in the name of living: to talk, to relax, to dance, to sit beneath the trees, to do the things that friends do. She seemed impelled by some irresistible force to push ahead, to wait for nothing. When Billy fell in love with her and knelt in front of her in a new suit of clothes that had cost him dearly, to propose marriage to her, she kept walking almost as if he were not there. He held out the box with the diamond ring that he had gauged more valuable than the last of his savings, extending it to her as a spring branch extends a blossom to the world, but she knocked it out of his hands as though it were a sin and kept right on walking. Her eyes seemed locked in a stare straight ahead, her arms swinging powerfully back and forth, like the arms of a power-walker in a race, like the arms of my marching soldier, like Billy's robot and Andrea's monkey.

We watched her in amazement, utterly beautiful, with the gear protruding from her back like a butterfly's or a fairy's wings. But the lovely wings were not wings, at all, they were, instead, an uncompromising mechanism which connected everything tender and original inside of her to the strong will of the hand that had wound her up, some distant time before we met her. Who was it who had wound the gear in her back, and set her down; and towards what destination was she pointed? Would the mechanism wind down soon, and then, would she be free to go where *she* wanted, liberated, at last, from the prison of someone else's intention; or would she merely *stop*, and cease to walk at all, cease to breathe, cease to see and cease to speak? Would someone else have to go behind her and wind her up all over again?

We began to feel, as time went on, and as the mechanism which drove her forward showed no signs of relenting, that she could not go on this way for very much longer. She was alienating too many people, isolating herself like a flower than insists on blooming in a swamp. Her friends could not get close to her. Whenever they approached, drawn to her radiance, those powerful swinging arms which she could not restrain, would lash out at them, striking those dearest to her, knocking them to the ground, or else scattering them like pigeons when a speeding car approaches: the kind of car that barrels through puddles along the curb, spraying torrents of water over pedestrians in the winter.

"Perhaps she is not who we think she is," Billy told us. "Perhaps, after all, she is only cold-hearted and unkind. If this is how she wants to live her life, what right do we have to interfere? If one cannot be her friend without being her victim, perhaps it is time to let her reap the solitude she has sown."

But Andrea was sure that Billy was saying this only because he felt hurt by her rejection. She said: "Have you stopped looking at her eyes, Billy?"

"Why should I look at them; to fall in love again? To suffer forever?"

"She is miserable," Andrea said. "You can see it in her eyes. She is in pain. She is not ignoring us, nor driving us all away, because it gives her pleasure. She is hurt ten times as much as we are by her indifference towards us. She is trapped by the terrible gear which is embedded in her back, to act against her interests, to obey someone else's will, to abandon the logic of her own life."

"What can we do?" I asked.

Billy said: "We can try to get hold of the gear in her back, and to stop it from turning."

"How do we know if we stop it—if we break it or just somehow stop it—that there is something inside of her that will continue to function? That she will know how to walk, to think, to breathe on her own?"

"You can see it!" Andrea reprimanded me. "If you look carefully, you can see the real her, which is like a hostage, held at gunpoint by the hand that wound her up. You can see who she is trying to be, like a prisoner behind the bars of who she is. She wants to get out of that prison! She wants to be with us! She wants to sing and dance and run with us in the woods! She wants to feel, to love, to hold a million hands!"

Acting on this assumption, Billy, who had loved her most, accepted the responsibility of his disappointment, and coming around behind her, seized the relentless turning gear in her back, and tried to fight against its rotation. However, it was quickly apparent that the mechanism had far more force than he did. He gritted his teeth and planted his feet in the ground to try to defeat it, but you could see the gear turning in spite of all his efforts, until, at last, Billy was thrown onto the ground and our friend kept walking forward, as the gear continued turning, triumphantly, in her back.

We regarded each other with despair.

"Perhaps, what is inside her can overcome the hand that wound her!" Andrea dared to think, at last. She took out an old copy of her favorite book on mythology and read to us the part where Ulysses sought to avoid going to war by feigning madness. He was plowing the sands on the beach and mumbling utterly senseless things to himself when those who wished to recruit him threw his naked infant son, Telemachus, in the path of the plow. A madman would have kept on plowing. But Ulysses, acting as a man with his reason still intact, and his love not obscured by sickness, swerved to avoid his son, whereupon the other warriors called him on his deception, and succeeded in forcing him to join them in their terrible ten year war, which ended in the pillaging of Troy.

"I will lie down in front of our friend's relentless march," said Andrea. "I will pit the goodness which she has, and the love which I know is inside of her, against the blind power of the mechanism which is controlling her life. I know she will choose me. She will change course, just as Ulysses did to avoid Telemachus! She will overcome the power of what is enslaving her!"

Stripping off her clothes, which thrilled both Billy and me, for Andrea is a beautiful woman who no one could avoid lusting for, or, at the very least, admiring as a masterpiece, like Botticelli's Aphrodite—she laid down directly in our friend's involuntary path. Andrea chose to do so utterly naked, not to compensate Billy and me for our friend's aloofness, but because she wished to seem as helpless and as vulnerable, as much like the infant Telemachus, as possible, in order to trigger our friend's resistance to the mighty, impassive turnings of the gear in her back.

All of us held our breath as our friend drew nearer.

"She's going to stop," Billy whispered hopefully. "I'm sure of it."

But to our horror, our friend barely seemed to notice the lovely exposed form of Andrea lying in her path. We saw our friend's eyes flicker for a moment with what might have been a trace of horror, but then, again, just as quickly, they were vacant as they often are, or rather, determined with nothing more than determination in them: no humanity, no concern. Merely that steady, bulldog-like gaze locked onto the leg of the horizon.

We rushed to Andrea, too late, who cried out in pain as our friend trampled her with no thought to all they had shared; without a shred of loyalty to the affection Andrea thought had bound them together, like sisters.

"Andrea! Andrea! Are you all right?" cried Billy, rushing to her side.

We saw her flesh already badly discolored, the terrible bruises that would take weeks to heal.

"She weighs a ton," Andrea groaned. "The lack of will inside her has the weight of a truck."

Our friend was no behemoth; she was of average build, and ordinarily, to be stepped on by a person of her stature would only have been a discomfort. But the sorrow of a captured life could crush metal flat.

"Now what?" we asked ourselves.

Though Andrea was hurt, she is the one who noticed that our friend was not walking in an absolutely straight line. "She is moving slightly to the left. Over a distance, you can see it," said Andrea.

We agreed. This was just like Billy's robot, which had tended to drift left as it walked across his floor. "Whenever I sent him somewhere," Billy told us, "I had to take that into account, and set him walking towards a destination that was actually slightly to the right of where I really wanted him to end up."

Now we began to wonder. Had our friend's slight drifting to the left been with her since the very start, or was it something new: perhaps, somehow, the result of her walking over Andrea? Billy thought he might have noticed it before. If that were the case, we wondered, did the drift signify some level of self-control still retained by our friend, an ember of autonomy that might be rekindled, some valiant element of her soul which was in conflict with the purpose of the hand that had wound her up, and might one day overcome it? Or was the drift merely some kind of defect, like a twitch or limp, or a broken wheel? Just as importantly, was it making her stray from the course which the hand that had wound her up had intended for her, or did that hand know of the drift, and had it compensated for it, as Billy compensated by starting his robot to the right of its intended destination? Was our friend headed towards the goal of the hand that had wound her, or was she drifting off course? If she was drifting off course, was that a good thing, a sign that she was finally gaining independence, or a bad thing—did the hand know best? The terrible hand that we all resented—was it merely a tyrant, or was it also wise?

Billy and I decided, one day that we observed our friend crying as she moved relentlessly forward, that the hand that had wound her up could not be wise, for what is right ought not to leave a trail of tears behind it; so we decided to try to stop her, or at least to slow her down, by moving obstacles into her path. "She needs to think, she needs to stop moving, to be still, she needs to see what is right here, in front of her, in her reach, not what is far ahead, and always a day away. The horizon kills the taste of the fruit in your hand. She needs to taste the bounty of life while it is here."

"Make sure you are not merely trying to get her for yourself," Andrea warned him.

"My love was like that at first," Billy said. "Now it is not. Her coldness has destroyed my self-interest; I am like a forest in the wintertime. There is nothing left here but majestic trees in the snow, the skeleton of the world without its green body. The branches have lost all their kisses. My lips have turned into thoughts. I see a part of the world that is crawling and I want to help it to its feet. That's all. That's what love means to me now."

I, who had never loved her as much as Billy, could not silence my lust like him. I could not rise above wanting her. She was so beautiful—but so difficult! I was only protected from her by my fear of complications.

Together, Billy and I pushed a huge boulder in her path and left it at the foot of a great hill. "She will not be able to get past this," he assured

Andrea. "We could barely move this boulder over level ground. She won't be able to push it up the hill. She'll have no choice but to liberate herself from the gear in her back, and to assume control over her own life. Otherwise, she'll be stuck there, forever."

But logic is, sadly, worthless in cases such as this. You build up amazing towers of belief which seem so well-thought-out, so in tune with the observed facts, and so internally consistent, that you convince yourself that there is not the slightest chance of failure. You are 100% certain that you have cracked the nut of the centuries and stand back to revel in the triumph of mind over matter. And then, against all odds, reality shows up. Reality, *not what you thought was reality*. What incredible strength is possessed by the things that hold us back! If it would take an elephant that could fly to prolong our unhappiness, we would soon be seeing elephants streaming through the sky.

Our friend came up upon the boulder and began to push it. You could see how it slowed her down, and, in fact, Andrea became worried that our friend might be hurt by the efforts we had made to help her. What she saw reminded Andrea of when she had held her wind-up monkey's arms as they tried to swing, and her father had warned her to stop, telling her that she might break the monkey that way. "You'll destroy the mechanism!" he'd told her. "After she's wound up, you have to let the arms swing free!"

"Maybe this isn't a good idea!" Andrea thought.

"She's ruining her life," Billy reminded Andrea. "We have to try to free her, at least to get her moving in a different direction—a direction that she will choose herself!"

Though it tormented us, we continued watching. Further and further up the hill, our friend pushed the boulder that was in her path. Though her life would have been so much easier if she could merely have stepped to the side of the boulder, and walked around it, *she could not*. It was harder for her to take that one small step to freedom than to push the massive weight of the stone all the way to the top of the hill that was the height of a mountain. Her tears made it that high.

We, too, were crying just as hard as her as we watched her struggling alone and tiny up the hill, as desperate and filled with suffering as Sisyphus must have been as he rolled the boulder of his sins up the hill whose summit he could never reach.

"What have we done?" lamented Billy. "We were wrong to try to save her!"

"No," I said. "She lives every day as though she were being vivisected. We are justified in pushing her. We cannot continue to accept the status quo. It is deadly!"

"The prison which holds her has more walls than we thought," Andrea said.

At last, our friend, covered with beads of sweat, her face looking ten years older from the effort, reached the top of the hill, and with a great shout of triumph, pushed the boulder from in front of her. As though frightened by her terrible commitment to her lack of freedom, the boulder fled from her at full speed, bounding down the other side of the hill with huge crashing sounds that were like cries for help.

Our friend continued her merciless march towards nowhere.

After a while, an old friend by the name of Gregory came up to us. He had done well for himself, become an engineer since we saw him last, when he, too, had been in love with our friend. But she had told him he was too dry, which was easier than saying she could not stop walking away from him.

"I have made some alarming calculations," he told us.

We looked at him with concern.

"If she continues on the path she is going, for another six months, she will come to...," he placed his finger on a map. "The canyon is five hundred feet deep, four hundred yards wide, and seven miles long, and has sheer sides from the direction she will be approaching."

"What are you saying?" Andrea asked, terror in her eyes.

"In six months' time, our friend will come upon an enormous, and impossibly steep cliff; if she cannot resist her trajectory by that time, and change course, she will invariably plunge into the abyss to her death."

"No!" Billy cried out, in despair.

I reminded them all about her drift towards the left. "Surely, in consideration of the great distance to be covered between here and there, the drift we have observed will lead her to outflank the canyon and to safely pass it to the south."

"I have taken the drift into account in my calculations," Gregory, whose keen powers of observation missed nothing, informed me.

For a moment, all four of us joined hand-in-hand in a brotherhood of despair, until at last I offered a ray of hope. "Well. Maybe it will be for the best. Maybe this is the kind of crisis that she needs to jolt her out of her fervent lethargy. The boulder was too slight an obstacle for us to pit against her lack of autonomy. But the canyon will be an insurmountable barrier. She will have no choice, when she comes upon it, but to overcome her captivity and to recover her will. What is inside her will have to overpower the revolving gear in her back, because there is simply no other choice."

"Except to keep going forward," Andrea whispered, "and to fall to her death."

While for his part Billy said, "Choice is not a part of her universe."

Trepidation remained. It was Gregory who proposed that we test the limits of her helplessness by putting up a series of signs in her path, long before she reached the canyon, which said: "DANGER: CLIFF AHEAD. BEAR RIGHT. WARNING: SHEER DROP, DEAD AHEAD. TAKE DETOUR!" Timing the speed of her progress, we put the signs up in a place she was due to arrive in after darkness had fallen, so that she could not see the terrain around her and discover our deception.

We then illuminated the signs with lights, and clearly marked the path of the detour with makeshift barriers such as are used at road-construction sites.

Then we gathered ourselves in nearby bushes to watch. To our horror, our friend was unable to prevail. True, she seemed to look at the signs and to wince. There was a moment of struggle displayed by the movements of her body, which were as expressive as the features of a face. She was trying to stop herself, but something inside her was missing, or else it shut down. The signal from her mind could not get through to her body. We witnessed a tormented soul imprisoned in a body that would not listen, and watched that body push forward, without any internal guidance except for a decision that had been made many years ago by someone else, past all the signs of warning, past all the protective barriers, towards the imaginary cliff we had invented to test her ability to defend herself. She could not.

"The cliff won't stop her," Gregory observed, on the basis of our little experiment. "She'll come up to the edge, and walk right off of it."

"My God, what are we going to do?" gasped Andrea, distraught. Her love was not diminished by the bruises on her body.

"We have six months to find a solution," was Gregory's grim reply.

Gregory, brilliant engineer that he was, soon came up with the answer. But it wouldn't have been possible if our troubled friend hadn't been so well loved. It turns out, literally thousands of people knew her and wanted to help. There were hordes of men who had dreamt of her and longed to have her as a girlfriend, as a lover, as a wife, as a friend to share the joys of life with, to pass time in museums looking at the treasures of history, or in humble eateries, sitting side by side sucking up sodas through a straw. Artists wanted to paint her in the nude, or even with her clothes on, scientists wanted to name stars for her, athletes wanted to become world champions so they could dedicate their victories to her, soldiers wanted her to kiss them so they could say they had lived before they died, filmmakers wanted to spread her around the world like a religion. Women loved her, too; they wanted to be her friend, they wanted to be tolerated by her, to catch drops of her radiance, to touch her hair and become irresistible to men. Children wanted to grow up to be like her, or to have someone like her at their side. Even those who she had tried her best to drive from her life, with insults and flailing arms and coldness she could not control, rallied to her cause on the basis of past affections, and in defense of the bittersweet illusions which she had inspired in them, which now lay like deflated balloons on the ground. Everyone knew she was more than she was. But they wanted to see that manifested in the world, not merely in their mind's eye.

And so they all came together, under the direction of Gregory, to fill the great canyon that lay in our friend's path, with earth, so that she could cross from one side to the other without perishing. "She does not have the ability to change her ways," Gregory informed the multitudes. "So we must therefore change the face of the earth for her."

No project of these dimensions had been undertaken since the days of ancient Egypt, when Cheops, in command of thousands of slaves, erected his enormous pyramid in the Valley of Kings. We were not slaves, but we were fighting to save a slave; and there were many thousands of us, breaking our backs under the hot sun as in the olden days, working as though our very lives depended on it, for, in spite of everything, she is what made our lives beautiful. Massive holes were dug in the earth in distant locations, which did not lie along her predicted path (otherwise she might fall into them), and vast amounts of earth brought from them in convoys of trucks to the edge of the cliff, from which the earth was dumped into the gigantic gorge. Workers inside the canyon worked feverishly, day and night, to pack the earth and to build it up to the level of the canyon wall—to undo God's work of ages in a matter of months, to heal the gigantic gash He had made in His world, and to replace what was missing with what we wished to be there in the place of nothing: to fill the great hole.

"Faster!" Billy urged the workers, as Andrea lent her sad, desperate eyes to his exhortations. Meanwhile, Gregory stood above us all, on the edge of the cliff, a map which he could barely prevent from being carried away by the wind in his hands, constant insights streaming out of his mind lifted up by love. "We need a ramp here, at once!" he shouted. "We must increase the angle! We need to import cement! I need reinforced steel, also! Time is running out! We have the base, we must widen the platform! Hurry! Hurry!"

I must admit that my body is not custom-designed for physical labor, but in spite of my slender frame, I pushed myself as never before, I worked like the powerful bear of a man that I am not, all because of my love for her, which did not equal Billy's or Andrea's, or Gregory's as I could tell from his new thinness; from his once well-ordered hair, now wild and unmanaged, and his face, bearded like a prophet's from neglect. All of us fought with every tool and every resource at our disposal, gave it everything we had and gave what we did not have, too.

"Hurry!" Gregory urged us, so much that his voice became ingrained in our minds, and we heard it even when he was not there, when we were trying to sleep, lying exhausted in the dark. "Hurry!" We heard it, ringing in our ears like an awful bell that made us wish to fight off our tiredness and climb back to our feet though we were on the verge of collapsing. "Hurry!" It drove us mad, completely mad; our only relief from it was to pass it on to others. "Hurry! Hurry!" in thousands of different voices. Echoes were everywhere. The canyon we were erasing was blessed to have ears of stone.

At last, at dawn, on exactly the day which Gregory had predicted, our friend appeared about two miles distant, coming down a sloping road towards the edge of the cliff.

"Is it ready? Is it ready?" cried out Andrea with trepidation.

"I believe so," said Gregory.

"You *believe* so?"

"There is some instability at the midpoint," Gregory admitted. "We didn't have time to reinforce the structure, and some elements are out of place, and only held together by pressure without a proper bond."

Andrea's eyes looked at him reproachfully.

"Look," Gregory said, sitting down exhausted. "We've done all we could. It's got to work. We can't have gone through all this in vain."

Now there was nothing for any of us to do but watch. We had partially filled the canyon with earth and built ramps and bridges at various points, at precisely calculated angles, to facilitate our friend's crossing. Now we held our breaths.

No one spoke as our friend came up to the canyon's edge. But we knew at once that our work had been justified, for though you could still clearly see that this had been a canyon and that it was not, in spite of all our efforts, advisable terrain to enter, our friend, without the slightest trace of caution or resistance, pushed forward. "If we had done nothing," Gregory said, "she would now be dead. She would have fallen off the cliff's edge and, given its height, struck the canyon floor exactly five seconds ago."

Andrea, feeling guilty for the six months of pressure she had put on Gregory, which had been motivated by fear and expressed through anger, put her hand on his shoulder. It was the best apology she could give, as we watched our friend work her way across the canyon, none of us able to utter a word.

At last, as our friend approached the other side, a murmur of hope began to escape from our lips.

"She's going to make it! She's going to make it!" Billy cried out, his eyes suddenly erupting with light.

Andrea waited a little longer; then she, too, began to jump up and down with joy. "She's going to make it! She's going to cross the canyon!

The structures have held! She's going to live! Gregory! Billy! She's going to live!"

And now, a huge cheer rose up from all our throats as our dear friend made it to the other side of the canyon.

"She's alive! She's alive!" we cheered. "We did it! We did it! She made it across! She's alive!"

For some time, we stood there, together, thousands of us, happy beyond words, utterly triumphant, knowing that we had preserved our friend, against all odds. Only after a while did the limits of what we had done begin to sink in, as we saw her disappearing in the distance, still bound to the terrible trajectory that had forced us to fill a canyon. With growing awareness gradually replacing euphoria, we watched the same sad body we had changed our lives to rescue marching onwards, with the huge gear still turning in her back. We had prevented her from falling to her death. But we could not stop her from continuing her endless walk to nowhere.

In the end, in spite of a thousand helping hands reaching towards her from the sky, she, alone, could decide when, if ever, her life would belong to her again and not to the one who had wound her up and set her down, so many years ago.

THE SUICIDE NOTE

Over the years, I have been constantly preparing to kill myself, to rescue myself from the misery that is existence. With this thought in mind, I have collected and accumulated, throughout my lifetime, a wide variety of deadly objects, from the .38 caliber pistol which I keep locked inside my desk drawer with 20 rounds, though I think that one will do, to the thick hemp rope which I maintain hidden in a box in my closet with which to conjure the hangman's noose, to the tiny yet overwhelming vial of cyanide which I have cleverly concealed in the battery compartment of an obsolete radio which I appear to be holding onto in slavery to nostalgia. It is an impressive arsenal, and often I wonder what it is that has kept me from experiencing its effectiveness. There can be only one explanation: the suicide note!

On the day I thought I would kill myself, I wrote the first draft of that note.

But I was not satisfied with it. The gun was already out, and the bullets on the table, when reading it over, I decided that it was actually imprecise. It did not accurately describe my motives to the world; the adjectives, I realized, had been chosen to be dramatic, not truthful, and the terror of being misunderstood without the ability to correct the misperceptions that might arise stayed my hand, which was already intimately familiar with the handle of the pistol. I tried crossing out the offending adjectives and replacing them with more modest and honest ones. But the physical corrections on the paper marred the aesthetic presentation of my final message to the world and seemed to reflect badly on the life that was about to be taken. Not wanting to perish in such a slovenly manner, I took out another piece of paper, white and fresh, and rewrote the suicide note, completing it, I thought, to my satisfaction, until rereading it I discovered that the new adjectives I had chosen to replace the old ones were, in spite of being more accurate, uninspired and flat and in no way worthy of the passion that had pushed me to the edge. "You have just castrated a work of art," I told myself. "No one who reads this note will understand why you did it, because the intensity is no longer there: the rage and despair that led you to point a gun at your own head have been cut out. With these neutered words, these pitiful concessions to the truth, you eclipse the greatest moment of your life, you belittle your end." Driven by these thoughts, I struggled to create a third version of my suicide note, which would accurately represent my state of mind and explain my reasons for ending my life without sacrificing any of the glory of the act. I wished my pain to leap as high as Nijinsky, to sing as boldly as Caruso. I would not leave the world as just another "John Doe." But this time, though I felt I got the language right, my hand faltered as I wrote. I was displeased by my handwriting, by the letters which lacked vigor and simplicity, and were not written with decisiveness, but seemed to gasp and wheeze their way across the page towards my demise. As I saw it, the weak, uncertain handwriting betrayed the brave and vivid content of my final message to the world.

Telling myself I was being overly perfectionistic, I picked up the gun. But looking at the note a final time before pulling the trigger, I was convinced anew that the words I had splattered across the page with my pen were spiritless. The "I's" were loopy and wide, they seemed to demean me, they were not the "I's" of a Tragic Hero like valiant Oedipus, crushed by Fate, or noble Brutus, despised by those he tried to save; and once more my "r's" looked like "s's," so that some who looked over my final message might have misread the word "sun" as "run." When I tried to make the "s" clearer, I ended up disfiguring the word entirely and was left with an illegible letter that might as well have been taken off the wall of an Egyptian tomb.

"Tomorrow, I'll get it right," I thought. I put my gun away.

But the next day, perfection continued to elude me. This time, I remembered an important train of thought which I had failed to include in my explanation of why I was about to kill myself, and I was forced to spend the rest of the day trying to work it into the existing text, without disrupting the flow of the passage into which the new material was inserted. Though I had completed my task after several hours, I then noted how one train of thought diminished the other, stole its thunder, so to speak, and to restore the impact of that, a massive rewrite was in order.

The following day, a beautiful metaphor occurred to me as I was about to finalize my message, and I decided I could not leave it in the air, but must give it a landing site on my page. My pale corpse with the bloody hole in the temple, which I had spent days imagining, would be mourned more passionately on account of it. But then, I observed how the metaphor grated with another in the subsequent passage. People might be confused by the one paragraph's use of the idea of "snow" as a symbol of purity and the other's reference to "ice," so similar to snow, as a symbol of indifference. What if the reader's mind was not as plastic, as quick to trade shapes, as mine? The rest of that day was, inevitably, spent on trying to overcome this problem, which, in turn, uncovered another even greater problem I had not previously detected.

And on it went. In this way, days turned into weeks, weeks into months, and months into years.

The suicide note expanded, became deeper, richer; it grew wildly, from passion, like vines in a garden, and was cut back by the ruthless hand of editing, which frequently went too far, requiring the planting of new seeds. The note seemed sometimes insufficient, other times beautiful, even magnificent; but always there was something more that was needed intruding on its finality, a new insight or thought given to me by the life I had not yet ended which must be included; an unexpected aversion to some part of it, to something written or something left out, which had somehow escaped my scrutiny.

At times, the thought of having to delay my suicide in a world so heartless drove me to desperation; twice, I determined to forget about the suicide note and to kill myself despite the lack of a worthy testament; to hurl the imperfect note which was impeding me into my garbage can, or feed it to the shredder, or even burn it, and just get on with things. But each time, the thought of an utterly invisible death repelled me; the idea of perishing without words in my mouth, like the silver coins which the ancient Greeks used to place beneath the tongues of the dead to pay for the trip to the Hereafter, horrified me. Such a black, empty death without bearings, without a gesture... To die so incomplete, like a tree which has borne no fruit, not even the fruit of explaining the emptiness of its branches...

I resisted the entreaties of silence, I persisted in my effort to perfect the suicide note.

And to this day I persist. When I look back on the drafts of the note I wrote in the beginning, filled as they were with clichés and superficial perspectives which I thought were wise, I cannot believe how far I have come since then. My message, now, is deep and poetic, the words that I used to stumble over fly like birds. But there is still room for improvement; every day I do not kill myself, I grow a little more and am left disappointed by who I was and how I have represented myself; and I realize that it is possible that this note I have before me right now, with which I am so pleased, may one day seem as sterile and as shallow as the ones that went before it. I am constantly bettering myself, transforming the trite into the profound, the drab into the colorful, the out-of-tune into the melodious. My pen thunders across the blank white pages, galloping new ideas, new and daring strings of words, into being. How could I dare to interfere with the development of this ever-expanding and luminous document, by cutting short the existence which feeds it?

There is still a gun and a packet full of bullets inside my drawer.

But there is so much left to write; so much to learn, and so many things I need to say before I die.

My suicide note is still only one half of what it could be.

TAKING OFF THE CAST

What a dreadful day! But its coming had been inevitable since the very first moment: nothing in this world lasts forever. It was time to take off the cast.

For eight weeks now, the heavy plaster encumbrance had clung to my leg, hugging it, like a mother embracing her child in a storm, like a python crushing the breath out of its prey, like a pyramid entombing a pharaoh, protecting his journey into the afterlife. Underneath it was the broken leg, a victim of wet leaves and a steep slope in the park, which was where the city left green relics of an old god, just enough to appease ancient longings that might otherwise return to overthrow it. Nature invigorates the soul, and for a brief few minutes, one might lose oneself in the woods, imagining that one was wandering through the rugged hills of the Black Forest or through the great timberlands of northern California, with their towering, centuries-old trees, which these bravely lingering New York trees could play the part of if one had never seen the mighty sequoias clutching at the ankles of heaven. *Swallow me up! Swallow me up!* The soul cried, running deep into the illusion of a forest. *Surround me, forever, with wilderness and rocks, hide me from sickening useless things, from battles of the deaf and dumb, won by men not sabotaged by horizons, won by men on their knees, don't give me back! Let me rush with the Fenians through untamed Celtic woods, let me hunt enchanted deer and fight invaders, let my thoughts be as tall as trees and my heart as pure as streams bled into being from the pure white snow of the mountains, let me be as noble as the tree ravaged by the storm that stands tall even with giant pieces of itself lying all around it on the ground.*

The park hurled one's spirit high into the air for a brief moment, in a forgetful cluster of thick trees on a fierce hill that had no ramp for the wheelchair-bound, until one suddenly burst through to see the distant road with lines of cars crawling along it, like a terrible anachronism, like the streetcar that inadvertently got into D.W. Griffith's scene of ancient Babylon. *What are they doing here? They do not belong!* But then the soul woke up, the spell was broken, one realized that the cars were real and that it was the freedom that was the dream. At first, it was incomprehensible. *In any house that demon or God ever formed, Fionn and the Fenians could not be in bondage.* But the rumble of the heavy engines of trucks, and the occasional sound of horns honking, like fireflies of sound flickering on and off, could not be explained away, they slowly brushed the half-sleep from one's mind, and brought one face to face, once more, with the world as it was.

When I fell down the slope, not realizing that the leaves were as slippery as they were, and that there was no real ground beneath them, just a thin piece of broken branch which had ensnared them and was wearing them like a wig, and a rock face, I knew at once that I was in trouble. My leg seemed to go straight down into some kind of pit and I heard the snap and felt an excruciating pain, before pitching forward and sprawling down a slope which I half rolled down and half slid down. By the time I came to a stop, I was in unbearable agony, yet also only half conscious from the pain. I tried to stand, but couldn't, was overwhelmed by dizziness, then tried to crawl towards a path, and vomited. For a moment, I thought of the idealistic, unprepared man from *In The Wild* who had abandoned civilization and set off to return to nature and live off the land in the backwoods of Alaska, only to end up becoming stranded beyond the reach of any helping hand and starving to death. Or the protagonist in Jack London's story, *To Build a Fire*, another victim of the unforgiving power of nature. But then I stopped myself, I reminded myself that this was not the Great North Woods or the unsparing Yukon in the wintertime, this was a park in New York City in early November, and all around there were people walking dogs, cyclists going by, and not that far away cars streaming by the thousands. Even though I was without a cell phone, this was not going to be the end of me. It was only an awful amount of pain, a stupid blunder, a terrible inconvenience, and pain, pain, pain! But there were painkillers, yes, they would give me a shot of something, a pill, once I managed to drag myself out of the woods into view and offer my misery to an ambulance.

I cannot deny that I felt terrible embarrassment as my lips formed the hateful word "Help!" at the edge of the bicycle lane, which I finally managed to reach like a lungfish crawling on land. The woman passing by on a bike stopped about twenty yards beyond me, half-stepping off of her bicycle while remaining on it, and peered warily into the woods from which I had crawled. After a while, detecting no trace of danger, she walked her bike back to me and seeing that my leg really *was* broken, removed a cell phone from her belt and made the call to 911. So she would not see, I turned my face away, which was contorted in agony with a deluge of tears streaming out of my eyes.

"They'll be here soon," she said. "How are you doing?"

If I had not been in so much pain, I would have laughed. Was she the kind of person who would try to strike up a conversation with a man's head on a pike? But she had made the call and it was my duty to be grateful.

At last, the ambulance arrived, and the EMS people were both professional and comforting. After what seemed to me to be an endless, cautious inspection, and a series of unanswerable questions which I responded to with grunts and gasps, they finally seemed to ascertain what they needed to know; they then handled my body expertly, lifting me delicately yet strongly onto a stretcher and carrying me into the back of the ambulance which I always thought of as a kind of morgue on wheels, a place to conceal the dying from the living, but which I now realized was a haven of hope in the midst of human panic and suffering. A female paramedic put her hand on my head and said something which I don't remember, but which was like a soothing ray of light. The trip to the hospital was slow, in spite of the siren, which I thought, in amazement, was wailing just for me. All the cars ahead were being pushed to the side to make room for *me*! As though I were the king, the emperor! *Make way for the Sun God! Make way for the Sun God!* My whole life, I felt like I had always been the last in line, the one who wasn't given a key and was left standing outside in the rain, the one who no one wanted to be on their team, the one who got a perfunctory and irrelevant, if not subtly demeaning present, while everyone else was jubilant and delighted on Christmas morning, clutching something they had always wanted. I was the forgotten one, the neglected one, the invisible one, the deserted one, the dried, toothpaste-filled spit you wash off of the mirror so that you can see yourself. But, suddenly, now, the whole world was bowing down before me, stepping aside that I might pass, strewing flowers of their own lost time in my path, carrying me on their shoulders by leaving the road open to the wailing ambulance. I was coming like a Roman general in triumph in his chariot towards the hospital, suddenly the most important person in the world! I was important! *I was important!* Thanks to a pile of wet leaves on the side of a precipice, I mattered!

Even in my wretched condition, and in the midst of my gratitude to those who were saving me, I could not suppress a tinge of disappointment to realize that I was not the only compassionate person in the universe, that the world was not utterly cold, self-centered and uncaring like I thought, and that I was not the sole crusader for humanity that I had believed I was. I felt jealous as the competent and caring EMS crew tended to me: jealous because the fruits of their kindness were so immediate and direct, not like my kindness, shaped into a maze of philosophy and politics through which my heart was slowly moving towards an incredible gift of gold for the human race, as meanwhile, thousands of people with broken legs cried and groaned in the gutters of my concern for the future. Why couldn't I be as necessary as these humble paramedics, as useful, as loved, and as appreciated as them? But I could not forsake the unseen and unfelt salvation of the multitudes, which I had dedicated my life to, for the quick fix of something tangible, for the satisfaction of receiving gratitude in my own lifetime! I had chosen to save more people, by saving no one in my own times! No, I must save humanity from the heart attack of war, the stroke of poverty, the auto wreck of global warming, the fall off the ladder of unsustainable lifestyles. I must load all my human brothers and sisters into my ambulance of ideas and drive it to a future of peace, prosperity, and dignity. I must study, read, network, build cities for tomorrow with the power of my intellect, struggle on a higher plane than that of the dying and the injured. These thoughts, I cannot deny, came to me in the back of the ambulance until I suddenly burst into tears again, which they thought was from the pain of my leg. And I fell off the mountain of my great pride, as I had fallen down the slippery hill in the park, hating myself, utterly hating myself, and frightened by the helplessness of being humble, of being less than these simple men and women who did not study history or philosophy, but lifted the wounded from the ground.

My wife came to meet me at the hospital, after the x-rays had already been taken, the nurses had given me strong painkillers, and the doctor had set my leg. They hadn't been able to reach her and she had found out from the message on the answering machine when she got home, and rushed to the hospital at once, completely disordered, exhausted from her work, and desperately worried about my condition, as though I had been shot down in a gun battle in Iraq. She was, as I can only think to express it, a radiant wreck! I managed a faint smile, and told her, "Sorry." Surprisingly, she hugged me, a most warm and beautiful embrace like something from the early years of our marriage. We had been having terrible rows lately, as I had been laid off from one job and was having tremendous difficulty in finding another. "You aren't really trying!" she had told me one day, in a fit of rage.

"I am!" I had responded angrily, matching her despair and premature visions of homelessness with my own protective fury, wrapped around the soft and vulnerable insides of my impractical dreams. "It is just that my past is catching up with me! Look at this resume! What can anybody do with it? I have no track record in anything except changing jobs; I am overqualified for any job that could serve as a refuge, and underqualified in terms of experience for anything I am suited for! Employers don't want interesting people, they want reliable people! They don't want birds that fly, they want rocks that stay. And they want their job to come first, they don't want to see signs that their job is only the unwelcome appendage of your violin or harp, or merely the money you need to buy paper so you can write your poems! They don't want to know that the stupid product they are trying to sell matters less to you than the world you are trying to save, that the idiot work they give you is nothing more to you than a ball and chain you have to live with as you try to walk towards something that is worthwhile. But they see it, they see it! In your face! They see it in the stilted way, you try to talk to them, they see your nobility afflicted with lies, like sores breaking out all over its face; the bad acting of your soul. They read it in between the lines of your resume! It's there blaring like a trumpet, shining like a spotlight on a prisoner; and when you think you've been clever and reinvented your past in a way that will satisfy them, they laugh at you, as though you were a child who had tried to cover over a pool of blood with white-out!"

"You'll never get anything with a defeatist attitude like that!" my horrified wife had exclaimed. "Do you want a job or not? That's all that matters! There is something called willpower. You are making it sound like you were cursed, like you belonged to the House of Atreus! You have to fight! You won't get anything just by sitting on your ass and sending out one or two resumes a week, one to be a brain surgeon and the other to be the director of NASA! Good god! And don't do anything stupid, like trying to be a messenger again, don't punish me with your exhaustion and Jesus Christ face! It's like going on a hunger strike, and it won't pay the bills! I hate my job, but at least I have one! It's not fair to dig into our savings this way! We need two incomes, this is New York City, god damn it! And cut this crap about saving the world! You aren't the Buddha, you aren't Oswald Spengler, and you aren't Pablo Neruda! I should burn all your books, I should burn them!"

But now that she saw me there, before her, worn out from my ordeal, only vaguely conscious from the exhaustion and the sweet mental caresses of the painkillers, with my leg in a huge white cast, her anger evaporated in an instant, she wept tears of guilt for not being a saint, and held me with tenderness that forgave me for my betrayal of the codes of pragmatism. She gently stroked my hair, and ran her hands up and down my face, looking into my far-off eyes that saw her through a cloud, a cloud that was like a swan with an arrow in its heart. She wept again. "Well," she said at last, making a joke that was a kind of peace treaty, "at least you won't be able to work as a messenger."

Of course, the injury was terribly inconvenient. It interrupted my job search, and it made it difficult for me to do many of the things I had done at home, things as simple as taking our clothes to the laundry, drying the dishes, and helping to carry the bags back from shopping. But with amazing good will and patience, my wife found ways to keep things afloat even as I sat at home as a cripple. She worked harder, complained less: the stoic strength of distant East European ancestors, strong women carrying great weights on their shoulders and backs, returned to her, she seemed at every moment to be spinning a web like a tireless spider, with eyes focused and loving like an artisan's on the task at hand. Then, when the work was done, she would sit down beside me and put her arm around me and kiss me on the cheek. She was the first one to sign the cast. "To Sir Edmund Hillary—not." After that, a whole host of friends and acquaintances took to signing the cast, whose vast white space could not be resisted. Soon, it was filled with all kinds of witticisms and well-wishes, ranging from the simple, such as "Get well soon," to the somewhat witty, such as "At least you could have been skiing," to the annoyingly wise, such as "The Universe teaches us through misfortune," to the dastardly, such as "I love Bush and Cheney" (I was a Democrat), placed in such a way that I could not reach it to cross it out, to the obscene, such as "Now, at least, one leg out of three is always hard," to the erudite: "For breaking the bones of a freeman, the penalty shall be 300 asses; of a slave, 150 asses." This, it turned out, was from ancient Rome's Twelve Tables, which were publicly posted in the city so that all might know the laws to which they were subjected, a revolutionary concept at the time. My cast, it seemed, had become a modern version of the Roman Forum! My wife's artist friend Regina added the finishing touches with a wonderful little painting of an angel with its leg in a cast, flying away from the earth towards a star, and another of little healing fairies, handing bones to each other in some kind of magical bucket brigade that was slowly reconstructing my shattered leg. "Just look at yourself!" my wife exclaimed one day. "You have become a walking mural, like something painted by Diego Rivera, or actually, more likely, by Chagall."

"Except for the fact that I am not walking," I said. But now, whoever came to our apartment stopped to admire me like a work of art, and to see if they could fit in some word of their own to leave behind on the cast that imprisoned me.

But, of course, it was not a prison! Sometimes, to be sure, it felt that way: especially at first, when the pain was awful, and all the throbbing was buried beneath an inviolable crust of plaster, through which I could not reach my flesh. At such times, I felt like my heart was in a cage with a lion, and I, on the outside of that cage, could not get to my own heart, and it drove me mad. I wanted to hold myself, to put my hands on where it hurt, to be my own nurse, but I was thwarted, thwarted by the savage discipline of the cast that held my leg together, preventing any stray blow or act of mercy from penetrating the ruthlessly loyal armor. Then, later, once my poor, suffering leg began to itch with a capital "I," it became even worse. My fingers wanted to rip through the cast, to dig through it to the treasure of relief, but the subterranean torment lay buried below the hard white shell of the cast. I felt like screaming and setting my leg on fire, to replace the itch with something new and different, something more ferocious and intense, to blot it out and to shame it as it destroyed it. If there must be destruction, let it be done by soldiers and not by vandals! And then there were the times when my immobility in bed drove me insane, when I needed to toss and to turn, to lie on my stomach and clutch the pillow, to face the window instead of the ceiling, but I could not. Hours passed by without a minute of sleep, hours of discomfort and exhaustion, made worse by the calm face of my sleeping wife beside me, who I could not disturb by shouting out and cursing, especially now that she was struggling so hard on my behalf. I felt like Gregor Samsa from the Kafka story, the human cockroach trapped on its back with its helpless legs wiggling in the air. In vain, I counted sheep, then horses. I closed my eyes, and saw myself on a beautiful tropical island with gentle waves washing up on the beach and palm trees swaying in the breeze, then I was lying down in a little cave in the ground like the kind of cavern found at the bottom of a tree, with roots for its ceiling, that leprechauns hide their treasures in, and I was resting there amidst emeralds and rubies and olden coins of gold, but still without the jewel of sleep in my hand. In angry, resentful mornings, I would sit up on the sofa with my leg on a stool, after half-walking, half-collapsing there, staring into space and telling myself, "Go on, then, die; if you can't sleep, you will die! You will die from exhaustion, go on, then, no use resisting! Go ahead and kill me with insomnia!" Who I was talking to, I do not know, but whoever it was seemed to listen and to feel sorry for me, for almost immediately, I would fall asleep and wake up hours later, refreshed, still sitting, on the sofa. "If horses can sleep standing up," I told myself, "Why not? If dolphins can sleep, in snatches, in the sea, which could drown them. Sleep—go to the surface for air. Sleep—go to the surface for air. Yes, I can survive this way." And the thought calmed me down, until I was finally able to sleep again in my bed.

But these inevitable drawbacks could not overcome the wonders of the new world that my injury spread at my feet like a carpet. From being a stubborn, impractical, maddening husband, a man who counted stars in the sky while dollars blew out of his pocket, I suddenly became a sorrowful victim, a precious, wounded soul, a magnet for any woman who had a mother or a nurse inside of her. My sins were forgiven, my faults overlooked, my blunders buried in the past, I was now the recipient of enormous sympathy, nearly constant attention, and renewed love; the absurd pressure of life which blinds us to souls was ruptured by my small disaster, and my dreams were pushed to the surface of the earth where their beauty sparkled like diamonds in spite of the pain they caused to those who must live in a world that is pointed in the opposite direction. My wife recognized my nobility once again, saw the silver lining of my foolishness; gently, she kissed my white plume, the first time in many years.

And the pain became manageable; it diminished, and at the same time, I got used to it. When you want to live, you can get used to almost anything. Little by little, I learned to get around, it was like learning to ride a bicycle, the bicycle of my body's heaviness and inflexibility, until finally I could get up and down without fighting like a gladiator, go to the bathroom and wash myself without risking death on the bathroom tiles, go up and down stairs without the terror of plunging down them like the baby carriage at Odessa, and walk on the street, flying gracefully like a pendulum on my crutches and moving so quickly and vigorously, in fact, that I cracked the hand support of one of them and needed to get a replacement. Though people who were well passed me by, it was as though I were traveling faster, or just as fast as them, because I was injured and they were not. We now lived according to different standards. Doing less on the outside, I was their equal, because I was doing more on the inside. It was an amazing feeling to lag behind them, and yet not to be considered slow, not to be despised by them and not to despise myself. And I thought: you cannot march to the beat of a distant drummer, only limp...

At the public library, which only one week earlier, before I mastered my condition, had been as far away as the moon, I got out some books that interested me, books I had wanted to read for a very long time, and lugging them home inside a backpack as I conquered the world with my crutches, I set down to reading them in absolute peace, without having to bear the stigma of irresponsibility or to face the charge of escapism as in the past. My leg was broken, what else could I do? I might as well read, I might as well blossom like a flower in my unrealistic garden before the world got me back!

In one book, a military history of the Western world, I studied and was amazed by the courage and brilliance of ancient warriors who had taken stands and, unlike me, materialized things in the world. I read about the battle of Marathon, and how a small Greek army charged down from the hills upon a vast Persian horde before it had been able to properly deploy after disembarking from its ships. The audacious exploitation of the perfect moment had delivered a victory that would not have been possible under any other circumstance. How could you be so ready, so ready to strike like lightning through the tiny windows of opportunity that fate provides to the nonconformist, to the true individual seeking to break free of the herd, to the democratic experiment in the midst of tyrannies? Then, I went on to read about the incredible exploits of the Theban general Epaminondas, who, with his unique oblique formation, overwhelmed the undoubtedly superior army of Sparta before it could bring its full force to bear against the whole of the Theban front. Concentration at the decisive point, this was Epaminondas' great contribution to the science of warfare; strike furiously with your strengths, while your weaknesses are kept out of range! Then there was Alexander the Great, who had the imagination of Scheherazade and the decisiveness of a falcon diving from the sky upon its prey, and Caesar who was both shrewd and bold, but more than that, a cultivator of loyalty, a man who won the love and trust of the human beings he turned into his weapon. Incredible tales: tales in some ways dark and sinful, yet somehow inspiring, written from the pit of human violence and from the peak of human accomplishment. Anyone can dig up a jewel on a calm and sunny day; who can find one when the whole world is crashing down on his head? I read these tales of ancient heroes and bygone struggles with glowing eyes, I flew beside the greatest heroes of history because I was crippled and did not have to take a step in the world.

Besides this passionate, strident book of extremes, I turned to a giant volume of Buddhist teachings and essays. It was a wonderful book, profound and illuminating, with something so clear and liberating in the style of the principal commentator, and even in the way the letters of his words were printed on the page, and the size of the margins, and the amount of white space left between the lines and between the words, and the thickness of the pages, and the way they felt as they were being turned, and the way they smelled… Just holding the book in my hands, I felt something incredible and powerful flowing into my soul, I felt that my life might be on the verge of changing, after years of stagnant daydreams of a new me. And for those few weeks I was injured, with nothing to drag me away from that book, I raced towards enlightenment, like a wind gathering force over the sea. In the monastery of being a cripple, I grew and grew, alone and sheltered from the temptations of the world and the terrible demands, which it recruited those who you loved the most to make on you. I did not have to fight with a boss, I did not have to endure the treachery, cowardice and indifference of coworkers, I did not have to climb into a can of sardines to get to work, or put up with the disappointment and grotesque visual of watching out-of-shape people rush for seats like miserable pigeons battling for a pretzel. I was here, by myself, in a temple of wisdom, saved by my broken leg, which was like the great tree the Buddha sat under. Without the world, I was the great, shining Buddha himself! Who was there to strike me with a stick and tell me I was wrong? Who was there to throw me off the bridge into the raging river, to gauge how deep were the waters of Zen? Passing from one chapter to another, I hardly noticed the poem: *Oh bird, what perfect wings you have in the tree!*

I did not doubt my resurrection as I sat there, alone, with my leg in a cast, I stood like the boy with his finger in the dike, keeping out the sea of everything that could crush me. I could sense its power, hear its roar on the other side of my time off, feel the wetness of my finger, but where I was was dry and I believed in that dryness in the upper stories of my mind, above the unspoken fears that crept about in the basement of my holiday, threatening to spoil the wonderful vacation of my misfortune! I could clearly hear rats, in the shape of clocks, searching for food in the darkness; anything precious to me was their food, they had a hunger for what made my life meaningful, they had always, since I could remember, preyed upon my dreams, sneaking into my world through the gap between who I wished to be and who I was. There, in the center of my unguarded soul, they ate the means to my ideals, but left my ideals standing as a source of torment, like the grapes of Tantalus. They left me with my words, but turned my most eloquent and impassioned writing into a Potemkin village. They left me with the ambition of Alexander the Great, but with the morality of a monk who is afraid to squash a fly; but in the end, my great and paralyzing morality was actually, as Nietzsche recognized, only the fear of not being able to get away with the crime! For surely no crime is graver than abandoning the world, than withholding one's gifts from it, and that is precisely the one that is the easiest to get away with, and the one I had committed, instead of any other that might have saved even a single life! Now, with my broken leg, I was blessed with the most beautiful amnesty; a white flag was flying over the no man's land between my divine purpose and my noncompliance with God. I did not have to solve the puzzle of how to walk over the flypaper of the world, as it was, to something better; I was sidelined, free of the flypaper and free of paradise! But the clocks were ticking! Regina's innocently cruel fairy healers were methodically rebuilding my leg, and soon, I would be hurled back into the great test of the world, thrown into the deepest waters of Zen, torn from the gentle place where you can be an angel because no one is beating you with a club and no one is stretching their hand out to you for help because you are stronger than they are. All over again, I would have to begin the hateful task of looking for work, I would have to put away my frivolous, beloved books, endure my wife's desperation, which would return, I would have to split in two, like Janus, with one face pointing towards what the world wanted from me and one face pointing towards my heart. I would have to keep my roses hidden or face real lions, I would have to jump out of the coffin of my diaries and poems and advance like Epaminondas against armies of simple-minded Spartans, with something that was hopefully peaceful but as real as a spear, or else admit that Epaminondas was far beyond me and become a creature of science fiction like Captain Nemo, plowing endlessly through the seas between my ears! I would have to make a choice between fantasy and the truth! With both legs back, I could no longer revel in the beauty and innocence of incapability! I would have to walk!

On the day the doctor finally took off the cast, showed me the x-rays, and told me, beaming with pride, "Your leg has healed magnificently, you're as good as new!" I could only pretend to smile back, as deep inside, my heart was flooded with an awful sorrow, in which I nearly drowned. I felt as though someone had just expired, someone very dear to me, someone who I could not live without. Books, books, how many beautiful books must be buried now; how many more would die in the plague to come? I thought of the precious objects in my room, pages with my handwriting, books held long ago by a dreamer's hands, and souvenirs from trips to places that time had made sacred, and I thought, "They are no longer yours. Once more, nothing belongs to you."

But then I resisted—I resisted the collapse of being well! Epaminondas! Epaminondas! I thought. He had marched his underestimated warriors into the field with the brilliant fire of his mind, the love of his city, and the will to emerge from his mother's womb; he had not clung to the semi-conscious visions and heroin-like comfort of the watery haven between her thighs. He had won a great battle because he had let himself be born. I felt a surge of utter terror, black and bottomless, rush into my heart and soul, I could walk again, I could walk again! The cast was off my leg!

God help me, I thought on the day I was finally healed: they've taken off the cast!

THE FIRST MAN IN THE VALLEY OF EGGS

He hardly remembered how it happened, but somehow he had been born. He realized this, one day, walking by the fragments of the shell from which he had hatched.

All about him, in the valley, stretching as far as the eye could see, he beheld the giant white eggs, thousands of them, lying scattered about on the ground; and something deep inside told him that from these eggs other beings like him would one day emerge, to rescue him from loneliness, and share with him the wonder of living beneath the wide blue sky, beside the little stream of water which nourished the gardens in the gray hills.

As time went on, he became more adept at living. He hungered less, for he knew better where to find food; he thirsted not at all, because he learned how to dig into the ground in pursuit of the stream when it disappeared into the mud in the summertime. His struggles diminished, and his joys increased. The desperation of his time was quieted by resourcefulness and replaced by curiosity and exhilaration.

But still, he was alone. When the rains fell, and his body shivered, though his mind rejoiced, for thirst was at an end, he was alone. When lightning flashed in the sky and struck the ground like a knife of fire, when thunder bellowed as though the sky itself had been wounded and was thrashing about with maddened claws, he was alone. After the storms were over, he would weep, and embrace himself, for there was no one to comfort him.

Years came and went, and he developed habits: he took to making rounds of the empty valley. At least once a month, he would span the enormous, drab expanse, walking among the giant eggs, putting his ear next to the silent shells, wondering how long he would have to wait until he was not alone.

As time went on, and survival no longer seemed enough, he began to study the flowers that grew upon the bank of the stream, and to emulate their colors with paints he made from plants and petals, from sands and pigments. He began to beautify his world. He imagined the beings who would one day hatch from the eggs and, for them, created brilliant and moving works of art from the primitive resources at his disposal. Then he invented words, and he began to write poems to the sky, to the water, to the rocks, and most of all, to the few brave trees that managed to stand in the sun-drenched valley, which was nearly as dry as ashes pulled from a fire. He wrote poems about the world he lived in, and poems to the beings who were soon to be born. He wrote of the dangers and the joys of the world they were about to enter.

Strange feelings also coursed through his body. For many years after it first awakened in him, he felt a terrible longing he did not understand; he stood naked by the giant eggs and begged for someone to emerge from one; he howled like an animal, and rolled in the dirt, until his mouth was filled with dust, he cried out with passion in the bushes by the stream and wept tears of sorrow in the wake of his ecstasy. He painted and wrote more than ever before.

Time went on—and on— and after a while, he noticed that he was no longer walking as strongly as he had at the beginning. His stride had shortened, he did less, and lost his breath sooner. "Something is happening to me," he thought. "Could it be that as I was born, I will one day die?"

With more fervor and hope than ever, he began to spend his days strolling among the unhatched eggs, listening for a sign of life. Once he thought he heard the sound of cracking coming from one of the shells, and his heart filled with joy. He sat down there for days waiting, but no trace of a fissure appeared, not even one tiny line insinuating itself into the perfect silence of the white enamel. He pushed his ear against the giant egg, he listened for a heartbeat, he tried to speak through the shell to whoever it was who was inside it, whose time of being born had not yet come. He invited them to hurry. He offered them the sky, the water, the majestic view of the valley, which did not know how to hold his hand. But nothing further occurred to raise his hopes. At last, he placed a marker beside this egg, which had raised his hopes in vain, and continued on his way, walking among the shells, day in and day out.

The weakness he had first noticed some time ago began to increase. It became harder and harder to walk. His thirst became harder to assuage. The sun seemed to grow hotter.

"Come! Please come!" he begged the unhatched beings inside the eggs. "Please come before I die, I want to see you!"

But all across the valley, they still lay as silent as the day he first became aware of their existence, thousands of them scattered like stones across the earth by the Creator of all things. Only his own egg lay ruptured, broken, in fragments on the gray floor of the valley.

Finally, he lost the strength to paint and to make poems. All the beauty of the world was no longer enough to give him the energy to lift his hand. His tired eyelids closed, and he lay down, in resignation, with only one thought to console him, now. *He would leave his work behind in the empty valley beside the thousands of unhatched eggs.*

He awakened and went back to sleep in solitude.

He was the first man, in a world that was not yet ready to come to life.

TWO WHO LEARNED TO FLY

Our town lies on a major convergence of thoroughfares, two great roads and a mighty river, which bring more interesting people to it than it deserves. That is, no doubt, how it came about that in a single year, we were blessed by the arrival of two amazing newcomers, R. and A., neither one of whom stood out immediately, although you could tell that R. thought highly of himself and, unless he was merely conceited, must have some extraordinary talent which he was keeping to himself. Some of my fellow townsfolk thought that he must be a famous writer who had written under a pseudonym and was utterly unknown by his real name. Perhaps he was fleeing from the burden of a pen that was dangerously ahead of its times, or an exotic imagination that would have offended simple people like us had we known the wild things it had conceived. Others, because of his accent, felt he might be some foreign dignitary forced to beat a hasty retreat from his troubled homeland: an exiled cabinet minister ousted by revolutionaries, or a member of some persecuted religion or ethnic minority. Many felt sympathy for him, as one does for a stray dog that no one recognizes, who seems to be looking for his home.

As for A., he seemed to belong to our own land, and we felt his story must be far less romantic than that of R. He was overly modest, as are people who think little of themselves, and usually such people have a good reason for viewing themselves as they do. He seemed a bit puzzled, yet in no hurry to figure out whatever it was that was puzzling him. Something in his soul was like a ship at sea when the wind is calm and the sails are useless, and for hard-working people like us, to see such immobility in a man's spirit is displeasing, like hearing the choir in a church singing out of tune. Mrs. L. suggested that perhaps he was at the point of changing directions in his life, and pondering which route he should take; and that if the choice he made right now might bind him for the rest of his life to a path from which there was no turning back, then surely, his hesitation was understandable if not laudatory. But then, Mrs. L. was always giving everyone the benefit of the doubt.

Both of our new arrivals made out well in the town, appearing to have some economic resources to sustain them through the long period of their inaction, in which rest and contemplation seemed to be their only objective. Obviously, A.'s finances were less impressive than R.'s, as A. eventually returned to working part-time at the shipping office's maintenance department. He had, we heard, experience and skills as a craftsman, carried with him from some populous city in the East.

But the purpose of this story is not to dwell on the appearance of two incidental strangers in our town, and their subsequent months of leisure. Our lives are not so miniscule that we must stoop to glorifying utterly ordinary men in order to amuse ourselves. No, both R. and A. shared an incredible ability, which justifies the writing of this account. Why they took so long to reveal it is not absolutely clear, but the way in which their abilities were discovered is well known.

With regard to R., I was standing out on the property beyond the warehouse, looking out towards the prairie, along with Mrs. L., Mr. and Mrs. H., and five young men from the warehouse, when, all of a sudden, we saw R. returning from his daily walk out on the prairie, where he could get away from us for a while. He cut a striking figure with his elegant, loose-fitting white shirt and stylish top hat, and the walking stick he carried with him, apparently only to mock it with his vigorous strides.

Mrs. H. was remarking on his intriguing and enigmatic presence when, all of a sudden, we saw him leap off the ground and soar gracefully, and practically vertically, straight up into the air. One of the workmen estimated that the angle of his ascent was well over 75 degrees, though it was certainly under 90, and another estimated that he attained a height of about seventy feet before he came to a stop, seemed to float for a moment in midair without moving, then, gently, but only because of the powerful and rhythmic flapping of his arms which acted as a counter to the force of gravity, fell back to the earth, on which he landed softly. Hardly had he touched down, but he was flying upwards again. We noted, this time, that he used a powerful downward thrust of his arms, to propel himself upward, and that two or three sufficed to raise him to an enormous height; many more beats were demanded of his arms in order to land safely.

"Is there any one of us here," Mr. H. asked us, "who has not partaken of alcohol today?"

None of us, in fact, had resorted to the spirits.

"By God," Mrs. H. blurted out, "we are in the presence of a miracle!"

All of us stunned, our bodies tingling as though we had received an electric shock from one of the many new inventions that the world is churning out these days, we looked at each other in amazement, searching for an explanation.

"God's work," said one of the witnesses.

"Or Satan's," said another.

But another, more reasonable and in harmony with the times we lived in, said, "A new breakthrough in science. We must get to the bottom of it."

But as we stood there, trying to shake off the astonishment which held us in its grip and would not let us move from the spot where our view of life had changed, we saw the second stranger, A., passing by along another path, that which runs beside the field that often succumbs to wildflowers. To our utter amazement, we saw that he, too, was not walking as an ordinary man, but rather flying; only his way of flying was utterly different than that of R.'s. Rather than taking gigantic, nearly vertical leaps into the sky, he seemed to float no more than a foot or two above the ground, except that "floating" is a word that makes his mode of travel seem too effortless. You could see the determination, by means of the tightness of the muscles in his face and the single-mindedness of his gaze. He went by, his two arms stretched out to the side, not flapping, but rather, tensed and rigid, and rotating at a steady velocity.

"He's not flying," Mr. H. speculated, or was it wished? For two men flying in but a single day, after thousands of years of human history in which not a single one had flown, seemed too much to bear, especially for a town like ours. "He's only walking. What a peculiar fellow!"

But after a moment, as he came out of the high prairie grass and we could clearly see the relation of his feet to the ground along the dirt trail leading past the warehouse back into town, Mrs. L. exclaimed: "Take it back, Mr. H.! His feet aren't touching the ground!"

And we all gasped, as though we had seen roses falling from the sky.

"Either it is the beginning of the end, and God's angels have come to usher in the final days, or else science has made God as obsolete as the horse-and-buggy," said one of our number.

We determined at once to gather more of us together, and then to march upon the two new arrivals where they lived in the hotel by the east-west road, to demand an explanation.

A., whom we cornered first, seemed surprised and somewhat alarmed by our excitement, in contrast to R., who, when he found us knocking on his door with A. a virtual prisoner in our midst, only smiled, as though an agitated mob was but a trifle. "Cigars?" he asked, opening up a beautiful, foreign cigar box and offering a smoke to any who would share one. A few accepted, and this practically drove out all the women, who have less of a stake in enduring overpowering clouds of smoke than men. However, Mrs. L. and Mrs. H., strong women that they were and proud ambassadors of their kind, refused to be flushed out of the room where they expected the explanation of a miracle to be divulged.

"Are you servants of God, or the Devil?" one man who did not smoke asked the two fliers.

Another of our townsfolk, after letting out a mouthful of aromatic fumes, asked: "Is there a scientific explanation, some invention behind this feat?"

While A. seemed pale and at a loss for words, R. replied: "Dear friends: there is no gadget, nor is this a miracle, so far as I know. Thomas Edison is not behind this, nor is William Jennings Bryan. I have merely mastered the art of leaping high into the air and retarding the effects of gravity, for the brief moment needed by my flight. Call it 'athleticism' or call it 'art'; as a form of ballet, it comes from the human body and is but a subtle extension of our normal physical capabilities."

Everyone looked at him, bewildered.

At last, someone said: "That is too simple an explanation! How is it that you can fly, and we cannot?"

"But I am sure that you can," R. told them. "There is no great secret to it, as far as I know. I learned how to fly on my own, by trial and error. It is important to perfect the timing of the leap and the first flap of the arms, and important not to let the subsequent flapping of the arms during the ascent re-inject weight into the body, which must feel itself light in order to continue rising. When coming down, it is important not to panic. The use of the arms must increase dramatically."

"But every little boy who has tried to fly..." protested another of our townsfolk.

"Children *play* at flying," R. said. "They do not apply the discipline, the will, the methodicality, the powers of observation of grown men to the enterprise, which are needed to succeed. They are not serious! By the time they are finally men, they are so convinced by what they have heard and read that it is impossible to fly, that they no longer try. Who would respect a man who they saw spending hours in a field, leaping upwards, flapping his arms, running and jumping, trying to lift himself off the ground, to fly?"

"It is Will," agreed A., finally daring to speak. "That is all. Will. Practice. The courage to try, to learn. Will," he said again.

Bewildered, the townsfolk regarded them.

"Will you teach us to fly?" someone asked them at last.

"Flying can't be taught," replied R. "You have to feel it with your body. Your body will instruct you. All you have to do is try. Try, try, and try."

"Will you watch us try, then?" someone asked.

R. smiled, delighted by the aroma of his cigar. "I don't see how I can help you," he insisted, "but if it pleases you, since you have been such hospitable neighbors, I will attend to your efforts."

*****

It hardly needs to be said that trying to fly has become the principal pastime of our important but overlooked town. Soon, the ball field to the east of the junction, and the prairie to the west of the warehouse, were filled with men, women, and children of all ages running, leaping, flapping their arms, and attempting to fly. In order to prevent them from becoming discouraged, both R. and A. would give periodic exhibitions of flying, the former thrilling audiences by leaping powerfully, yet almost delicately, from the ground, and hovering for a moment, high up in the air, in the manner of a balloon, before finally descending to the earth with a dancer's grace; the latter more slowly and ponderously floating above the dirt with his feet dangling, sometimes only a few inches from the ground, the soles of his shoes in danger of scraping the earth. In spite of the fact that R. provided exhibitions only when compensated, for he felt that otherwise he might be taken advantage of and worn out by our enthusiasm, he was vastly the more popular of our two fliers, and the one who everyone wanted to learn from, even though he had already warned us vociferously that he could teach us nothing. The drama and decisiveness of his triumph over the limits that bound the rest of us excited us beyond all measure, while A.'s laborious method of flying, which seemed more of a struggle than a liberation, seemed hardly to be flying of all. "He goes no faster than a man walking," someone complained, "and rises only inches from the ground."

Another said, "If one were in danger, being pursued by wild beasts, for example, or by bandits, such a means of flying would not serve one at all."

"I fly that way in my dreams," another complained. "I can't go any higher, and usually I am being pursued by a pack of wolves; I cannot elude them and, in fact, they are merely excited by my dangling feet."

"WILL!" R. told the frustrated people gathered around him. "WILL! That is what it comes down to! How badly do you want to fly? Obviously, not badly enough!"

"I *have* Will!" protested a man, nearly angry, except that being angry at a man who could fly did not seem right, and probably, neither was it wise. "I was in the war, back in the days of cavalry, and I charged up the hill with bullets flying all around me."

"You're that old?" someone joked.

"I have Will!" the man insisted.

"You had Will to ride a horse, and Will to fight. But do you have Will to fly?" demanded R. And he leapt back into the air, crushing the frustration with a new display of his prowess, which transformed feelings of impotence into renewed aspirations. A man who had once saved ten of us from a terrible flood when the river forgot its purpose for a week, rushed up to give R. the top hat that had fallen off his head as he flew above us.

I, admittedly, to my credit or eternal shame, was one of the first to give up trying to fly. I felt the world demanded too many ordinary things of me, which would, if neglected, soon become overwhelming, for me to lose valuable time attempting to bypass them by means of flight. My existence, as it was, offered me too many tangible forms of moderate satisfaction for me to risk euphoria. To live for all or nothing is a luxury of the rich, whose nothing is to merely live like the rest of us; or else, it is, perhaps, exclusively the domain of the brave. I felt myself to be in danger of losing the harvest of humility, which I knew I could depend on, by attempting to imitate these two, the only two men I know of who ever mastered the power of human flight. I preferred to be reliable rather than glorious, since the one thing seemed sure, and the other a hundred times as uncertain.

However, one thing I could not suppress, during the year my town was caught up in the throes of its flying craze, was the desire to know more about these two very different men who had learned how to fly. They were so absolutely different in temperament, and in the technique and style of their flying. How is it that each of them, in his own way and by his own method, had learned to do what the rest of us, try as we might, seemed unable to do? And so, I set out to interview them both before they left, for all of us began to suspect that they would not remain with us forever. We seemed to bore them, or merely to impose ourselves too adamantly upon them. I am afraid that the thought of flight upended our politeness. Surely, our minds and our amusements did not interest them; they had come only for the peace and quiet that attends mediocrity, and not for the mediocrity itself. Once the peace and quiet were gone, what could induce them to stay?

I interviewed R. first, after paying him what was the equivalent of two months of my salary for the imposition, and as I shared one of the last of his cigars (perhaps he had made up his mind to leave town after the last of them was smoked), he told me: "As I have said a hundred times, the secret of my mastery of flight was WILL. All the subtle movements of the body and techniques for focusing the mind, which provide the basic mechanics for flight, came into being only because my Will demanded it. I do not tell you this to mystify you, but because it really is that simple."

Not wishing to part with so dear a portion of my savings for so meager a scrap of information, I insisted: "Surely, R., there must be something more. Perhaps it is what inspired you to have such a Will. Here, for example, I feel that many of us possess considerable willpower, although you may feel that if we did, we would not be living in such a backwater. However, I have noticed that what motivates us to wish to fly is mainly the wish to fly. There is something beautiful and glorious in the idea. But perhaps you had a stronger motivation?"

At this prying question, a flash of light came to R.'s eyes, and his foreign origin became more obvious. He had a different kind of passion, a fierce romantic streak burning inside him that is missing from our practical land, so much stronger than his, yet also so much drier. I imagine in his country that the people drink all night, dance until dawn, then shoot each other with pistols in the morning on account of some insult which such a lifestyle can hardly fail to provoke. They live in shabby, semi-civilized imitations of our cities, which are poor and cold, but write great novels. "Good for you!" R. exclaimed, enjoying me almost as much as his cigar. "You are the first one, in all this time, who has made an inch of progress!" And thinking for a moment, with eyes that darkened fearfully, then seemed to waver in purpose, then finally to rebel against fear and follow a wild impulse that might or might not be lethal, he told me: "Please promise me that what I tell you now you will tell to no one else, at least until after I have left your town. Even though there is no extradition treaty between your land and mine, I do not need the embarrassment."

Not certain if it was right to agree, I nonetheless did. "You have my word," I informed him.

Regarding me for a moment, with eyes that showed both hardness and cleverness—a frightening mix—he leaned forward, nearly as close to me as a lover, so that I could smell, besides the smoke, the alcohol on his breath, and he said to me: "Where I live, there is a large building on a hill, in which the wealthy live. It is like a fortress, ten stories high. On the level of the street, there are guards, and there is an iron gate through which no one who is not known can pass. But," he said, "Above the second story, there lie all the other floors, with windows left open and unlocked in the summertime. And behind those windows, extraordinary wealth: safes filled with money, with jewelry, with gold, with bonds from the ancient days. For years," R. went on, "I looked up at those windows and I thought: If only I could fly! If only I could make a mockery of that fence, those guards standing by the gate with their weapons, and simply fly straight up, over the fence, then again, up the side of the building—hover there, by a window—open it—crawl in— clean the place out, and get away!"

I looked at R. with horror. How perfectly molded was his way of flying to the task which had motivated him to fly, to the longing which had made his Will billow, like a ship's sail! "You were—you were poor," I suggested, not wishing to fear this man whose face was leaning next to mine.

"Not at all," replied R. "I belonged to the middle class, what there was of it. My father was hardworking and respected in his profession. We were able to live comfortably but not extravagantly. Do you know the difference between the women of workers and the women of aristocrats? The face, the waist, the manners? Do you know how different the food of the rich tastes? While you are trudging through the winter snows, which step on our cities as if they were bugs, you think of those who are lying on some sunny beach, in another country, who will only return to their homeland when the sun returns. No, my friend, my life was good, but what is good next to better? Their windows were open!"

I did not know what to say. R. was boisterous, excited, jubilant, and savage, all at once. "Do not tell anyone what I have said," he warned me. "I will be gone soon enough, anyhow, and then you will not have to feel you are keeping a secret from your friends."

I agreed again, and feeling faint, whether from the smoke or the terrible force of the personality of our town's hero, I staggered out to the street in search of air.

Two days later, fearing what I might hear, I proceeded to go through with the interview I had scheduled with A., in his hotel room, only one floor removed from R.'s. Somehow, I felt in mortal danger as I entered the building, but I knew it was unlikely that my trepidation would be validated, for R. was as intelligent as he was amoral.

A. did not at all provide me with the drama, nor did he speak with the flair, of R., but, nonetheless, we soon got to the bottom of his power of flight, which like R.'s, was driven by Will, which had a very specific motivation. "Back East, I worked in a large shop," A. told me. "We worked at tables and did skilled manufacturing that was not produced from a mold, but hand-cut to a standard. With work of this kind, we should have had a better boss, but he, always in mortal fear of going under, overlooked our skill and treated us badly. Morale fell, and disrespect seeped into our hearts. We learned from him to be bad to others. Well, it so happens that there was a cleaning lady in our shop, a Mrs. Kelly, and not being pretty enough to tease, nor imposing enough to fear, we afflicted her like a pack of dogs, mainly by walking over the floors which she had freshly mopped. True enough, her work and our sense of freedom often clashed, for we did not like to be bound to any one place by a wet floor that needed more time to dry. But it went beyond that, to the point where we would often leave our tables when we did not need to and find some excuse to walk over the floor she had just cleaned to make it dirty again; and for some reason, we found it amusing whenever our boss came by and chewed Mrs. Kelly out for not properly performing her duties. 'Do you call this clean, Mrs. Kelly?' he would demand, and we would snicker."

I regarded A. with curiosity, and a trace of disgust.

"Well," he said, "one day it happens, as I did my part to make Mrs. Kelly's life utterly miserable, that she looked at me, with fury and despair in her eyes which she could not express, and finally said, what of it she could get out of her: 'Mr., do you know I have little ones at home? Do you think it will be so funny if they cannot eat?' And it hit me then, right then, how far I'd fallen from being a decent man, and how needless was this cruelty which I had been weak enough to let myself learn from others. And I decided, then and there, that I would learn something new—a way to be kind. And as I saw it, in the environment in which I was, that was to be done by not walking on Mrs. Kelly's freshly mopped floors until the water had dried. And so, that is how I learned to fly, and from that time on, I never tormented her again."

In amazement, I regarded A., wishing I had one of R.'s cigars in my hand to do something while I wondered what I ought to say, if anything. As R.'s manner of flying was exactly molded to the purpose for which he had developed his power, so was A.'s perfectly molded to the humble task of avoiding Mrs. Kelly's floors!

"Will you be staying much longer?" I asked him at last.

"Not likely," he admitted. "I came here for peace, and because I was recovering from an illness and wished to surround myself with air that was pure. Out there on the prairie, the wind smells like flowers, and the sky is everywhere... Perhaps I shall continue traveling west."

*****

The days which our town had for retaining our two fliers were dwindling; as each had come to our town for his own reason, so, now, was each on the verge of leaving for his own reason. I spent the last days of their presence in our town, studying them as they flew, and watching my neighbors watch them.

I saw how eagerly my friends raced after R. as he leapt into the air and floated above us all. How excited they were by his impressive style of self-elevation, how ecstatic and fervent in their desire to emulate him. When he landed, he barely had a second to himself, before they were all over him, touching him, congratulating him, practically bowing down to him, although, in this country, we have not bowed down since, over a century ago, we applied our foot to the back of King George's pants. In sharp contrast, as A. flew, barely getting off the ground and traveling at such a low speed that we could match it by walking, and easily outpace it by running, enthusiasm waned. No crowds followed him, no young girl begged him to run away with her, no married woman dreamed of dishonoring her husband on his account; he did not have to fear the buttons of his jacket being torn loose, or the hairs pulled from his head like relics, as though he were a saint. There was clearly no comparison between the two means of flying, the one utterly melodramatic and the other mundane; the one splendid and defiant in the face of human limits, the one barely noticeable and in some ways inferior to our everyday modes of transportation; the one exhilarating, the other merely interesting. The difference was so great, in fact, that A.'s way of flying now, to us, hardly seemed to be flying at all.

I stood there, for many hours, watching the two men fly, and watching the people of my town reacting to their flying.

And for the first time in my life, I realized that I was no longer in agreement with those among whom I had been born and raised.

I saw less beauty in the high, majestic leaps of R. than in the struggling, low-level flying of A., who barely seemed able to get his feet off the ground.

I saw less beauty in the flying itself than in where the flying had come from.

THE VIOLINIST

When he first came into the town from the other side of the river, he didn't know what he was about to face. He thought he knew, but how wrong he was!

Usually, when people saw the well-protected, polished case, shaped tight-fitting around the instrument, they rejoiced, they came out of their homes to greet him, to offer him handshakes and drinks, to invite him to parties noted on their calendars, usually more than he could attend, and to weddings, and to beautiful gardens underneath balconies when the moon was shining.

However, when he stepped off the boat this time, he found the townsfolk strangely cold. It was as if they knew him from before, and he had done something terrible he could not remember. No one spread a carpet underneath his feet. No one handed him a flower. No one introduced himself or gave him an invitation. When he asked for a match to light the hand-rolled cigarette he had brought from across the river, no one could find one, not even the old men whose pipes were alive with billows of smoke, curling upwards into the gray sky. They were such a cozy group, gathered about the little fireplaces in their hands, but when the violinist came the mirth in their eyes fled, leaving grim faces and speechless lips as the traveler's only landscape.

In the old hotel, the clerk behind the desk gave him the key to a room that was at the far end of the establishment, in an isolated wing, all by itself. And he told the violinist that no music was allowed in the hotel, as it might disturb the other customers. This, the violinist could understand; after a long journey, the sweetness of sleep was sometimes more to be treasured than the sweetness of sound. But notwithstanding his understanding, the clerk felt it had to be said one more time: "Sir, may I remind you, no music is allowed." One could sense ferocity behind the polite forms of speech with which the clerk's brain had been indoctrinated.

The violinist spent a restless night in a silent room, then, as dawn broke through his tattered window shade, which refused to cooperate with the darkness it was intended to protect, he got up to wash his face, went down to have some breakfast in the hotel eatery, and wandered out into the street with his cherished companion of four-strings, searching for an ear to pleasure. He found nothing but empty streets and windows tightly closed.

When at last he found a young couple who seemed very much in love, sitting beneath a generous tree which scattered its leaves and fruits like alms to the world, he smiled, and opening the case that was like the oyster in which a pearl rests, removed the brilliant violin, its fine wood aged like wine, glistening with light which seemed to be golden sweat streaming from its pores. He thought to play a piece by Tchaikovsky, intense and moving like a fire that burns two hearts at once, or else something by Chopin, melancholy like a soul surrounded by a moat, transferred from keys to strings. With the mere touch of his bow, he would draw from the strings a declaration of the obvious that would make it eternal. But the couple was unanimous in its disapproval; its intimate bonds were expressed by the stern harmony of its frowns.

"Please, don't!" the woman protested.

"No!" the young man said. "Don't play, don't disturb us here!" And he indicated the beauty of their setting, underneath the caresses of the tree branches.

"It's for free," the violinist told them, thinking, perhaps, that they thought he wanted money from them. "I play for nothing more than the love of music, and for the love of man."

"Didn't you understand us?" the man chided him. "We want you to go away."

"Yes, please go away," the girl told him.

"But music," the violinist told them, trying to explain. "Music is the heart of man. Love, without music, only walks. Love, with music, flies."

The man stood up, with anger in his shoulders, which were used to carrying heavy things, his sweet eyes suddenly hard.

"No, please," the violinist told him, as the woman stood up also, upset as though he had just spilled something over her. "Don't lose the moment you're in. I apologize. Go back to each other. Your love is so great, I am sure you do not need my music. Pardon me."

Perplexed and disturbed, the musician wandered on, surprised by the impervious aura of the lovers, until he found sitting on the stone rim of the town's ancient well, an old man who was nearly as old as the history of the place he lived in. The man's eyes were sad, like an endless fall, the violinist could tell that he was the last vestige of something noble that was gone; he could see in the man's eyes a beautiful young woman who had become old and died in his arms, and a wild host of friends who had danced and laughed the whole night long, many years ago, but who could now no longer be found no matter on which door he knocked. The violinist saw the last leaf of a great tree, once gloriously adorned with green, about to float to the ground, and thought it should not drift to the earth without a requiem. And so, he took out his violin again, to play a homage so deep and true that pain and loss and failure would seem trivial things, that brevity would realize it was nothing but immortality's lack of self-knowledge, and that separation would discover it was only walking in a gigantic circle back towards its days of happiness.

But when the old man saw the violin come out, he waved his withered hand at the musician who dared to try to honor him, and shook his finger at him with all the decisiveness his faltering body could muster. "Leave me alone, young man!" he told the musician, who was young only by comparison. "Let me age in peace! Do not demean my trials with a concert, as though four strings could compensate a hundred years: thirty lonely ones that have damned the seventy that went before. Do not try to remove the weight that these breaking shoulders bear with wisps of air engendered by your bow."

"But, good sir," the violinist told him, "I come only to hold your hand. Only to part the clouds that cover you with gloom, to let the sun in."

"Do not degrade my last days," the old man replied, with a firmness the violinist could not reject. Amazed, for a moment, he realized he could not change the vision of this man who had lived long enough to earn the right to intransigence. Sadly, he left him to wither.

And on it went in this strange town as the musician tried to make a friend, tried to lend a hand, and found himself pushed away and denied time and time again. Sometimes, it was mere aloofness; other times, outright hostility. He felt, sometimes, as though he and his violin were the most outrageous sinners who had ever lived, who the town would stone to death if it were allowed to. And yet, he knew it was not because these people were frozen and shut to joy. He saw them kiss, he saw them embrace, he saw them looking at the flowers and standing reverent underneath the stars that sparkled in the sky above them, he saw them writhe like fish on a line as they told each other jokes, and heard them singing when he was not around.

"Perhaps it is only that they do not love strangers," he thought to himself.

After a while, he decided that it was pointless to stay on. He had come to enrich their lives, because that is what made his own life worthwhile, but they would have nothing of it. And so, he decided, at last, that it was time to go.

He finished paying off all his bills, turned in his keys at the hotel, and walked sadly with his violin to the shore of the river awaiting the arrival of the weekly ferry. As he waited, and as the ferry drew near, he heard, all of a sudden, drifting from the open window of a distant building which served as the town's concert hall, the sound of instruments playing. "Good Lord!" he thought, grimacing with discomfort. There were violins and cellos, and instruments of brass, and drums and flutes. The strings were all badly out-of-tune, and on the violins particularly, the bows were grating, squeaking like torture devices with all sense of beauty lost; for their part, the brass and flutes were playing discordant, clashing notes, utterly out of key, and the drums had not even the concept of a beat, they seemed to be thrashing about in their own world like hallucinating dancers in the middle of the street. The concert, it appears, was more of a formality than anything else, the town's commitment to have "art," since it seemed from the abundance of people elsewhere, that the performance was poorly attended. There was an orchestra here, but not a public for it. —And no wonder! "Good Lord!" the violinist gasped again. "If Armageddon had a sound, this would be it."

The ferry boat arrived, and as the violinist boarded it, in part drawn irreversibly onwards by the certainty he had felt in the morning, and in part pushed forward helplessly by the crowd in which he was imbedded, hurrying with its bags to claim a seat, he realized: "No wonder they would have nothing to do with me and my violin while I was here! *This is their only experience with music!*"

And suddenly deeply troubled that he was leaving, as the ferry boat began to stir up waves from the sea and to hurl trails of white foam to both sides, he took out his violin, and began to play a haunting melody of parting to the receding shore that did not know what music was…

FETTERMAN

James High Eagle, Ed Best, and Jim Fishes From Above were an odd trio, the one young and bold, with sharp eyes, broad shoulders and a sweet heart, but a terrible temper; the other a middle-aged, non-stop drinker who liquor never got the better of, because he grew silent instead of boisterous; and the last one, a hard worker with nothing to say unless it could make you laugh, who was inseparable from his baseball cap (which had a football logo) and his hand-rolled cigarettes. But one thing they shared in common was that they were all Oglala Sioux, which is how they ended up together in the parking lot of Brewster's in Rapid City, getting out of Jim Fishes' beat-up Chief Cherokee. (Everything Jim used had some tie-in with Indians, whether it was the Chief Cherokee he drove, the Washington Redskins cap he wore, the "Homeland Security" T-shirt with the picture of Geronimo and his Apaches which he donned underneath his blue-jean vest, or the Sacagawea dollar coins which his wife had sewed into his belt, alternately exposing the sides with the beautiful Shoshone guide and the eagle.)

"Back in the 60s, Dad said, this joint had a sign up that said 'No Indians Allowed'," Ed reminded them. "This is where Upright Bear got shot."

"The sign says 'Beer'," Jim Fishes said. "Isn't that what you want?"

"Come on," said High Eagle, waving them on good-naturedly. "No one can tell us no, just because we're skins." It wasn't that he was naïve; he only had a sense of justice that didn't bend.

"There's another place, about two miles from here," said Ed, too late, as Jim followed High Eagle into the bar.

All three of them sat down together, right there, in the front, while white men at the tables behind them stopped talking. The pool players in the back also stopped, and the faces of the men at the stools in front of the bartender, who the three Lakota sat down next to, grew strained.

"Three beers," Ed said. "Off the tap."

After a while, the bartender asked: "Which beer?"

"Budweiser will do just fine," Ed said.

From the tables, an interrupted conversation started up again, and someone sitting at the bar, beside them, went back to complaining to the bartender about the GPS chips auto manufacturers were putting into cars and trucks now.

"Emergency tracking systems," the bartender said. "Do you know that guy who got stuck in the snow and died in his van 'cause no one could find him? The old guy with the eight grandkids? They could've saved him."

"The government's going to use the chips to keep tabs on us, that's what they're going to do. Won't be no privacy or freedom anymore. The government is growing like a monster, bigger and bigger every day. Tax us to death, spy on us. When will it stop? The spirit that built this land is on the way out."

The three Oglala men received their beers. It looked like everything was going to be all right. It was just like a day in the forest, different kinds of animals going about their business, birds flying around in the tops of the trees, bears scratching their backs on the trunks. Nobody getting in anybody's way. But then, someone had to say something. They just had to.

"From my cold dead hand," someone was saying at a table.

"Easy, the Supreme Court's on our side," another voice reassured him.

"No, but now they want to limit assault weapons. It's nobody's damned business how many rounds I can fire and how fast! You got all kinds of creeps around these days. Crazy kids on drugs come around to the farm in a stolen car and shoot folks up or steal money for a high. Prairie-land junkies and drifters from the East. You heard about that little girl they found? What a damned shame! Flames of Hell ain't hot enough for the son-of-a-bitch who did that! And then you got that crazy alcoholic lot of Indians out there, on the res, who are always on the verge of snapping. For them, every white man is Custer all over again. Never know when they're going to show up to pick a fight, or steal your car, or shoot holes through your window. Politicians don't know! From my cold, dead hand, pal, from my cold, dead hand!"

"Don't pay it any mind," Ed told High Eagle, who he could see was flustered by the man's comments. "He's ignorant, that's all."

But somebody happened to overhear Ed calming down High Eagle, and suddenly, the loud voice behind them was saying, "Who called me ignorant? The Injun over there? Which one? That one? They both got blue jean tops. Which one? That one?"

"Maybe we better get out of here," said Ed quietly to his friends.

Jim Fishes, since he had nothing funny to say, just stared ahead with the kind of inexpressive face which used to infuriate treaty-makers from Washington whenever they came to swindle Native peoples with offers which any reasonable man was supposed to fall for.

They felt a presence looming behind them, as other voices were calling out: "Easy, Bruce, don't start nothing! Let it slide! They're just a bunch of stupid Indians!"

The three Lakota turned around.

"Someone here call me ignorant?" Bruce demanded. Two friends got up to support him.

For a moment no one spoke. The silence seemed like giving in.

"Good," said Bruce, a bear-like man with a rough beard and huge, agitated arms. "Glad you know your place. We won," he said, beginning to head back to his table.

Ed didn't speak because he was prudent; Jim kept his mouth shut because he was disciplined and knew that, after a certain point, he might not be able to control himself: being taciturn is the best defense against passion which burns too hot. High Eagle said nothing because when he was furious, he couldn't speak, only stare with eyes that were like hot coals. But as the lumbering white man headed back towards his table, thinking his race superior, High Eagle had to do something to rescue his spirit. "I said 'You are ignorant'," he lied.

As the white man turned around in disbelief, Ed corrected his friend. "No, he's not the one who said it. I did."

"Well, I'm saying it now," High Eagle said.

Now, five white men in the bar were standing. The Lakota were also standing.

"No one calls me ignorant," the white man said. "Not in my own country. Do you understand? You lost. We won. Wounded Knee mean anything to you?"

"The law says this country belongs to us as much as you," said Ed. "We come here to drink, just like you do, we pay our money, just like you do, and we have our constitutional right to think what we want, just like you do; and I just exercised my freedom of speech by saying that what you said was ignorant. Now you can keep right on saying it, if you want to, but that's my view."

High Eagle found Ed's rebuttal far too tame. "First of all," High-Eagle said, "this isn't your country, it's ours. So don't go around acting like you own it. Secondly, don't start up about crazy Indians, fact is, you bring more hell to these parts than we do."

"Fact is," growled Bruce, savage and hateful, "you're all a bunch of drunks and slackers. Rob, drink, do drugs, f**k, sleep, and wait on government handouts. Cry about being poor, about what we stole from you; fact is, you couldn't use it, couldn't do nothing with what God gave you except to ride around naked on horses, so he gave it to us instead; you're all a bunch of bitter losers, that's what you are. You don't need to come to this bar." And he added, looking at the coins which featured Sacagawea on Jim Fishes' belt: "Pretty little Indian ho. They really bend over backwards to make you feel good about yourselves in Washington, don't they?"

High Eagle started for Bruce, but Jim Fishes' powerful arm caught him and held him back. Ed jumped in, too, because High Eagle's sense of righteousness was twice as strong as his body.

"What, you want a piece of me?" Bruce demanded. "You want a piece of me? Let him go, let Chief Dumb Ass try me!"

Everybody was excited now, as High Eagle shouted, "White trash! You're just the kind who would have murdered women and children at Wounded Knee!"

"And raped them, too, if your bitches weren't so ugly," he said. "Didn't Columbus say they had the faces of dogs?"

"Hey, Bruce," one of his friends told him, "show him the post card! Show him the post card!"

By now, Jim and Ed could barely keep a hold on High Eagle. He was thrashing around like a fish in the claws of a bear, his eyes like raging fire. "White trash!" he shouted again. "Let me go, let me kill him!" He would have said more, but his anger was burning all his words into nothing, they were turning to steam before anyone could hear them.

"Calm down!" Ed was shouting, while Jim was torn two ways, a part of him wanting to let High Eagle go.

Bruce's friend came back with the post card from the rack of post cards and souvenirs which the bar kept in a corner, just in case one of the thousands of tourists who swarmed all over Rapid City like black flies wandered in. On the post card was a reproduction of an old photo from

Wounded Knee, featuring the crumpled up, frozen figure of Chief Big Foot lying in the snow, taken when the cavalry came back for his body after the blizzard which followed the massacre. The friend of Bruce held it up to High Eagle's face, as High Eagle's friends held him back.

"Yeah, there's your history lesson for the day," Bruce said. "Now get the hell out of here. Find some other place to get your firewater. Now be a good little Indian boy, and go back to Pocahontas; oh, that's right, she ran off with John Smith. Smart girl. Moving up." All the white men were laughing now, but suddenly, one of them exclaimed: "Look out, he has a knife!" And they all drew back in fear.

High Eagle, in fact, had a small knife, and had managed to pull it out.

"Stop! Stop!" Ed was yelling.

"Cool it, buck!" Jim was shouting.

Tables were overturned, and chairs and bottles were seized as weapons. A white man ran out to get a rifle from the back of his pickup. But the bartender already had a shotgun out from behind the bar and was pointing it at the wild, writhing pile of Lakota men, shouting: "Get the hell out of here right now! *Right now!* Get out, *now*, or you're all going to end up in the pen, god damn it! And you can spend the rest of your lives with Leonard Peltier!"

"You're taking their side?" High Eagle raged, whirling around in the direction of the bartender. "They start with us, and you're going to blame us, just because they're white like you? You don't have any sense of right and wrong, not even in your own bar?"

"Listen, you god damned Indians all stick together," the bartender said. "Get out of here, and don't come back."

"But this *wasichu* dog, except that dogs are better than him, started this!" High Eagle exclaimed.

The bartender said, "Everyone here saw *you* start it. Understand? Now get out, this is your last chance." His arms were shaking, and the shotgun was pointed right at High Eagle's head. High Eagle smiled like Lakota warriors used to when they looked death in the eyes.

"Go on," he said. "Shoot me. I won't get lost on this path. Many have traveled it before me."

The white man who'd run out returned with a loaded assault rifle, a semi-automatic with high-caliber shells that wouldn't leave much of a man at this range.

"Let them out!" the bartender ordered. "Move away from the door and let them out. I don't want a killing, I don't want police! Not here or in the parking lot! I just want them out!" Then, turning to the Indians again, he said, once more: "Get out, and don't come back! You're not welcome here! Ever!"

"Yeah, get your red asses out of my bar!" Bruce thundered, as Jim and Ed dragged the scowling High Eagle, whose madness cooled only one or two degrees at the sight of the weapons, out of harm's way.

"Shut up!" barked the bartender to Bruce. "I don't want police reports! I don't want blood on my floor!"

Out in the parking lot, the white man with the assault rifle who came out after them stood by as they got into their Chief Cherokee, and backed up, hastily, over the gravel.

"Racist sons-of-bitches!" Ed snarled as they swerved backwards off the gravel and onto the road.

Jim said nothing, but the windshield wipers didn't work the next day, and Ed thought that maybe it was because of the way he was looking out of the vehicle at the white men as they left.

For a moment, High Eagle sat there impassively, haughty, you could even say, worn out by his struggle and choosing, at the very least, to disdain his enemies if he could not kill them. But suddenly, an irresistible fury rose up in his breast. "Let me out," he said.

"What?" Ed demanded.

"I have to take a leak."

Jim slowed down.

"Real bad."

They were a few miles from the bar now, so that Jim thought it was safe. He stopped. The stretch of road they were on was pretty empty.

"What are you going in the back for?" Ed demanded, alarmed.

"I need the light you got there."

"What for?"

"In case there's snakes in the grass."

Ed was fooled for a minute, but Jim guessed what was happening, and said, "Don't."

"Son of a bitch!" exclaimed Ed. "No, *kola*, don't!"

But High Eagle had Jim's hunting rifle and the paper sack with the shells in it, and a blanket in which to wrap the rifle until he got back to the bar. He slashed one of his friend's tires so that they'd lose time putting on the spare, and started walking in the darkness, along the side of the road.

"No, stop!" Jim shouted, driving his wounded car off the side of the road.

He and Jim jumped out to restrain High Eagle, but by now High Eagle was running away from them so that they could not catch him.

"No, for God's sakes, stop!" Ed cried. "Don't *kola*, they're not worth it! They're stupid, ignorant white men! You'll spend the rest of your life in jail, for nothing! Think of your friends, your relatives! What about Sarah Hears Voices? You haven't noticed the way she looks at you? I can tell she'd be a good wife."

"The sacred tree will never bloom again if all the people are in jail!" Jim Fishes From Above cried after him. "The people will dry up, like an old woman's womb!"

"Sorry about the tire," High Eagle shouted back to them. "I have some money in an envelope in my trailer. It's yours."

"Come back!" Jim shouted. "Don't be a fool! Don't throw your life away just because white trash has a big mouth!"

"These are the people who took away our land, and killed our people!" High Eagle said. "Thanks to them, I've never really known what it is to be a Lakota. Now, I'll finally know."

"No! Not this way!" Ed shouted. "You won't know nothing except what it's like to be a piece of meat in a white man's jail! Or else a dead fool lying in a parking lot, who didn't change a thing. Crazy Horse died as a warrior, not as a punk!"

"Come back!" said Jim, again.

But High Eagle, his mind made up, had turned his back on them for good and just ran faster.

Ed and Jim, unable to match him, ran back to the Cherokee, pulled it back onto the road and tried to drive after him, in spite of the flat, but another tire was also low, and High Eagle was too fast and elusive for them, and also picked a shortcut which took him off the road. So, once more, they pulled over to the side of the road. Though Ed had a phone, it had no more minutes on it, and they didn't have a CB on board, so it all came down to how fast they could get the Cherokee up and running.

"Come on, help me get a new tire on! Hurry!" Ed urged Jim. Ed seemed to know Jim's vehicle even better than its owner, maybe from all the times Jim had lent it to him (which was how it had got so many dents).

All the while, as they jacked up the back, and worked on the tire with a wrench, Jim kept his head up, looking at the cars that passed.

"Pay attention, the boy's life is at stake!" Ed practically wept. "This has got to be like an Indianapolis pit stop, god damn it!"

But Jim had been praying, and when he saw a beat-up pick-up passing by with some tired skins in it, he waved at them, and shouted out to them in Sioux. They slowed down, and waited on the other side of the road. "Need help, *kola*?" the driver asked him, while a family with blankets wrapped around them, in the open air in the back where cargo is usually carried, looked at him with expressions that revealed nothing except that it had been a long day.

"Yeah, *kola*, you've got to help! This kid I know is going to shoot up a bar, because white trash insulted him, and he's going to ruin his life forever! You've got to drive me there, I've got to get there before he does, and maybe I can stop him!"

Suddenly, everybody in the pick-up was wide awake.

The driver, said, "Hop in! What about *him?*"

"Leave it on the side of the road, we'll come back for it!" Jim urged Ed, even though the car was still in the air.

Not even bothering to lock up, just leaving the flare there behind the car, and taking Jim's keys with him, Ed leapt into the back of the truck with the family.

"Hurry!" pleaded Jim. "He must be almost there! He runs like Billy Mills."

The driver stepped on the gas, and they almost had a head-on, as some fool tried to pass someone in the other lane right as they were coming on.

"Careful!" a woman's voice cried out from the back. "We could've rolled over, with all the kids!"

"Well, we didn't!" the driver said.

For those few moments, as they tore through the night, Jim wondered how he would ever be able to stop the enraged youth from killing the white men in the bar. In some ways, Jim was proud of the boy because High Eagle wasn't about to kill a man because *he*, himself, had been insulted, but because *his people* had been insulted. More than insulted, because they had been ravaged, and these white people were still reveling in the crime. But vain or noble, the end for High Eagle would be the same. "How do you stop a kid like this?" he wondered. "He's pumped up, his blood is burning, he's a young buck. In the old days, this righteous rage would have made him great. Nowadays, it will make him the lowest of the low. In the old days, it might have saved his people; nowadays, it will weaken his people, it will deprive them of a warrior, and it will give power to those who despise them." But High Eagle would not listen, he was sure. He was a Lakota brave in a world made for cowards; until he proved himself, he would not be at peace with himself and could not be at peace with the world. And there was no way to prove himself in a world made for cowards, except by going against it. Jim knew that that was suicide.

"Why is it that the most beautiful ones can never learn their limits from others?" Jim wondered. *How could he stop the boy?*

And that's when he remembered the trip. The trip he had made eight years ago with High Eagle's uncle and aunt, and High Eagle and his brother, and two other Oglala men, who wanted to see the battlefield outside the old site of Fort Phil Kearney in Nebraska, where Red Cloud had won his greatest victory in 1866. In those days, an arrogant cavalry captain, William Fetterman, had declared that with 80 men he could ride through the whole Sioux nation. Red Cloud had given him the chance. Attacking a band of woodcutters outside the fort, he lured Fetterman and a detachment of cavalry out in relief. Fetterman duly rescued the wood cutters, but had orders not to pursue the enemy beyond the line of sight of the fort. At this point, he should have returned to the fort. But as a band of Native decoys, including Crazy Horse, taunted him and insulted him from a distance, slapping their buttocks and waving blankets at him, he could not restrain himself from disobeying his orders and leading his forces after them, until they were finally led into a deadly trap. From all sides, Lakota, Cheyenne and Arapaho warriors raised up a triumphant, furious howl and sprang out of hiding, showering him and his invading army with clouds of arrows which decimated them, before finally closing in to finish off the last of his troops at close quarters with tomahawks and war clubs. It was a bitter cold December day, and not a single white man lived. Jim remembered old One Horn, High Eagle's uncle, telling the boy, who was very much impressed by the tale: "Fetterman was a fool who couldn't control his temper. He didn't respect us. He thought he was more than a match for us, that we were nothing but cannon fodder for his glory. When he saw Indian braves, he didn't see danger, he only saw a medal on his chest. And that's why he died and bore forever the shame of losing all his men." And the old man had told High Eagle: "Fetterman was the perfect enemy, because he did everything we wanted him to, when we wanted him to; we owned him because he was not the master of himself. A warrior must have spirit, but he must also know when and how to use it. There is a time to charge, and a time to hold back; a time to fight, and a time to look. What may be behind that hill? Think! He who throws his life away for nothing betrays his people, because they will surely need him down the road, and then, where will he be? Fetterman, what a fool! He was the perfect enemy!"

"Nothing will make him stop!" Ed was lamenting, as the pick-up driven by their new friends rumbled onto the gravel in front of Brewster's, just as High Eagle was coming into the lot with the folded blanket concealing the rifle in his arms. "He's got it in his head that he has to do this to be a man! He's a young buck!"

The driver wildly honked his horn and Ed and Jim jumped out, and also one of the women from the back cried out, begging the boy, "Brave one, don't be foolish, don't let us down—tomorrow we'll be alone!"

The woman's voice distracted him, but only for a second; you could see the savage determination in his eyes and body, this was going to be payback for everything, for all the massacres, the broken treaties, the stolen way of life, the dead, the lied-to, the poverty and alcohol, and diabetes, the trailers and shacks in the dust, and most of all, the shame of not being able to be a man. He would join Crazy Horse now, and all those who had lived under an endless sky riding through prairies without fences, even if it was only by charging into a bar filled with racists and drunkards.

"Stop! Stop!" the people were crying.

High Eagle's face was hard, Ed and Jim froze in their tracks; the kid was beside himself with rage, mad in his intention, he had swung the rifle towards them, to keep his way to the door open.

"We're your own!" a woman cried. "Because they insulted you, you're going to shoot *us*? You've lost it!"

Furious, High Eagle turned away from them and made ready to crash through the door. That's when Jim Fishes yelled: "Fetterman! Go get 'em, Fetterman!" He could see High Eagle stop, stunned, he could see his whole body flinch. High Eagle tried to shake it off, he began to barrel forward again, but again Jim yelled: "Go on Fetterman, you can do it! You can ride through the whole Sioux nation! Fetterman! Yes, FETTERMAN, that's *you!* That's what I'm going to write on your gravestone! FETTERMAN!"

You couldn't have told High Eagle not to do what he was going to do in any other way, because he would have thought you were trying to override the Indian in him. To steal away his loyalty to his people and himself, to eclipse the identity which he knew he had to hold onto. But by comparing him to a crazy white man...

While High Eagle stood there, amazed and confused, Ed ran up and grabbed him, and then Jim came up and took away the gun, and the brave woman was also there, saying, "Don't deprive us of a good young man, we need every one we've got!"

And High Eagle stood there, tears in his eyes, as Jim, passing the gun back to the woman, put his arm around his friend, and said: "That's not how a warrior fights, *kola*. That's not the world we live in. If you are fighting only for yourself, selfishly for yourself, well, go on, then, turn that god-damned bar upside down. But if you're fighting for your people, there's other ways to fight, and other times to fight. Your people are living in poverty, in degradation. You can't help them from a jail. Killing a racist won't do a thing. It will only make more racists. Do you want to help us, or only to die?"

High Eagle looked distraught. By now, they had him packed in the back of the pick-up, and were pulling out of the parking lot as a band of white people began to emerge from the bar, attracted by the racket and expecting some kind of trouble. They already had a gun with them.

Jim was in the back sitting with High Eagle. "Stay calm, *kola*. Stay calm." Not quickly enough, the bar disappeared into the night.

"They got the better of us," High Eagle said, at last.

"No, they didn't. They lost the spirit that makes a man a man a long time ago. They've got guns, they've got that stupid bar, where they drink and hate; and I guess you could say they've got the world, too; but they have nothing *wakan* inside them. They are like empty shells, without life. We have souls, High Eagle. Their world is dying. It is from our souls that the world will be reborn, if it is its fate to live. That's our battle, now, High Eagle. To stay alive, and to remain men as we do so. To be brave in a holy way. Not as drunkards who fight in a bar, but as men who hold the world in our hands."

The friends in the pick-up came up to Jim's car, still propped up on the jack. No one had messed with it in the time they were gone. "The Great Spirit has stood by our Cherokee!" Ed said, really meaning it.

Everyone stayed around until the tire was back on. High Eagle is the one who made the final turns of the wrench, and unwound the jack so that the wheel touched the road again.

"Sorry," he told Jim, another time. "I'll pay you for the tire I slashed. I'll pay you twice its worth."

"We're doing an *inipi* this weekend, out in the hills," Jim told High Eagle. "Sweating is a great way to start over."

High Eagle nodded.

"You've got to fly higher, Eagle," Jim told him. "Will you join us?"

After a while, High Eagle nodded. He was still excited, but his heart was beginning to slow down at last, to the calm pace of a man who is going to last for more than a day.

The friends said goodbye, after inviting them to drop by sometime for a visit. It turns out, they only lived thirty miles apart. Jim gave them a stash of his best tobacco, and Ed gave them a compass, which they said 'no' to three times ("go on, the kids will like it"), until they finally accepted. In return, they gave the three men, whose car was now ready, some food they had gotten at a fair, and the woman gave High Eagle a dreamcatcher, which, even though it was from a crafts store catering to tourists, had the good energy of having been hers.

"Good-bye!" they said again.

The road was dark and lonely, as Ed Best, Jim Fishes From Above, and James High Eagle drove back towards Pine Ridge in silence.

The world rarely notices things that don't happen. But sometimes, they are more powerful than a whole newspaper full of things that did.

GRACIELA

Graciela. I wonder if you remember me, after all these years, or if I was nothing to you. I wonder if you ever think of me, and if you do, if you do so with the slightest understanding of how our encounter changed my life. I wonder if you really knew what you were doing when you spoke to me on that fateful autumn day, twenty-five years ago, or if you were just playing with me, like a child who destroys an anthill with a stick, for the pleasure of seeing the desperate ants rush out to rebuild their city. Most of all, I wonder: did you stay true to the flag you unfurled in my heart that day? Or did you leave me alone, to walk this beautiful empty road without a single friend—even one unseen?

I was young back then, curious, alive, filled with energy, seeking something to do with it. That is why I left my suburban home, and my elite university, where the privileged play and are rewarded with open doors, to visit Mexico, to see something different, something that could make me feel I deserved what I was born with, by giving me a reason to have it. I guess I was like many of my age, and times, rejecting the benefits of my background, while living from them, empowered by the gift of being able to study, yet feeling powerless from shame, for not being destroyed like the rest of Humanity, for escaping from the place where so many other people had died. And so I came to Mexico, pursuing, perhaps, an idealized vision of the poor and oppressed, seeking to be forgiven by an angel from the fields, an angel from the slums. Seeking to give something, though I did not know, then, how little I really had to give.

It was on the campus of UNAM, the National Autonomous University of Mexico, in the capital of the ancient Aztec nation, that I met her: that I passed my momentous day with Graciela. Impressed by the gigantic murals of Siqueiros at Chapultepec Castle, and the murals of Diego Rivera at the National Palace, I had decided to come to UNAM to see the murals, the library, and the Olympic Stadium. It was on a weekend, so I was free from the little college where I was studying Spanish; free, with nothing to do. My friend Nelson was with me, with his camera and girlfriend.

"According to my map," Nelson was saying, "the *Escuela de Extranjeros* should be this way." What an awful accent he had for Spanish (even I could notice)! We had just gotten through seeing the famous Rectory mural by Siqueiros, and circling the magnificent library, which was simply overwhelming, like some kind of Aztec Ka'ba, with fascinating pictures of Mexican history and powerful symbols that seemed like they might be an occult message that could save the world. Now Nelson, on his second roll of film, was leading us towards the university's "School for Foreigners," hoping to get some information about courses and tuition costs, to see if UNAM might serve him better than the place we were enrolled in now. But, of course, it was closed. Weekend.

That is when I saw her, sitting on the steps of a silent building. A striking young woman in a white dress, wearing an open, black-leather jacket, that made her look something like a cross between Elvis Presley and Adelita (the Mexican folk heroine/gun-slinging revolutionary, cartridge belts draped over her peasant's dress). The woman's very 1970s dress left a lot of her legs showing, and I took everything in in one mesmerizing blow—the legs, beautiful, but a little uncomfortable, trying to find a way to protect themselves from excessive attention without becoming too Catholic, too virgin. The eyes, piercing like a hawk's, that seemed to be watching the world from a higher place; lines of laughter, lines of crying, lines of idealism in her face, something special about her, that you couldn't explain, a kind of fire that could heal as well as burn. Very dark-skinned, a *mestiza* (mixed blood), but with more Indian than white. Long black hair, with waves in it, a look of curiosity coming onto her face as we approached.

Nelson was already asking her, in his awful Spanish (when I first became aware of the fact that I was staring at her), if everything was closed today. She asked him where he wanted to go, and he said, "Anywhere that's open," in English, and she responded in broken English ("not much," she was waiting for a friend who had to do some work inside one of the offices in the School of Economics). "Nice university," he said.

"Thanks," she replied, "but I didn't build it." (Now I don't remember when we spoke in English, and when we spoke in Spanish, or when we struggled to speak in something in between.)

"What do you study?" Nelson asked her, after a laugh, that was all about buying time.

"Sociology," replied the girl.

"Oh—society. I guess there's a lot to study."

She nodded and asked if we were Americans, and Nelson replied, "Yes," and for a time there was a little probing back and forth, in which we discovered that her name was Graciela, and she learned our names, too. Nelson asked her if she'd ever been in the US before, and she said no, the closest she'd ever come to was the Monument to the *Niños de Chapultepec*, something he didn't understand, but his girlfriend did. (It was a monument to young boy-cadets killed during the Mexican American War in 1847.) "Come on," Nelson's girlfriend urged him, "let's get a coffee." (They were going to try the Student Center, which Graciela told them might be open.)

"Would you like to come?" Nelson asked Graciela.

"No thanks," she smiled quietly, like a discreet millionaire being offered a peso.

"I'll meet you later, at the Stadium," I said (we had left it for last).

"All right," Nelson said. "Or if not, back at school."

"Right."

"Bye."

"Bye."

Graciela, then, raised her eyebrows and regarded me as though I were a stranger, knocking at the door to her house, at dusk.

"Look," I said. "I know that the US and Mexico haven't always got along so well..." And that's how we got into the conversation: a conversation which lasted for maybe an hour and a half until her friend had finished his work inside the School of Economics, to which he had a set of keys, and came walking out, bent over to the side, with a briefcase full of books and papers nearly pulling off his arm.

Honestly speaking, I don't believe I am a masochist. But neither am I blind. And the way you learn to see is often by listening to other people and not turning away from the painful things they have to say. Sometimes, of course, you already know what it is they are going to say. Your mind has the knowledge and is just waiting for another human being to personify and embody it, to turn it into something you cannot ignore or forget. It is as if the knowledge were an electric light switch, and all the wires that connect it to the bulb tie it in with the wiring of the house, which is fed by the power lines outside. All of that complexity, all of that potential to shine, is there already. But it is the action of a human hand that turns it on and fills your room with light. For me, Graciela was the one who did that: the one who gave her face and beauty to the knowledge that I already had, and made me fall in love with it, unable to leave it.

It is hard to remember everything we said that day, and maybe what we said wasn't really what counted. I do recall that she complained about the US and its policies in Latin America, and I countered with something about Russia and Cuba, and she brushed this aside, and began to talk about poverty, and some field work she had been doing in one of the slums of Mexico City, and how the people were struggling there, and I asked what this had to do with America, and she began to talk about corporations and debt and international relations, and lost me there, maybe because she was speaking in Spanish, then, or maybe because it was just too complicated for a day of sightseeing, on which Mexico was supposed to have given me something, without asking for anything in return. Ideas aside, which I forgot, anyway, my memory numbed in her presence, it was her intensity and sincerity that impressed me, which burned something into my heart that nothing could ever take out. Especially when she began talking about Tlatelolco: October 2, 1968.

She hadn't been there, she was quick to say. She was younger then, at the age when you are just beginning to rebel and see things for yourself, or at least differently from your parents, but can still be controlled by them. Graciela's parents had told her she could not go. Her friend's parents had said yes. And that is how the deep wound had entered into the fabric of her Destiny. "Antonia was like my twin," Graciela told me. "We called ourselves Xbalanque and Hunapu [the hero-twins of the *Popol Vuh*]. There are blood families, and soul families," she added, saying, "Antonia was the sister of my soul, made of the same *materia*. If she had not gone there on that day, we would be sitting side by side right now, and you would be talking to both of us."

According to Graciela, on that day, a huge crowd of students and activists had assembled in the *Plaza de las Tres Culturas*, the heart of Tlatelolco, to protest government policies in the days just before the scheduled opening of the Olympics. "They only wanted change—a better Mexico," she insisted. But others thought they wanted more or thought that that was too much. And so, the army and police opened fire on the unarmed crowd with machine guns and automatic rifles, as helicopters illuminated the carnage from above with flares, one so beautiful, according to witnesses, that it seemed like some stolen, misused Star of Bethlehem. Penned in by buildings, by a church whose doors were locked shut against the blood-stained people crying out for sanctuary, and by advancing troops, the demonstrators screamed, ran, laid flat and prayed, and left behind chaos of purses, shoes, and pamphlets calling for a new day, as well as their lives, still so little used. Tanks and ambulances filled the streets, and before the night was over, three hundred people were dead, many more wounded or on their way to jail to be interrogated and tortured, or just contained, like refugees from another country, which this one had no room for. Later, there would also be cases of *desaparecidos*, or people just grabbed up by secret bands of armed men in the night, never to be seen again.

"It was window-dressing for the Olympics," Graciela said, bitterly. "The political equivalent of sweeping the streets: sweeping them clean of protesters and dissenters. So the world wouldn't see how tormented we were. How divided." And a tear slowly formed in her eye, and began to work its way down her cheek, as she remembered hearing how Antonia's parents had found her inert body lying on top of a cart in a hospital hallway, the white blouse splattered with blood, the jeans ripped from crawling over the stones or pavement, or maybe just from falling down, the body strange, as though it were trying to rise and walk away but were frozen by a spell, the face quiet, but somehow not at peace, waiting for something... Graciela, whose parents did not let her see her friend in this state, only saw her at the *funeraria*, lying in the casket, made up like a princess before her wedding. "And I cried—and cried," said Graciela, more tears beginning to fall, children of the tears she had cried on that distant day. "To have my sister stolen from me like this. To have so much of the joy that God gave me, in her form, taken away... Even to see her dressed up like a princess, like the girls she used to laugh about, who only want rich husbands; such an ironic departure for an intellectual and a rebel."

As a result of this, Graciela, whose grief gave birth to the flower of an implacable conscience, made a vow never to abandon the ideals which the army had tried to gun down that day. The ideals that 'freedom, justice, and dignity' should be more than words; that poverty should not be given such a long time to fade away, nor should its defeat be entrusted to prodigal dynamics of selfishness that had already used up generations, and wanted more; that compassion should replace self-centeredness, and that solidarity should replace hypocrisy, not only in the hearts of a few harmless people, but in the heart of an entire nation. "This is my purpose," she told me. "To never forget. To never give up. To try to end the pain, which may be the pain of a plaza filled with dead dreamers, flowers cut just before they opened. Or the pain of a normal day, without land or a job. Sometimes," she went on to say, "this is a struggle which may bring me into conflict with your country; sometimes with my own country; sometimes with human nature," she admitted.

I cannot tell you who were not there, what Graciela's energy was like. Nor would it, necessarily, have been the same for you; for what was coming from her that day was what the Universe had sent me to her to be filled by. It was my destiny to receive it. Like rare mating moths, who couple for a moment in the sky as they try to reach the moon, then vanish into the night, their purpose for meeting completed, so our minds and souls shared something sacred, intimate, more fertile than sexual union. More lasting than a home and family.

I told Graciela that I was sorry about her loss. I am sure my eyes were moist when I said it, because her pain was like an electric current that traveled along a connection between our souls, that was far stronger than holding hands, than embracing. I told her I wanted to do something. Nothing foolish, nor crippled by ideology. But something real, something human, something that I could do. She looked at me, earnestly, carefully, then, looking away, she brushed aside her hair (which had moved as she turned her head), so that she could see something that wasn't me. "I believe you're sincere, now," she said, staring into space. "But don't forget. You're only a student. Me, too! —But I'm living in the middle of something I can't get out of. And my sister's ghost is never far away, to remind me." She paused a long while, while words began to drift to her on the current of what she was meant to say, like leaves carried along by a slow stream. "You'll go back," she said, at last. "Back to your country. Back to your world. There, you'll forget about us. The time for your rebellion will end - the time when your difference can be tolerated - and then everything you do, that is not what is expected of you, will start to have a price. Probably, you'll try to go on for a little while longer. To remember. You seem honest and genuine. But one day, you'll get tired—and our faces will start to grow dim, and to lose their hold over you. Too many things will pull you away from us." She thought for a moment longer, then nodded her head, agreeing with herself. "No. It is a beautiful stage you are going through, but that's all it is. It won't last. It can't. That is the strength of your country, its greatest weapon, more powerful than its bullets or bombs—its power to make the rest of the world disappear from your minds."

I protested, and Graciela apologized, saying, "Maybe you will be different," but not meaning it and not doing this in an effort to manipulate me, but really feeling it and sad about it. Nor was she blaming me, as an individual, only gauging the power of forgetfulness, and the might of a land whose abundance was like the gravity of a black hole that keeps all its light trapped within itself, sharing nothing with the universe but darkness.

"Well, I can't foretell the future," I told her, "But I think I *will* be different."

I remember her looking at me, then, not arrogantly, but with a kind of loneliness that had nothing to do with having friends, or not having friends, or going to parties, or not going to parties, or having political companions, or not having political companions; a loneliness that goes with a certain level of sincerity, that is almost always sure to be disappointed, feeling abandoned even in the midst of thousands of demonstrators shouting the same slogans, carrying the same signs. I saw that she wanted to believe me, that her heart was trying. But she had a mind also, a formidable bastion of logic, the product of a desperate society which was too controlled for violence, whose outrage, therefore, took the form of analysis. In her intellectual background, personality counted for very little, barely denting history; instead, it was social structure, economic and social relations, and material conditions that defined reality. And so, she looked at me, trying to see a precious Quixote, a fighter of windmills, a hero beyond the reach of his environment, but not allowing herself to. 'Structure' returned - the power of my land, and its satisfaction - and she could find only the temporary rebel in me, the man of promises who would one day go back to worshipping the sun, which was brightest in his sky, and stop looking up in the night at a distant star.

"If you really mean what you say," she told me, at last, as her friend began to struggle out of the School of Economics ("José, are you starting up a library, or what?")—"then make a promise to yourself, that you will never wear a suit and tie."

"I promise," I told her, as though she had asked me to take a vow before her, to swear to *her*. What a tiny thing to promise, in this world of so many hardships! What a brilliant structural approach (I was to discover).

José, grateful to put his briefcase down for a moment, shook my hand, and Graciela told me how much she had enjoyed talking with me. I wanted to ask her for her telephone number, but I thought José might be jealous, even though something told me they would not be together for very long. And I could sense that the specter of his jealousy also inhibited her; while he was only distracted. (Most Mexicans, in this situation, would have made some form of generalized invitation for the future.) "Well, nice to meet you!" he said as he started to struggle away.

Graciela came up to me, and offered me her cheek to kiss, and we shared a kind of shy half-embrace that I keep dreaming about, even to this day, wondering how I was once so close to such a magnificent woman, and yet, just walked away and let her disappear forever from my life. "Good luck," she told me, warmly and with caring in her voice. "I know you have a good heart, and I know you will try to make this a better world, in your way."

Turning to watch them go, I saw her open José's briefcase, as they were walking, and remove several books. I saw her —trying to convince him of something—finally get him to put his briefcase down, allowing her to close it (after she first put the pile of books she was carrying on the ground), whereupon he picked up the briefcase, and she picked up the books, and they continued on their way. Looking over her shoulder, one last time, she erupted in a beautiful smile that was only to torture me, in years to come, with an even greater sense of loss. And that was it. My one and only day with Graciela. How, I wonder, could it have changed my life so drastically!?

I did not notice at first, of course. Everything seemed the same about me, except for the longing. (The longing drove me to visit the university campus several more times before I came back to America, hoping to bump into her, hoping that Destiny would, somehow, help me overcome the odds. I even sat on the steps where we had talked, and a terrible pain surged up from some place I did not know and could not defend against.)

Back in America, I continued to be as I had been before—idealistic, with more fuel to keep the fire lit, more experience. At my university, I was active in several organizations championing social justice and human rights, and then I graduated.

And it is then that I began to discover the power of Graciela, the depth of her impact, beyond nostalgia, beyond obsession, beyond the moments of life turned into mourning, which anyone who has once been young carries hidden inside him until he dies. I turned down an entry-level opening, with tremendous potential, in my field, because it was a little "off," not morally perfect, not something I would not have some misgivings telling Graciela about, should I ever encounter her again. For a while, I did jobs "beneath my status," telling myself that I was learning and growing all the while. During that time, I met a beautiful woman who became my wife, for a man cannot live forever, loving a woman who is only a dream. He needs to feel a body, to hear a voice, to be with someone who is more than his own imagination, trying to forever manipulate and shape a few treasured memories into something new.

My wife and I had a great love, but economic pressures began to build, and soon, survival drove me to look for better jobs, to leave behind the days of "working below my station." And that is when the vow I had made to Graciela, never to wear a suit and tie, began first to exert its force.

"Aren't you wearing a suit and tie?" my wife asked, as I prepared myself for a job interview that could lead to a better life for both of us.

"No," I said.

"Why not?"

"I hate suits and ties," I answered.

"Well, I could get you a new suit. But for today, why not wear the one you have?" (An old one, which I had never thrown out.)

"No-I-I don't want to."

"But honey!" my wife pressed, puzzled (since I seemed so reasonable in other regards). "This is a *job interview*. It makes a big difference. It's expected of you..."

"It's against my principles," I replied, my tone of voice becoming almost cruel.

She backed off, no doubt feeling mistreated, though she kept it to herself; but when I didn't get the job, all her suppressed anger roared back to the surface, and she demanded to know more about these principles of mine. And what could I tell her? That I had met a girl in Mexico, and talked to her for 1-2 hours, long ago; and that, in her presence, I had sworn to always remember the truth of the world, and to never wear a suit and tie? What would she say? How could I make it make sense to her? And so I just said something about "cramping my style," which she told me was a form of rigidity and selfishness; and stung by guilt, I wandered out into the night, trying to ask myself just what it was I was doing?

'Who is this Graciela?' I thought to myself. 'And what has she asked of me? Or did she even ask it of me? Why not wear a suit and tie? What is the problem? Why shouldn't I?' And I found myself far from home, in a place where strange and sleepless characters roamed, seeming to look for pieces of gold that had fallen out of the pockets of the happy, whose carelessness was the only way God could bring life to the sad. I ended up in a bar where some loud drunk was busy telling everybody he was a knight, and so I asked him, "Tell me what are the conditions that others place upon knights, and why do knights accept those conditions?"

Surprisingly enough, the drunkard's incoherence seemed to make sense, as long as he stayed on a subject that had no visible connection with our own times.

"The Lady," he said, overjoyed, at last, to have an audience, and somehow seeming to know that a woman was the secret behind my question, "is the Knight's light. His wars, his quests, his suffering, his loneliness—are all for his Lady, who has become his heart. Without her, he is dead. With her, he cannot die, for by dying, he becomes *her* heart, and beats within her till the end of time. My friend," he said, passing me a glass of beer, "everything you see here, in this world, is for the Lady, though only drunkards know it, having lost the minds that hide her. The millionaire wants her and tries to buy her. But his jewels and diamonds buy only whores, and he passes through them, night by night, thinking he is only lustful, never realizing it is because he is still seeking. The soldier fights for her. Though he says he is fighting for his country, it is for her that he really fights, for her that he tries so hard to remain a knight, in spite of the tanks and aircraft that suffocate his courage. The musician who sings—he is but a bird, singing outside the Lady's window. While the dreamer who dreams— it is she who is truly the center of his dream, and everything else, but the palace he is building for her to live in! A cure for cancer! A Nobel Prize in Literature! World peace! It is all for the Lady!"

Tears in his eyes, the man pushed another beer in front of me, which he would not let me pay for. "It is in us all," he said, "but only a few understand. Only a few have vision enough to find the Lady who is meant to be *their* Lady, and the purity of heart to be faithful to her, even if they sleep with whores!"

For a moment, he choked on his beer, then, waving away my concern, said, "You asked another question?"

"Why do Ladies sometimes impose conditions?" I agreed. "I think you have already answered why knights do not betray those conditions."

"Conditions? Sometimes? Well—perhaps," he said, "though, often, it is the knight himself who imposes his own conditions, the codes of conduct that preserve his worthiness in the eyes of the Lady, whose ideals are too high to accept a prize captured without greatness. For to the Lady, the prize is not a Grail or a Jewel or the horn of a Unicorn, but the path the knight traveled to get those things *for her!*" And narrowing his eyes, another giant beer glass nearly empty, he said, "A condition is but a way of loving—it is not sex which binds the Lady and the Knight, but something beyond sex—and in that love, the condition takes the place of the kiss; it is the way the Knight's and Lady's souls entwine." And eyes drifting, to a warm place, not of this world, he asked, looking far past me: "And you have found her—*your* Lady?"

"I don't know," I said, confused, thanking him and leaving him there, drunk and rambling on, telling the world, "You can see it in their eyes when they have found their Lady!"

Back in bed, that night, beside my wife, who could not help but be awakened by my clumsiness, she only said: "This had better not become a habit. I won't put up with a drunkard!" And I laughed, the laugh that could only be laughed by someone who has no fear of losing his woman, because there is another one he is carrying around inside of him.

And yet, I could not help but wonder if this drunkard's simple vision of 'The Knight's Lady' really explained Graciela, after all. Time went on, and my ban on wearing a suit and tie began to affect us more and more. I was shut out of many jobs and fired once when new management took over and introduced a 'dress code.' My wife and I could not escape from a life of economic uncertainty, always struggling just to make ends meet, never rising out of tension and anxiety, never attaining a sense of peace or freedom or stability. It began to wear us out, and to undermine our relationship, especially since, to my wife, it all seemed so pointless, so stubborn and unjustifiable, on my part. And the sketches did not make it any easier.

Probably as some kind of uprising against the unfulfilling jobs, the unrewarded tension of living day to day, the burden of being all alone with a secret world that was too strange to share, I took up art—drawing—taking advantage of some free adult education classes, and some low-cost workshops. Little by little, I began to develop the capacity to make sketches - amateurish, at first, finally bordering on competent. And, of course, I began to try to draw her: Graciela. Thinking I was being clever, I also drew many sketches of butterflies, horses, buildings (old brownstones were particularly interesting), famous people whom I copied from photographs, all to "hide" the Graciela pictures among. But my wife was no fool. She noticed the recurring sketches, primitive at first, gradually beginning to evolve, from my first crude efforts that could have been practically anybody who had a face, into a well-defined individual, with a distinctive look and personality, at first mechanically reproduced, then beginning to radiate an energy that revealed a deeper understanding of her, a more intimate level of contact.

Suspicious, she asked me: "Who is that woman? She looks Latin..."

"Just a woman," I replied. "Her look is very conducive to my art."

That made my wife even more suspicious; that, plus the fact that I framed and hung up one of my sketches of Graciela between two imitations of details from a Siqueiros mural: stylized peasant soldiers in *sombreros*, wearing cartridge belts, advancing in a menacing, righteous way; and an outraged mob holding up the body of an unjustly slain man. For me, it became a kind of altar, but for my wife, it was something more of an insult.

"Are you having an affair with that woman?" she blurted out one day.

"Wha—what?" I gasped, astonished that she could think like that, at the same time that I realized that it was, in some ways, true.

"Who *is* that woman?" she demanded. "Stop playing games with me. Stop treating me like a fool! Obviously, she is somebody you know, and you are very much obsessed with her. I have a right to know. Is there someone else besides me?"

"No, no," I insisted, like a desperate man covering up, home late from work, smelling of another woman's perfume. "She's—she's just a woman that I've been seeing in my dreams - maybe some kind of guide, or disguised angel. It's very personal. You're the only one," I reassured her.

My wife then demanded to know about the dreams, and I could, in fact, tell her something about them without lying, because I had been seeing Graciela frequently in my sleep. "Well," I told her, "in one dream I saw myself walking up the steps of a gigantic building. It was sort of like the old pavilion at the 1964 World's Fair that they built up for the US presidents - huge, rectangular, greenish-bluish. And I came inside, and there was a huge, expansive floor, and that open space extended all the way up to the ceiling which was many stories high, and there were elevator banks and corridors that you could faintly see ringing the edges of the open space from the second floor to the top, and beyond them, unseen floors filled with books, even though the building seemed, at first, to only be a giant lobby. In fact, from the inside, it reminded me, in many ways, of the NYU Library - only it was far more spacious and impressive, and on the ground floor, there was nothing but emptiness and an information booth; and the woman was there, waiting to receive me. She told me this was 'the Ministry of Indigenous Affairs.'"

My wife blinked (waiting for more, but there was none), and then agreed, "She seems like some kind of guide. Does she have a name?"

"Umm—not that I know of," I lied. (I felt that if I said too much, something of this magic bond might die, like something prematurely born, not yet ready to survive outside of its sacred womb.)

For a time, my wife was appeased by my pretense of openness, even interested. She said I should pray to the mysterious dream woman to bring us prosperity. And I pretended to do it.

But as time went on, and the conditions of our lives failed to improve, my wife began to react again. "You're destroying our relationship," she wept, when I had to withdraw from consideration for a job due to the fact that 'corporate attire' was required, and not negotiable. We entered into a crisis, which at last drove us to a marriage counselor, and ended up landing me in psychotherapy, as a last resort to save my marriage. ("If we can barely pay our bills right now, how are we going to pay for a shrink?" I demanded. "Once you get over this crazy limitation, we'll more than recover our investment," my wife replied.)

I remember the therapist: a rather pale, large man who seemed, somehow, very threatening, eyes glimmering with brilliant intensity, but something not quite right about him, as though he planned to perform some kind of painful surgery against my will, and was enjoying the prospect. Friendly, at first, though it was really only like he was adjusting the sights of his sniper's rifle, he talked to me about the difficulties of marriage and the rewards, also telling me about his own life. "No kids?" he asked.

"No," I said. (At first, my wife had not wanted any, but much later she'd changed her mind. Now, however, our economic and personal situation was far too unstable to go ahead with that, though I think she believed that by having a child, I might be forced to come to my senses. But I didn't want that. To have a child, only to make me give up. Not for the joy or sacredness of it.)

"So—you have an issue with wearing suits and ties?" he began, at last.

"Well—yeah."

"What's wrong with suits and ties?" he laughed. "I'm wearing one and it's not killing me! Now," he said, smiling even more, taking off his tie, "they've got clasp-ons. You don't even have to tie them." (He put his back on.) "Great, for lazy people like me. As easy as 1-2-3."

I watched him, coolly, like I would watch a magician who's not the best. Sensing the hostility behind my silence (for I already knew how he was planning to treat me), his aggression began to manifest.

He asked me to close my eyes and had to struggle to get me to do even that (for I thought he planned to 'hypnotize' me and try to brainwash me to have his way). Instead, he only asked me to go back to my childhood and tell him everything I could remember about the clothes I wore and the clothing that the people in my family wore. Much to his satisfaction, he learned that, at the age of ten, when I was transferred from a formal school where white shirts and ties were required, to a public school, where everyone was wearing T-shirts and jeans, I had continued to wear formal clothes - and become the object of bullies as a result. "Your mother forced you to continue wearing those clothes? I see," he exclaimed, delighted, it seemed. (I heard his pen scratching wildly on a piece of paper.) Eyes open, sitting up again, he told me that my problem was one of control, an extended effort to reject my mother's authority and to escape from the punishment of the bullies, "a drama which your psyche is stuck on, and replaying, over and over again, out of context." Feeling he had discovered the root of my problem, he, nonetheless, called me back for another appointment.

In that one, he subjected me to a session of 'free association', asking me to say whatever came into my head, as he rattled through a list of words that included "mother," "school," "wife," and, predictably, "suit and tie." For "suit and tie," the words that popped into my head were "submission," "insult," "hypocrisy," and "betrayal," and like a hunter excited by the footprints of a lynx, made only an hour ago, he got to work, something about him seeming like it wanted to impress me— and if it could not impress me, to crush me.

"That's a lot of emotional baggage for a suit and tie," he grinned, superficially sympathetic.

I just sat there, giving him nothing, no sign of cooperation.

"Let's start with 'submission.' Now that's an interesting word association. What do you think it means? A suit and tie—and 'submission'?"

"You're the psychologist," I said. "You tell me."

Well, I know that wasn't called for, but I couldn't help myself, and that pretty much set the tone for the rest of the session.

The doctor told me that going to a job was not "submitting," it was "participating" in the world of work, in an activity which united individuals, forged societies, and produced economic benefits for all. He went on to say that rules were a necessity for any organized, cooperative form of human life, and that following rules was only a way of making cooperation possible, just like making roads and stoplights to give form and order to the flow of traffic makes a large-scale and effective transportation system possible. Rather than "submission," he suggested that I might consider following rules to be a form of voluntary cooperation in the construction of something greater and more useful than anything a single human being could accomplish on his own; an expression of "social responsibility" and "maturity," as opposed to the "immaturity" and even "infantilism" of acting out a "delayed-reaction rebellion" against my mother, and prolonging the nightmare of my childhood flight from bullies.

I cannot tell you how hot my blood became on that day. I regarded the psychologist with nothing short of contempt, matching his sense of superiority, without batting an eye. "Traffic rules are somewhat different, if you stop to consider it," I told him. "They prevent car crashes. What is the purpose of wearing a suit and tie?"

He replied with something feeble about symbols of group cohesion, then, observing (burned by) my disgust for his effort to "cure" me by making me more like him, he demanded: "Well, why don't you tell me what putting on a suit and tie means to *you*?"

And so I did. I told him: "A suit and tie, for me, is like raising up a white flag; like coming out of your fortress with your hands above your head. It is like being manacled and chained, and led behind the chariot of your conqueror, put on view before his people, who glorify him because you are naked and in his power. It is like bowing down and kissing the feet of a man who stole another's throne and dares to call himself a King. It is like being branded with the word 'Slave'; like wearing the uniform of an army that deserted its post in the night, abandoning the people it was supposed to defend. It is like being told to get on your hands and knees and crawl if you want to be fed."

The psychologist, simultaneously stunned and overjoyed (to have such a far-gone patient), said, "Sort of like wearing the Mark of the Beast?" (hoping I would go that far).

I replied, "Everywhere, here, people talk about the land of the free; freedom, freedom, freedom! The individual, the individual, the individual! They used to rail against Chairman Mao, and the 'little blue pajamas' worn by the Chinese Communists. Meanwhile, they were all wearing their suits and ties! Strange," I said, bitterly. "Without the appropriate uniform, you are just out of a whole level of work, a whole level of income. You are free, only so long as you do not attempt to be yourself, even in so little a regard as wearing the clothes that allow you to feel alive. Meanwhile, this whole society of 'free' individuals, wearing the clothes that they are forced to wear, that turn them into extensions of somebody else, something else, which absorbs them and carries them, is just rolling along, like a boulder falling down a mountainside, smashing places of incredible beauty it doesn't see, heading towards places of incredible horror it does not know. Hypocrisy!" I raged, in conclusion: "Tyranny, whose deadliness is not made of force, but of subtlety."

Rather bewildered, the psychologist regarded me. He started to say there were many different kinds of ties, then stopped himself—his eyes vacant, exhausted, like a computer that is slow to download something from the Internet. Then, at last, he said, "Well, like it or not, suits and ties are a social reality that affects the quality of life in our times. Adaptability is one of the most important aspects of mental health." And he added something about how only children believed they were entitled to have everything they wanted, when they wanted, in the way that they wanted. Still somewhat at a loss, he finally brought up the word "betrayal," which I had mentioned earlier, when we were doing word associations. "Betrayal of who or what?" he asked, hoping for one more chance to prove his abilities.

For a moment, I toyed with the idea of telling him about Graciela. But then I thought - what will this practical, ruthless man, whose vision of mental health seems more alarmed by nonconformity than injustice, have to say about her? About the woman I met years ago, whom I knew only for a single afternoon, and who defined the trajectory of my entire life? I thought of Graciela, sitting there on the steps of the building where her life became imbedded in mine - beautiful and idealistic, demanding because of her great love—and I looked at him, huge, unkind, his eyes with the perceptiveness of a microscope, but useless for finding the planet where I lived with Graciela—and I decided, not to let him into the sacred place. Not to let him come through the door, like a rapist, to see Graciela in her beauty, to soil her with his intellect, that was like a form of lechery, contamination, poison. No, he would never have her as a target, never go there; never would I show her, in my sky.

Of course, the psychologist believed that I ought to keep seeing him, but I canceled my next appointment and never went again. As I asked myself whether the ideas I had told him really mattered to me, or if they were only my mind's way of legitimizing something utterly incomprehensible, my mind's way of trying to disguise Graciela's shocking influence over my life, by making her imposition seem like my own philosophy.

Naturally, my wife was infuriated by the failure of the psychotherapy. She accused me of sabotaging it, which I guess I did, just like a kid who is told by his parents that masturbating will make him go blind, sabotages his parents by going right ahead and doing it. Of course, our lives together became more and more difficult. My wife felt hemmed in, trapped by my stubbornness, shut out of the better life that just a little flexibility, a little willingness to bend, on my part, could have put within our reach. She became colder, crueler, as I became more withdrawn and inaccessible. She replaced confrontation with contempt, and I replaced defensiveness with indifference. But I was not, during all this time, as much of a stone as she believed. I suffered, I blamed myself for ruining her life. I feared to see her reach menopause without a child, I feared the weight of destroying a life for something I did not even dare to mention, I felt like a thief, who had stolen something precious without a reason that I could expose (for it would vanish into dust should I try to bring it into the light); I felt like a "cheater," like a faithless man who had hidden an adulterous affair from his wife for so many years, never coming "clean." I wanted to make her happy. So much. I wanted to fill her world with the things that make life comfortable, enjoyable, secure, beyond the shadow of stress and fear. I wanted her not to lag behind her friends, not to suffer, not to go through life with the spirit of a desperate sailor, bailing water out of a lifeboat, praying for a rescue ship to appear on the horizon. "God—what have I done!?" I thought, tortured, like a criminal, by guilt.

And yet—neither could I drive away Graciela. She was like a fire, burning inside me, that I could never extinguish. Whenever I came to the edge of the fire, dirt in my shovel to put it out, I faltered. I could not do it. I realized, to my horror, that the image Graciela had impressed into my soul's eye, in only a single instant, was more compelling than the image of any other person I had ever met or could ever meet, even one I had lived with for years; and it made me feel like some kind of madman who, listening to "voices" inside his head, murders real people - although this whole thing began as a homage to real people, who were never given a place to live on our planet. Real people, who I had sworn never to let become "fantasies."

I remember, once, the last day I tried to defeat Graciela, standing by the mirror, all alone in the apartment, determined to break the fatal spell, and live my life—my real life, with my real wife. I began to put on clothes that could have changed our destiny and brought us back from the edge of the world, where we watched it, not belonging to it. I had the trousers on, the white shirt, and got so far as to put on the jacket and to take the tie up in my hands. I looked at myself for a minute, then, and even felt a bizarre twinge of pleasure, maybe like a transvestite feels as he begins to put on a dress and women's jewelry, finally destroying something too hard to maintain. And then, nearing the end, I began to arrange the tie itself, flipping it over my neck, crossing the two strands, and pulling the one strand under and up... But that's as far as I got. For suddenly, it seemed as if I were tying a noose about my neck, and something in me rose up against it, not to save my life, but to save the most beautiful thing in it. "Go on. Do it!" I tried to force myself, one more time, reality trying to reclaim me—maybe some invisible protector of my wife. But once more, I balked, like a horse that will not jump over an obstacle, no matter how hard his rider tries to push him.

Astonished at myself—amazed and bewildered—I gave up. Instead of finishing the job, I began to go back, to strip. I threw the clothes that, to everyone else, were just clothes, to the side, until finally, passionate and alone, I stood there, confronting a naked man in the mirror, who even I could not understand.

"Graciela!" I cried out, at last, surprised by what I was saying, but not interfering. "Where are you? I want you! I need you! All these years alone! I want to feel your hands on my body, even if it is only for one night—I want to see you—make love to you! —All these years—I need something! All these years in bed with another, longing for you! All these years of suffering... destroying myself! I want—one more night with you—I want you to love this body, that is the home of a soul that never left you!" And as I stood there, by the mirror, the clothes of my salvation laying at my feet, for a moment I thought I could feel her mind, her soul, her heart, pouring over my naked body like water, like light, caressing and bathing it with a kind of recognition, like the love of lovers who have gone beyond loving; and eyes half-shut in ecstasy, I stood there like a plant in the sun, until the moment passed, and I became aware of the ticking of the clock, and the fact that my wife would be returning soon.

Not surprisingly, my marriage did not last much longer. (If anything is surprising, it is the fact that it lasted as long as it did.) "It's not going to work," my wife told me one day, in a moment of calm that I knew was neither an overreaction nor a mistake. The social and economic pressure had grown too much to bear, especially as youth's reserves of euphoria and powers of resilience had given way to the tiredness, sense of limits, and vulnerability of middle age. Deep inside, my wife felt that I did not love her, or I would have made greater efforts to protect her, to respond to her cries for help. For her, I was like a man who would not accept living in a house and forced her to sleep in the rain and snow with him.

Strangely enough, I cannot deny that I felt very much relieved by the divorce. I was relieved to see my wife go free, to see her escape from the shadow of my foolishness. I also felt as though a great weight had been taken from my shoulders, a terrible burden of guilt and failure that had afflicted me, like a terminal disease, for years. Until I found some of her old things in the apartment, that she had failed to take with her when she left me to start a new life, to make something of the years she still had left... And once more, I felt a crushing blow of sorrow for what I had done to her hit me in the guts, and in that asphyxiating sorrow, that overwhelming nostalgia and mourning for missed opportunity, I once again was forced to confront the mystery of Graciela: a woman—from the first day more memory than woman— who had pulled my life away from the people I was with, and led me to sacrifice it on behalf of a person I would never see again.

Graciela—who was she? A spirit? An angel? Antonia's ghost? The soul of a wounded people, the face of all wounds? Was she, perhaps, my Lady—the woman Destiny placed in my path not to have, but to light a fire in my soul that only she could light, and then disappear forever? And was I her Knight, after all? Or only a fool?

Or was Graciela, when all is said and done, only a caring and brilliant woman who needed allies in another land, and who—seeing the power of that land to swallow up its dreamers, to tame its idealists, to defuse its heroes - conceived a masterful "structuralist" solution, just what one would expect of a radical Latin American thinker: which was to bind me to a "dress code" that would exclude me from the center of my society, bar my ingestion, and force me to live and work on "the outside," experiencing poverty, injustice, rejection, and hypocrisy for my whole life, eternally fueling my hunger and my capacity to be outraged, keeping the wounds open that would connect me to the wounds of the world. That would prevent me from ever passing through the Door of Distractions, to the Place of Forgetfulness. That would thwart me from ever gaining those things which turn the whole world into the fear of losing them, and transform justice into a threat.

Perhaps, when all is said and done, this is all that Graciela was. A brilliant and insightful "structuralist." And yet—with what charisma did she incite my loyalty to this masterful plan, which was so doubtful of heroes, built, instead, with a trust in the formative power of social conditions to shape the beliefs of individuals? What was the magic within her science, the spark that ignited me, that turned her challenge into a vow I could not and would not break, even as my life, and the lives of others, fell to pieces around it? How did she get me to accept this deadly limitation—to trap myself within the structural mechanism she had designed to keep me pure, to prevent my idealism from flickering out under the airless cloud of success?

I wonder. And never cease wondering.

Sometimes, I ask myself if it was her beauty. But the world is filled with beautiful women, and I could have many if I were to travel far away from her, on the road of shining surfaces.

But perhaps, hers was another form of beauty—another dimension. Not merely the vast sexual potential, hidden underneath her moral and intellectual demeanor, yet visible to any man with desire. (As a hunter, by seeing tracks on the ground, can envision the magnificent animal he is in search of, so a man with passion can see the tracks of love and lust in the subtle gestures, and eyes, of the most discreet of women, and know where there is a fire waiting for him.) Although Graciela had this unmistakable potential, I am sure that it was something more—so much more. The kind of resonance in a singer's voice that can shatter glass... That was it! Her beauty, like a voice, unique in pitch and power— my soul, the glass, so in tune with it—that in my brief moment with her, it shattered and changed me forever! Soulmates, some people call this level of connection, that may use bodies but is beyond them— perhaps the three of us— Graciela, Antonia, and me—like some kind of bizarre triad, fulfilling a purpose none of us could ever hope to understand, one by dying, one by remembering, one by learning.

Still, I wonder—why is it that I didn't just let it all go, once it began to ruin my life? Why is it? Did I think, perhaps, I might one day meet

Graciela again—was it the hope of a magical reencounter—and my effort to preserve my chances with her, should such a meeting ever take place? Not to face her in a suit and tie, rich, polluted, "just like everyone else" who had had a dream and left it behind once it got in the way? The sad fulfillment of her prophecy? Or was it that Graciela was somehow inside of me now? That her image, in my mind, was alive? That now I took her with me everywhere I went, and felt her watching everything I did? Had she become like a ghost haunting my conscience, not with the threat of terrorizing me if I did not obey her, but with the threat of leaving me if I disappointed her?

I cannot say, I only know that somehow, this woman has become a part of the texture of my soul. That, as water is neither hydrogen nor oxygen, but both of them, bound together, so I am not myself, but myself linked to Graciela. We are, together, a drop of water in the universe, though I do not know whose thirst we are meant to quench.

And I know, as the night deepens, and my pen, amazed to finally reveal the story, prepares to sleep, perhaps forever, that I would like to call out one last time to her, and tell her what is in my heart. And I would like to say:

Graciela! Please tell me that you have remained true and not sent me on this road alone! Please tell me that you never succumbed to what you thought would conquer me!

And I would like to tell you: Graciela! I have never abandoned the road you showed me. Your inspiration has kept me on it, though I wonder what either of us has gained. For the purity it has preserved, it has no tools to fight with! And the heart it has kept true is on the edge of the world! Men with suits and ties have both harmed and helped, but I—I have merely disappeared into the night, understanding, but with my understanding locked in silence. I have given little things— grains of sand thrown into the wind. And nothing more, but my dying.

Graciela! Do not judge me, harshly, for failing—or for trying! It was my choice—my decision to serve the beauty of your soul. I accept the consequences. The burden is mine, the glory belongs to you.

Graciela! The years have not passed easily. Tonight, I am like a swimmer in the river, which I have been swimming in ever since I met you. My stamina has deserted me—it is that time in life: and now there is only my heart, thinking of you like a man, dying, thinks of the great love of his life. And I ask that you pray for me as I try to reach the shore of the dream you gave me, just by sitting on the steps. Graciela! Pray for me one time before you release me to the night!

And I ask you, Graciela, that if tonight should prove to be my last - that you will not deny my patient soul one embrace, once you, too, are in Heaven, where I will be waiting in the shadows, to see the beauty that Death will never be able to extinguish, nor God to take the place of!

I FELL IN LOVE WITH A SLUM GIRL

I don't know how it happened. How I fell in love with a slum girl. I mean, not that there's anything wrong with it, but just, I wonder, how did it happen? Was it pity? Was it compassion? Maybe just a part of me that wanted to be different, to be able to tell my friends, "I'm going with a girl from the slums." Or was it just the desire to experience something unknown, to cross an emotionally charged barrier and get the life that came out of that, or to show that I believed in people more than in position? Or could it be that, in the end, when all is said and done, that it really *was* love: that mysterious bonding force that overshadows nation, class, and race, that makes everything that should discourage it irrelevant, that makes dove and crow lose their whiteness and their blackness for a moment of fatal foolishness, tying their hearts together, even if their hearts have no future together but to be broken?

I remember, on the last day, walking through the Neighborhood Gate, from my part of town into hers. It was like a gate between planets, really, not just a door from one block to another, and there were not that many from my part of town who would walk through it these days. "Too depressing," was the usual defense. "Too sad." And who could say they were wrong? But I, as a social worker, had, of course, made the decision to bear the world's pain upon my shoulders, whether from guilt or nobility, I cannot say. And, of course, that is how I first met her.

Diana was her name, and now that I thought about it, on my way to see her, something about her had impressed me from the very first day. But what it was, exactly, is something that is not easy to put into words. Yes, she was pretty, of course, at least to me, with her whitish, pale skin, so tender and outdated, and her long black hair, which was often abused by elaborate hairdos that did not seem to recognize the greater beauty of her hair when it was just left alone. But then, the world is filled with "pretty girls." Why this one—and from the slums, of all places!? Was it, perhaps, her laughter and intelligence that you could imagine lighting up a party, back on your side of town, if you could ever manage to bring her through the gate? Maybe. —But then, there are so many women who are lights, who could fill up the empty night inside of a man. Or could it be her slightly strange comments that sometimes left you feeling like the witness of a genius, like you were catching a glimpse of some great artist or thinker, not yet recognized, who saw the world on an entirely different plane, before she suddenly disappeared in a puff of smoke, leaving you, again, beside an ordinary person; who you still, somehow, could not quite accept as ordinary. (You were left wondering if she was a diamond, or just a piece of glass, but overwhelmed by the luster of whatever she was.)

What it was about Diana, I just can't say. If it was her, or my hunger for an image. Her, or my longing to be compassionate. Her, or my creator's eyes, always turning the world into art.

"Golden Boulevard—next right," the sign said. What names they gave to places in the slums! Right now, I was on a thoroughfare known as "Showcar Drive" and it was lucky I was in good shape, because this route was really made for wheeled vehicles, the big kind that used to drive all over the place; and I was just a small man, like an ant in this desolate neighborhood, walking on such a huge and empty road.

"Diana—what a beautiful name," I recalled myself telling her one day, this memory for some reason pushing itself into my mind as I continued on my way towards her apartment, thinking of her, thinking of us, on the last day. Why had I said it? I wondered now. Why had I crossed the line? Why had I started things off? Why had I been so unprofessional?

Of course, she responded. What slum girl wouldn't have? Lonely, left out... then suddenly touched by a smile, offered a moment of not being ignored by someone from the other side of the Gate? For a woman like this, a kind word is like a sexual advance; and Diana was soon opening up like a flower in my presence, spreading the perfume of her desire, and before I could find some way to stop myself, I found myself naked in her bed, crying out in ecstasy, overwhelmed by the taste of forbidden fruit; overwhelmed by the naked, desperate love of a girl from the slums.

And from then on, my visits had ceased to be a job and had become a kind of secret tryst, in which we both forgot what we were supposed to do during these encounters, and remembered only what we had done before, and could not stop ourselves from doing again. Crazy things. Things you don't talk about (unless you are a writer), but which, nonetheless, become the center of your consciousness, creating a kind of barrier between you and the rest of the world, a kind of permanent distraction that makes everything else seem trivial. Eating cherries and grapes, passing them from one's mouth to the other's with passionate kisses (and how red her lips became); sprawled out on the floor together, on the sofa, in front of a door left wide open at dawn; contorted in insane positions of love, that made the limbs of our bodies seem absurd, twisted together and sticking into the air at strange angles, like pieces of wreckage that were warm and alive. Shaking and crying out each other's names, along with promises not planned or considered, that just came out and built great mountains of hope out of an accident. It was wild, and addictive, and, somehow, much deeper than it seemed. And then, of course, at the end, burnt out but shining, still wet and glistening from the shower, whose moisture had replaced the moisture of our sweat, we would sit down together, over a cup of coffee, and have to invent the day's report, agreeing on what we had "done" and "documenting" Diana's progress: her economic and psychological advances against poverty, which is both a social condition and a state of mind.

Well, though I am a man who is sometimes a captive of my heart, and subject to the dangers and abuses brought on by passion, I am not without a conscience. And given enough time, it *will* kick in, no matter how far I have fallen, to free me of the wrongs I have committed, and set me back on the path towards what is right.

Maybe this was what was on my mind, on that last day, as I turned off Showcar Drive, and began the long walk down Golden Boulevard towards her home. Maybe I had decided, at long last, that it was time to stop playing the role of Prince Charming, the one who had come to rescue Cinderella, and actually to do something real for her; something more than letting her illusions turn her into my whore, to be used each week, then left behind, in the place where desperation fills bodies with the explosive longing to escape, and turns love-making into something even bit as intense as the struggle of predator and prey, wrapped about each other and rolling in the dirt, with life, itself, at stake.

Yes, it was time to move things to another level, time to stop treating Diana as a life-giving secret, stashed away in the safety of the dark, time to bring her out, into the light of my life, my world.

Looking back on that day, now, I can only view my walk down Golden Boulevard with sad nostalgia. For it was to have been my triumphal march, the last part of a long, unplanned journey to unite two hearts, one from the poor part of town, one from the rich part of town. A march that would have shown the whole world, through her and me, that the divisions that keep us apart are only in our minds, and that we really *are* one, after all.

I remember it all as though it were only yesterday. The giant towers rising up on both sides of the spacious boulevard, like huge stacks of disks piled one on top of the other, each disk being an immense apartment, shining brilliantly like gold whenever the sun was there to ignite it, each tower filled with vast rows of windows peering down at the city, the higher windows so mesmerizing to look out of, that it was almost like seeing the city from an aircraft, as it comes in for a landing. The tops of the tower roofs, of course, had once been used as air-vehicle landing ports, and giant elevators, darting up and down the transparent central tower shafts, with spectacular views of gardens on each floor, and forest-like lobbies far below, had always astonished those rare visitors not accustomed to seeing them every day, who had a chance to glimpse them.

Of course, this part of town had not always been "the slums." Once the heart of a fabulous, pulsating city, brightly shining with golden reflected light by day—blazing with what seemed to be an electric war against the night as the darkness tried to fall—it had been the stronghold of the privileged and the rich, an "exclusive neighborhood," a place where the poor were not welcome, and seldom allowed, except after careful scrutiny. As a poet of olden days had written, it was, "The place where all the treasure of the earth was gathered, the pinnacle of history, on which only a few could stand."

But, of course, times have changed. Slums, which have a strange way of moving around, once encircled the golden towers of the city. But now, it was the abandoned core of the city that had become a slum, and the wealth of the city had moved out to the edges.

Passing underneath a giant, elevated tube, snaking its way around the city, the deserted pathway of the ancient "tube train," my heart soared —on the last day— because I knew Diana's tower was but a few minutes away. "Diana," I whistled to myself, inventing a tune or maybe just putting words to one I already knew, "I'm on my way to you; Diana, our hard times are through." Past the tube and its shadow—past the giant Jewelry Center, locked shut like a fortress, though nothing was left in it, now. Past the Paradise Hotel, and then the next block of golden towers, 551, 553, 555, and hers, at last: 557.

I remember smiling as I came to the perimeter. The once-electrified fence, now dead, a door that nobody cared about, left open, an abandoned guard-post, inert, lifeless cameras poised all about, which had one watched every approach like snipers ready to fire, the disengaged alarm fields that you could just walk over, now, even jump or play on if you wanted to. All the blunted, fallen thorns around my beautiful rose, Diana!

Entering the lobby, I felt, as I often did, the grandeur of the fallen world of the towers. The giant marble floor that gave the impression of being a cloud at the end of time, the ring of high doors leading to the elevator section, the beautiful footpaths, now overrun by plants, winding through the little forest (people who wanted to could ride the horizontal elevators instead), and the gigantic transparent tube rising upwards like a beam of light, like man's ambition to be more than he is. It did not work any longer, of course, and so I was compelled to use the service elevator at the back, hidden away from the eyes of the people who no longer lived here, like a shameful family secret.

"Diana," I said, hitting a buzzer before I got on board, to announce my arrival over the intercom. "I'm here. I'm on my way up!"

For a moment, there was no answer.

"Diana," I started to say again.

"Come and get it," I heard her say, in a teasing and seductive voice, and then her end clicked off, and I found myself riding up the ancient, rumbling elevator, praying that this would not be the day it finally decided to say, "Enough!"

Well, of course, I had come to broach a very serious topic with Diana today, which was nothing less than our future together. But as I entered her apartment from the rear, through the door left open— left open for me— I felt that it was not going to be easy to shift the trajectory of our relationship, to wake up from the dream that led nowhere, yet gave constant relief, as it headed towards an ending of heartbreak and emptiness.

"Diana!" I called out, feeling like a burglar, or a person about to be robbed, I couldn't tell which. "I'm here! Diana?" Walking around. "Diana?" Obviously, she was playing a game, and though there was very little surprise regarding how it would turn out, there was, undeniably, curiosity about the variation it would take. Not to mention the fact that, in this case, what was predictable never got old!

"Diana? Diana!" I called out, wandering through the 'library', a giant room with shelves on every wall, filled with statuettes, vases, trinkets, postcards, video disks, and a few old books that you were afraid to touch, because it looked like you might end up destroying them. "Dearest Elizabeth," I read, turning to the back of a postcard which had a picture of the Pyramids on the front. "Quite lovely, the pyramid of Shopes [sic], too bad he was already dead by the time he got to live in it. We are all sunburned, and Regina fell off a camel. But the desert has provided welcome relief from all the beggars, thank God, they cannot chase after us without water. Hope you are well, kisses to Poochie, Love from Auntie and all." Of course, it wasn't Diana's card; it was just something left from the past.

"Diana!" I called out again. "Diana! Where are you?"

"Here, baby!" I heard her voice giggling, not far away. Pushing through a beaded, seductive curtain—two of them, in fact—I found myself in a giant bedroom. But the huge, circular, cushioned love bed which waited there, like a new lover wanting to join in a threesome, lonely and ready, was all that was there. Throwing open the doors to all the closets, I only ended up finding a speaker in the wall, left in the 'On' position, and I knew that Diana could be anywhere, still, near or far.

"Diana!" I said. "Come on! Stop playing games! Where are you?"

Drifting out of the bedroom, I passed next through the 'gallery.' Paintings hanging along the walls, which were once said to have had some value, though to me, they really weren't much to brag about. Some squares, some cubes and triangles, signed by somebody who knew how to blow his own horn, and a few uninteresting portraits of people who did not look very appealing, even after the most blatant attempts at flattery. And yet, this whole room had once been rigged with alarms and even had steel gates that could be used to 'lock it down,' as though it contained all the brilliance of the Louvre.

Descending a little spiral staircase to another level, I came upon 'James.' We'd met before. He was the 'robot', the servant, who once upon a time could actually cook, clean, serve drinks, put on videos, and even 'think', or at least respond to questions, which, for lots of people, is the same. According to Diana, years ago, she had been able to talk to him, and she recalled asking him questions like "Why does rain fall down instead of up?" And he would give interesting answers, like, "Would you like an umbrella?" In fact, she had passed many nights talking with him in this way, just to hear a voice that seemed, in some way, to be connected to her. But, of course, his batteries had finally run down. And there seemed no way to get replacements. Now, the only trace left of his deeply missed self was the small orientation disk, recorded in his voice, which Diana could still manage to insert into one of her disk players whenever she wanted to remember. "Hello. My name is James. I am your Class 7, B series, All-Purpose Service Robot... No more salaries to be paid, no more worries about having your valuable property stolen, no more anxiety about how that all-important dinner will turn out... And no more rudeness, or envious looks; I am programmed to be happy for you, and to admire your phenomenal success... Thank you for letting me be a part of your world."

"Bye, old fellow," I said, with some emotion, though what it was all about, I'm not quite sure.

Walking past James, I entered a narrow passage, peeked into a bathroom (where Diana and I had often taken showers together), and went around to another room, a viewing room with a giant couch along the whole wall, offering a spectacular panorama of the city below. And I wondered if this is how God saw the earth. Still, no sign of Diana.

"Diana! Diana!" I called again, leaving behind the spell of the mighty window. "Why are you playing with me? Where are you?"

"O take me! O take me!" she was crying out, and I was yelling out, "I love you, I want you!" and she was also saying, "I was thinking about you the other night," and I was saying, "In our times, poverty is a state of mind..." and she was replying, "Like an animal! Do it like an animal!" It was the Echo Room, a small, dimly lit room, something like a dark globe, that somehow recorded and was able to replay all that had gone on in it before, bouncing it back and around and surrounding you with it, for as long as you wanted. Mixing the sounds and the memories was real art, and Diana was quite good at it, now. Bursting into the settings room—a closet-sized compartment filled with knobs, dials, and switches, where I thought I might find Diana—I only found the chart she'd set up, the dates and times she'd fed into the mix, and the volume levels and sequences. Overpowered by a sudden rush of curiosity, as her mix began to repeat itself, I saved her work and began to play with the controls on my own, setting them back to 10 PM, 100 years ago. And then I stepped back into the dark and mysterious globe where nothing was ever forgotten.

"And what are you going to do about the diamonds?" someone was asking.

"What do you mean?" another voice replied, with the spirit of a tiger growling, that will not allow an intruder into its territory.

"I mean—that whole war over there is about diamonds. The child soldiers, the massacres..."

"So you want me to stop marketing diamonds *here*?" the tiger demanded. "Look, I'm not asking people to kill each other for control of the diamond mines. That's their business."

"But you'll buy from them, no matter what they do? No matter how they come by the goods?"

"Look, Max, I'm a diamond seller, that's the bottom line, what am I going to do without diamonds?"

Then there was a click, as though an audio disk, or even a video disk, had just been put on, and I heard a moving piece of classical music wrapped around the following words: "Show you love her with diamonds. Cover her with proof of your love. Make her sparkle like a diamond!" And the tiger was saying, "What a gorgeous, elegant babe," and the other guy, Max, was saying: "Now, that woman has class!"

Back in the control room, I returned Diana's mix, "Do it to me like an animal!" and continued in my search.

"Diana? Diana—where are you?" I called, feeling rather foolish as I made my way through the giant apartment in the clouds. God, was I grateful for her short attention span, because if I was running out of patience, by now, she must be ready to crack! And sure enough, my surprise was not long in coming.

Suddenly, as I entered the bizarre circular mirror room, she sprang out of a closet, naked except for a mask, and said, "Tell me who I am, and you can have me!"

God, was she hot! Standing there naked and totally out of her mind!

"Diana!" I said, desiring her, her body burning with the fever called life, so exposed, and rapidly becoming my entire universe. (That body—what madness is it in our human genes that makes Woman overwhelming to Man? What power, what helplessness? In the mirrors, all around, angles of her hips and legs, and the wild symmetry of her curves, like a dancing harem, hypnotized me whichever way I turned. God, we human beings are mad, I thought! Builders of rockets, writers of books, and yet, when all is said and done, it is this which moves us most!) "Diana!" I cried out again.

But she held off and kept me waiting. "How do you know it's me?" she asked, like some inebriated, difficult reveler at the Carnival, who had drunk enough to be standing right at the line but needed one more drink to cross it. "After all," she said, "I'm wearing a mask."

"Of course it's you, Diana!" I said, forgetting the seriousness of the day. "Your voice! Your body."

"Are you sure?" she asked me. "Are you sure, without seeing my eyes?"

"Diana!" I implored.

"Or perhaps I am someone else," she suggested, "here to test you— to see what it is you really love about Diana."

Unable to restrain myself, I leapt at her, and in a flash we were both lying on the floor, me kissing and craving her, she playing difficult just a little bit more, saying, "What if Diana comes in and finds us?" before giving in and reprimanding me— "I could just be anybody, couldn't I?" —and beginning to kiss me back with the force of a tigress, being hunted and hunting at the same time. Images of us flying about like spirits in the mirrors.

"Diana," I said, both of us in bathrobes, now, perched high up in one of the viewing rooms above the city. "I've been meaning to ask you something, for quite a while."

"Yes?" she said, distracted by a pain that, no doubt, had to do with the recklessness of our lovemaking.

"You know how much we enjoy being together..."

She made some kind of noise that was an assent. Very sexy, at the same time.

"Once a week," I said.

"Yeah."

"Well—what about if we could spend more time together?"

At that, she looked up hopefully. "You mean, you could work in another session? Make it two times per week?"

"No, Diana, I mean—well—what about if we could actually *live* together?"

Diana's eyes lit up, now, dramatically, like the fires that suddenly leap into being underneath rockets before they begin their ascent to the heavens. "You mean—you could come here to live with me?" she gasped, a wild thrill entering her voice, transforming it.

"No, no, no, wait a minute!" I warned her, trying to calm her down. "Not that. I mean - what about if you could come back, to live with *me*?"

She sat for a minute, regarding me, her eyes confused, ideas of all kinds racing around in her head, until at last she got a fix on what I had just said, on what I meant. Now, even more than me, she tried to calm herself. She wanted to be clear. "What?" she asked, in that tone of voice slum girls sometimes use. "You want me to come back with you— through the Gate—to *your* side of town?"

"Yes, Diana," I said. "I want—I want to take you back with me."

Speechless, she looked at me for a moment. Then, restless, disturbed, she stood up and grabbed up a hand-held scope, just to do something with her hands, just to give her a weapon against the awkwardness. "Baby," she said, beginning to look out over the city with the scope, peering into the windows of apartments across the street.

"It's not that I don't want to - or that it might not be good—but—well, all the people there, on your side of town..."

"You mean the 'rich people'?"

"... They might not accept me," she said.

"But they will, Diana," I protested, alarmed by her resistance. "They will. Their hearts are open!"

"But - like the way I am?" she asked, continuing to sweep across the city with her scope, like an explorer studying a planet.

"Well—"

"No," she said, angrily, hurt, before I could think of a way to lie, "they don't understand. They don't and they won't and they can't! They just expect everybody else to be like them."

"Diana - "

"Or to begin trying to be like them, like what you already are is some kind of curse, some kind of horrible disease, and you need to be cured!"

"But Diana, there's no one way you have to be," I protested.

"Fine!" she retorted. "There's a million different ways not to be me!"

"Diana," I said. My heart, heavy and stunned, words out of my reach, in awe of the beautiful dream that was falling apart before my eyes; the beautiful dream that had never stood a chance, that our laughter and sex had only passed through, never turned into a home. I wanted to tell her she was wrong, but I did not know how to—and deep inside, a part of me was waking up to the fact that she might be right.

"Diana," I said at last, as she hid from me, staring out of the window through the scope. She did not answer, but some attitude in her body seemed to correspond to "Well?" so I said: "Diana. Tell me—looking out over the city—looking into the apartments across the boulevard - what do you see?"

For a moment, she thought I was joining in on the ancient past-time, 'scoping,' the craze of the old 'voyeurs,' whose social lives had slowly receded inwards, inside the towers, leaving Humanity on the other side of telephones, and computers. Until voyeurism had become the last act of social behavior left in the city: staring into the streets below, and into other people's apartments, with the life-giving scopes. And in its heyday, neighbors would even oblige, becoming each other's objects of desire and mystery, sometimes staging elaborate shows in front of their windows, for the benefit of other voyeurs: orgies, or fights, or 'accidents,' or invented rituals, or dances, or whole 'insane' personalities, anything to make life more interesting and give it some meaning. "Well," said Diana. "I see three big sofas in the apartment I'm looking into, right now, and a giant aquarium tank—but I can't see any fish or lizards or anything. Not even plants in there. There's a hole in the wall with some wires sticking out, and a vent, and a doorway…"

"And what about people?" I asked Diana, carefully, meaningfully.

"No," she said, hypnotized by the image in the scope, because it was someone else's apartment she was seeing, not her own. "No—no people yet," she reported.

"And no people later," I reminded her severely - trying to reach her, somehow. "Diana!" I shouted.

She looked up, startled by my voice which was as close to giving a command as I could come.

"You don't see any people - and you won't see any people!" I cried out, ferociously. "They're gone! They all left!"

"You don't know that!" she protested, her eyes teary, rushing back into the scope, trying to escape from me. "You don't know that! There might be somebody!" she insisted.

"They've all left," I repeated, not heartless, but with the cruelty that compassion sometimes needs. "Left. Because the world could not endure these golden towers, that used all the earth to raise up an island on which only a few could live. Because the rest of the world left these towers standing, by themselves, and discovered the wealth of living free, in the company of other human beings, in friendship, not fear, in ways that could be sustained, not ways doomed to perish after an age of glory. Because these towers, which were once the center of the entire world, were abandoned and left behind like empty shells of a time of ignorance, once the new wealth of human life was discovered; once the treasure of really living was found by the awakened consciousness of the world."

"'Rich is he who has true friends; poor is he confined to emptiness that hides 'neath gold,'" began Diana, cynically, reciting a poem of the world's change. "'Rich is he who has done right; poor is he who stands high, upon a broken soul. Rich is he who gathers love; poor is he who owns others' tears. Rich is he who lives outside the shining palace of treasures, made of solitude and fear.'" And she jerked her body, involuntarily, as if struck by a whip, then said, in a mocking, but highly defensive tone: "Is that what you mean to say to me?"

"Diana," I said, gently. "You are living in the slums. Life has moved on. What was 'rich' yesterday is 'poor' today. Outside, we have what we need—"

"You live in shacks," she countered, a trace of the arrogance of bygone days coming through her voice, to cut me. "You have nothing!"

"Not in shacks, in homes," I said. "We have what we need. We have each other. We have life. We have a world. We have hope."

But once again, she said, "You have nothing!" And suddenly, in a tantrum, screaming something unintelligible, she threw down the scope, smashing it to pieces, and ran off towards the Game Room, with me right behind her, still trying to find a way to make it work. "There are others!" she cried out, as she ran. "I'm not the only one!"

"Yes, a few," I agreed. "Scattered here and there. Holding out in their towers. All alone with what used to be called wealth."

"Others," she panted, throwing open the double doors and bursting in amidst the treasure-trove of her beloved amusements.

"Diana!" I said.

"Look," she protested, utterly wild, now, like someone on fire with drugs. "Look at this!" And she began pulling levers and punching buttons to initiate a gigantic pinball game, nearly half the size of the room. "Look! Look!" she cried out, as it came to life, as though somehow, this enormous game might bewitch me, might win me to her side. Lights began to flash, and bells to ring, buzzers went on and off, as balls flew up and down the pathways of the game, bouncing off of barriers, disappearing into holes, scoring points. "Look at this!" she cried out triumphantly, like a pilot in a war, saving the world. "Score! Now watch—now watch and tell me," she said, trying to release a few words to me without breaking her concentration. "Do you have *this*, back on your side of the Gate? Do you?"

"We have games," I said.

"*This* one?"

No, I thought. Not that one, nor the air-inflatable suit that enabled one to float around the city like a balloon; nor the brainwave projector, that allowed one to record and watch one's dreams; nor the endorphin stimulators, that could turn a person into a walking drug factory, nor the exotic love dummies, nor the vision-sharers, that allowed you to see what other people were seeing, if you could convince them to have a doctor place the implants—the retinal-taps and transmitters (and in those days, it wasn't hard to find takers. People outside the golden city would do almost anything to get a little money, just to live. And then you could watch them eat and work and have sex and go about their insect lives.) All of these amusements came with a gigantic price tag, of course, each one costing more than the lives of a village, a town, or sometimes even a city.

"Your games are nearly all broken," I told Diana, walking quietly among them. Picking up a lonely soccer ball, seemingly misplaced amidst all the extravagant entertainments, I told her, "We have these."

"What good is it?" she asked, glancing at it, then turning away so she wouldn't lose track of the ball bouncing around inside the giant pinball machine. "You just kick it. *And???*—So what!?"

I wanted to tell her something—but maybe too many things wanted to be said, all at the same time, crashing into one another, until nothing was left to say. I felt desolate, as empty as her abandoned city; I knew I had to get back to my part of town, to my side of the Gate.

"Diana," I said. "I think it's time to go."

"No—wait a minute," she said, putting her game on pause. "Wait a minute,"—checking to make sure it was on pause. "Are we going to do the report?" she asked, coming over to me.

"Diana," I told her. "I want—I wanted—and still want—you to come back to live with me. I'm just asking," I said quickly, "I'm not judging you. And I'm not telling you what to do. I just love you [or some part of you, I thought], and I thought you might like—"

But her expression cut me off. Not that it was angry or rude, just a look like I was torturing her, that made me feel cruel to ask again.

So I asked her, "How is Emilio?" ('Emilio' was her still-functioning love doll, the one that said, 'Hello, señorita, how would you like me to show you around the town?')

"O, just fine," said Diana. "So 'guapo.' That means 'handsome.'"

I nodded, as though I had learned something new, and as if I was happy about them.

"Well, Diana," I said, "maybe it's time for me to be going."

"And the report?" she asked.

"I'll write it up, later, don't worry."

Silently, Diana followed me—strangely, I thought, like some demure woman of olden days trained to serve—as I went to find my clothes.

"You'll be back?" she asked.

"Maybe," I lied. "But they might be sending another social worker instead."

"Oh," she said, with an innocent acceptance of the fact that cut deep into me, like a knife. "That's too bad. I was—used to you."

"Yeah," I said, feeling tears well up inside my eyes. "Yeah - but - the most important thing is how the work goes."

"Yeah. 'In our times, poverty is a state of mind,'" she said, trying to prove that she'd learned something during my time with her, after all.

"Yeah," I agreed, struggling to appear satisfied.

I slipped out of the bathrobe and for a moment she touched my naked body, then watched me dress, like she was watching a loved one leaving from the airport, not just saying good-bye at the departure gate, but sticking around to watch the aircraft taxi onto the runway, and finally take off and disappear, glittering with its tiny flashing lights, so brilliant but so alone, into the sad enormity of the night.

"Well," she said, holding my hand as we walked together towards the door, past the enduring memories of the Echo Room - sounds of old love that had, in its moment of being lived, been the most important thing in our lives: "I think I'm going to miss you..."

"Diana," I said, stopping to kiss her one last time, feeling like dying as I spoke, trying so hard not to cry. "If you ever change your mind—"

She nodded quickly, to spare us both, and said, "Yes. Maybe one day. But not yet."

I touched her hair and felt such an excruciating pain that she did not know her true worth, nor how easy happiness was to attain, once you let yourself realize that you were sad.

"Good-bye, Diana," I said.

"Good-bye, Case Worker," she replied.

And it was only outside her apartment, hidden inside the ancient creaking car of the descending service elevator, leaving in the same way that janitors and delivery men had left, that I began to weep and weep, as though my life had just been taken from me.

"Diana—why?" I cried. "Diana!"

Outside, alone, once more, on the giant deserted road, the ghostly barren boulevard whose day had passed, I looked up towards the windows of the golden tower where I had left my heart. And sure enough, high above me, I thought I saw her shape, standing in a window, watching me walk out of her life, forever. A princess, who no knight could rescue, trapped by no one but herself. And a new eruption of weeping surged up from my breast as I fled, broken-hearted, from the waste, back towards the gate where life began.

THE CASE OF THE MISSING CHEERIO

Who would have believed it? A single, sloppy mistake—a lone, donut-shaped cheerio falling off the edge of a spoon and plummeting, unmistakably, to the floor. (We both know it did; we heard its impact on the floor and saw it bounce once, out of sight, though he is now saying, in desperation it seems to me, that he only *thought* he heard and saw it fall.) And yet that cheerio - that single, blundered-away breakfast bite—*fraction* of a bite, if you really think about it, for it began its aborted journey towards my mouth in the company of several others of its kind, the bunch of them immersed in a half-spoon of lowfat milk—has come to assume the dimensions of Sir Isaac Newton's apple. It shook us to the core and forced us to confront the overwhelming mysteries of the Universe, when all we had intended was to eat an ordinary breakfast. It changed our lives forever. *—Or did it?*

I know you're curious—at least, by now, you should be—and I would like to satisfy your curiosity the proper way—the time-honored way—by beginning at the beginning. The only trouble is, I can't find the beginning. Not anymore, not after what happened on that fateful morning. In fact, the more I think about it, the more possible it seems to me that the beginning may actually be located at the end, or even dissolved, "in solution" as it were, throughout the entire tale. If so, then I suppose I might as well just start.

His face. That seems as good a place as any to jump into the chaos, fertile confusion. *His face*, staring at me from across the breakfast table, eyes propelled like rockets from the lenses of his 1950s glasses: brilliant eyes, fiery eyes, the eyes of a genius, or psychopathic killer, that somehow always come out blazing red in photographs. Eyes in love with science, addicted to marvels, but only those that science has brought within reach. He looks like one of those flight technicians from the movie *Apollo 13*, analyzing data from a computer at Houston, Mission Control. He likes *Star Trek*, the vintage reruns, and can put up with its minor anomalies and scientific errors because it's in the ballpark, emotionally if not technically. But fairies and elfin folk irk the hell out of him. For him, Thomas Edison is "Merlin enough," and much beyond that gets his eyes blazing like a WWII machine gun nest.

Across the table, his son, looking like a prematurely aged and washed-up Druid. That's me. A brief romantic stint as a bike messenger that veered out of control and somehow turned into a full-time career. Another Kerouac down the drain, and now, sitting in the temporary refuge of his once-rejected home, a very private kind of detox, where his dismal wages and professional history are somehow being linked to his political and metaphysical beliefs. If p, then q. Name the subject, one false move and it will go up in a boom. The Zapatistas, crop circles, the death penalty, Gingrich, past life regressions, welfare, alien abductions, the pyramids on Mars: it's like smoking on the *Hindenburg*. It's like being Richard Jewell.

I guess in that kind of atmosphere, what happened was pretty much inevitable. There, in the powder magazine of the pirate ship, what else was to be expected from an accidental, careening cheerio, from a tiny breakfast mishap, than absolute disaster?

It fell off of *my* spoon if that makes any difference. At the time, it did not seem to, but now he is making a big deal about it. I do not think he is trying to strike below the belt in this regard. I think it is simply a matter of desperation, a kind of metaphysical thrashing in waters too deep, a frantic grasping at straws, to try to recover dry land by banishing my missing cheerio to the realm of Dawson's Piltdown Man. Be that as it may, the facts of the case are simple, and in my mind, there is no doubt as to what occurred, nor is there in his, though we have, in our moments of fury and frustration, exchanged scathing insults, he consigning my account of what transpired to the same "false memory syndrome" that has produced accounts of the mass rape of kindergarten classes, and I, attributing his own panic-stricken reworking of previously acknowledged events to the advent of premature senility. What we both acknowledged, at the time, is that a cheerio rolled off of my spoon as I was lifting it towards my mouth. He had just, in typical breakfast fashion, proposed an air and sea blockade of Colombia, in order to "protect our nation from international drug dealers," and I had responded with a critique of modern American civilization, which, I argued, made life so unbearable for its citizens that they had turned to drugs *en masse*. "It's a problem of demand, not supply!" I raged. ("You ought to know," he said). In other words, conditions were not favorable for the smooth passage of my spoon, overloaded with cheerios to begin with, to and (even more importantly) *into* my mouth. The hand wanted to gesticulate. The mouth wanted to rave, to right a million wrongs, to overpower a whole world's misunderstanding. And there they were, the poor cheerios, caught in the middle. No wonder that one of them fell. You could even say it was a miracle not more of them fell. (But best to leave the word "miracle" out of it, otherwise, he will accuse me of opening up a new front.)

Plink! It was as simple as that. The cheerio hit, derailing my counterattack at the decisive moment, discrediting me somewhat. It was a soft, but unmistakable bouncy sound, puny but clear against the floor, seemingly superfluous and trivial, although it had already ruined the eloquence of my political counterstroke. We looked, we both saw a momentary hint of movement, something rolling, seeming to flee our presence at the breakfast table, vanishing beyond our fields of vision. We could have leapt up and strained to follow its course, but it was all so obvious where it was headed. Into the corner, and against the wall. I would have to get up, pick it up, and throw it out. That's all. Then the two old rams could lock horns anew, in their eternal, inescapable staging of the Oedipal conflict.

His eyes twinkled as I stood. That I remember as clearly as the sound of the falling cheerio. A kind of laughter emanated from his eyes, as though that fallen cheerio were a muchly deserved, if overly subtle punishment for my insubordination; as though that fallen cheerio, in and of itself, represented some kind of fatal flaw in my arguments (and life in general), some kind of glaring inconsistency, or blatant fallacy. (People carry umbrellas when it rains. Therefore, carrying umbrellas makes it rain.) But the twinkle in his eyes would not last for long.

"Having trouble?" he asked, still in the ecstasy of my discomfort, as though savoring a delicious fruit. I was down on my hands and knees now, in the corner of the kitchen, scouring the floor for any sign of the missing cheerio. It was as though I had lost a contact lens. I remember feeling deeply irritated, even outraged, as the light increased overhead, the dimmer switch turned slowly up to augment the morning sunlight, filtering in, now, through the windows; for the increasing light seemed a mere extension of his laughter. I, after all, remained alone on the floor, on my hands and knees while he stood, gloating, by the light switch.

"It's not here," I said at last, tired of feeling ridiculous.

"What do you mean?" he asked, as I stood up, finished. "Of course it is. You dropped it."

"Yeah, well it's not there."

"Maybe it slid into the crack underneath the wall," he suggested, as though that idea might not have occurred to me.

I just said, "I looked there already."

Still slightly amused, and perhaps even saddened now (by the incomplete transmission of his genetic material), he struggled down to his hands and knees to look for himself. But what would have been welcome a moment earlier as a show of solidarity, now seemed like a mere display of killer instinct, and so I walked away, to distance myself from the inevitable, "Here it is!" The inevitable, "This is how it's done, son. This is how you find a missing cheerio."

To his undying credit, however—what followed, notwithstanding—he *didn't* find it. He could have produced a fake cheerio, taken one from his own bowl while my back was turned, in those first moments of confusion. But my humiliation and banishment to the wilderness meant less to him than the legitimate solution of a scientific mystery, than the search for a genuine answer to the case of the missing cheerio; and for that, I am grateful and owe him the deepest respect.

The first sign that something was seriously wrong - seriously wrong for *him*, I should point out—came as I saw him, eye at floor level now, still down there, lying on his stomach, tracing methodical search patterns with his finger as though he were a coast guard pilot searching for fragments of a shipwreck, or the beautiful orange life preservers of survivors bobbing in the sea. He was stiff— painfully so—and probably besieged by cramps. His legs were like boards, and his teeth gritted, as though he were an archaeologist crawling in a tiny shaft beneath an Egyptian pyramid. I felt sorry for him, even though it was his own fault that he had opted to continue relying on an outdated exercise manual from the 1950s, rather than to take up yoga as I had requested. He was getting older, no longer the mad sprinter who had once left me in the dust, and it softened me, for a moment, till I remembered Clint Eastwood in *Coogan's Bluff*. "What color is pity? —Red. The color of my blood on the floor." No—you could never take it easy on him, or he would simply take advantage to swallow you up, like an ameba engulfing you with his pseudopodia, to turn you into his breakfast, or his clone.

"What is this, your imitation of a snake?" I said at last, recovering some of my dignity in his debasement.

"It's odd," he said, an understatement of vast proportions, for he was reeling, and he later admitted, dizzy by this time. "I can't find it."

"Can't find *what?*" demanded my mother, suddenly appearing as a phantom in the kitchen, like a specter of the conscience who could never be evaded, from whom no dusty bedroom, no failed test, no lost job, could ever be hidden.

"A cheerio. Nostradamus, here, dropped a cheerio onto the floor, and I can't find it."

"Jay, you should help your father," my mother insisted, leaving his slight untouched.

"I already did, it's not there."

"It *must* be there!" he insisted, gasping the words out as though he were a trapped passenger in an overturned, sinking bus that had just gone off a bridge, trying to pry open an emergency exit. "What do you think—that it vanished into thin air?"

My mother has always been a practical woman, like the ancient Romans. While my father and I argued about strange things like the ancient Greeks— (*Could* Achilles catch the tortoise? *Could* you step into the same river twice?)—she built aqueducts and roadways. It was not soon before we two were left alone, again, with our missing cheerio.

"Well, you know," I said, beginning to sense his metaphysical discomfort, but still only playing, not fully captivated myself, as I soon would be, "the world's a lot stranger than you think. I've been telling you that for years. Maybe this is what you need. Like the apple that hit Sir Isaac Newton on the head. Maybe, now, you'll stop insisting that you and your beloved science know everything there is to know about the Universe."

His eyes looked up; at that instant, he seemed a strange cross between a Christian martyr and one of Dr. Moreau's regressing beasts. "Are you seriously—?"

"Yes," I said, guessing his weak spot. "The cheerio did exactly what you said it couldn't possibly have done. *It vanished into thin air!*" And I left him there, piled underneath the crumbled ruins of his worldview. I had things to do, another unpublishable novel to start on. How could I have known? Half an hour later there was a loud knock on my door. Without waiting for a response, my mother burst in, demanding to know what I'd done to my father.

"What do you mean?" I asked, actually alarmed for a moment. "Is he all right?"

"He's still crawling around on the floor, with a flashlight, now! He's moved the refrigerator. He's all covered with dust!"

I knew the crisis was entering a new phase.

In retrospect, I really think I would have passed the missing cheerio and its cosmic implications by, losing that *satori*, that "Eureka!" forever, had it not been for my father and his stubborn obstinacy, his relentless desire for closure. It was he, after all, who searched every nook and cranny of the kitchen, who positively determined that the cheerio was nowhere to be found, that no remote and inaccessible hiding place, no crack, no corner, no piece of furniture, no coloration or design of the floor itself, no oversight remained, unexplored, to harbor it. His face began to grow dim as the day grew old - my mother thought from physical exhaustion, but I knew better. He took on the appearance of the parent of a missing child, as the days begin to pass with no word, no clue, hope fading and eventually withering into a duty, but losing its inner light and warmth, a kind of mummy of the heart.

"It couldn't have vanished," he muttered to himself, over and over again.

"Not according to the laws of science," I agreed, helping him, now, but delighted to find nothing. "Science, as *you* understand it." I then tried something on him I'd heard at a New Age seminar, something about quantum physics, electrons disappearing or jumping from A to B with nothing in between; multiple dimensions, wormholes, time travel, parallel universes—the *new science* that was really just a mathematical form of Buddhism and the ancient truths.

At least, that revived the color in his face. If I were to reproduce a transcript of what followed, it would rival those government reports of UFO investigations for the amount of material that had to be blacked out. In a nutshell, and mercifully, it can be categorized as something best left out of any story—even this one. The bottom line was that since I didn't understand the equations that described the basic functioning of an electric light bulb—do you, does anybody? —I had no right to be talking about perturbations in the texture of space-time. The assault was, I must confess, piercing and degrading, and left me feeling utterly foolish and incompetent (my father was an expert in producing these feelings in others)—completely paralyzed and worthless—until I realized that I did not need to remain pinned down on *his* battlefield, but might find more success, if I were able to maneuver back to mine. I, therefore, returned to my forte, as one always must when hard-pressed, and simply threw his equations to the side, "the cryptic walls of formulas," I said, "that barricade us from ourselves, our fullness, and our life." I told him that his form of science was nothing more than a new religion, filled with fanaticism and intolerance, "a dogma, without the redeeming factor of God." I told him to go shave his head and climb a ziggurat. We, the "Captive Jews" of Science Land, had *experience*, and *being*, to teach us of reality, I insisted—mystical experiences, shamanic visions, past-life regressions, out-of-body journeys, synchronicities; we did not need the gates of our reality, which can only be reached through our perception of what is possible, to be controlled and limited by a sterile scientific elite, a *new priesthood* of guarded mysteries, categorizing our experience as valid or illusory depending on how well it fit into their latest model of the universe, one of many such models which have been built by the ages, only to be torn down, after ruining the lives of those who made the mistake of living too much inside of them.

As the moments passed, and the cheerio remained unfound, I must confess that my initial thrill as a rebellious son began to metamorphose into something higher, a feeling of euphoria and ecstasy, a kind of NDE without a hospital bill. If a cheerio could defy the known laws of science —just vanish into thin air, without being launched through a particle accelerator, or hurled into a black hole—just by falling down onto the kitchen floor—mightn't it be possible for alien beings to walk through walls and levitate abductees into their spacecraft, as John Mack said? Might there not be a hollow earth, after all, an inner earth dimension to harbor elves and fairy folk? Mightn't the light barrier be breakable, and the doorway opened to other galaxies and times, both past and future? Might we not have souls independent of the mortal matter of our brains? Might I not have lived before in ancient China, or Egypt, or Greece, or Rome? Bless the missing cheerio, suddenly transformed into the key with which I might unlock the prison door of my hemmed-in life!

My father called me partial, as though my wishes might somehow be acting as a cloaking device, rendering the cheerio, which should lie in plain view, invisible. He said something about "selective perception" and "negative sensory hallucinations," obviously meant to refer to me, while lamenting the declining condition of his own eyes. "Of course, I understand how much your fantasies mean to you," he said, "considering . . ." Yes, of course, considering my life of dismal failures, my depressions and paralysis, my poor showing and lowly stature on the playing field of reality. Yes, the cheerio, he thought, was like false gold, pyrite, in the hands of a fool, or a needed opiate, perhaps; morphine for a cancer patient. He was sorry to have to continue his search.

But continue he did, for the only alternative was to risk a repeat, in our own times, of the decline and fall of the Roman Empire, "destroyed by superstition," or so he said. A catastrophe that did not permit him to spare his son, who was, after all, only one person. (Had I been Telemachus, he would have plowed me over, I thought.)

Of course I did not spare him my own barrage of psychoanalysis, delivered broadside as in some ruthless battle on the Spanish Main. Why so fearful of a missing cheerio? Why the palms and knees practically scraped away down to the bone, why the hours-long search more befitting of a medieval penitent than a modern man of letters? "It is because, in the end," I said, "you are more magical, even, than I. That cheerio, for you, is like the finger in the dike, holding out the vast and terrible sea of the unknown, preventing it from rushing in on you. For you, that cheerio is a charm to banish demons, a fire to frighten away the dead. It is the child's sheet, pulled above his head to shut out the monsters of the night. Beneath all that rationality, all that science which you deploy, all that facade of complexity and reason, is a primal desperation, like the chanting of frightened cavemen during a thunderstorm. You need to convince yourself that you understand the universe, in order to survive in it," I accused him. "You seek to tame it with false knowledge, with premature conclusions, to confine it inside a box that you think you are the master of. And anything that gets in the way of your defense, even the truth, must be destroyed!"

He flew into a fury, of course, proving my hypothesis all the more, at least to me; and we did not speak for several days until a bizarre new twist occurred, which temporarily gave him the upper hand, and restored his will to communicate. That was the rediscovery, at long last, of the missing cheerio—or so it seemed. He came upon it in a corridor leading out of the kitchen, and held it aloft as though it were the greatest archaeological find of all times—after first calling me down from my hunchback's garret to witness it, of course, in its original "sediment". ("Look - down here—what do you see?!") He even clicked off a roll of Polaroid snapshots to celebrate his triumph (the kind that the camera insultingly manufactures, one by one, each photo needing sixty seconds to dry before the image materializes on it), while I just stood there, bewildered, at first without emotions, which finally began to well up, however: a stinging sense of humiliation, like being beaten in a wrestling match by someone twenty pounds lighter; then, on its heels, a sense of devastation, like finding out your girlfriend has had enough of being with a poor man. I cursed myself for ever getting mixed up with this falling cheerio in the first place, for contaminating and undermining my faith with it, for allowing my faith, which should have sufficed of itself, to become *dependent* on it, so that now that the cheerio had finally been found, my whole world, my whole life, could be taken from me, like water draining from a tub once the plug is pulled.

But suddenly, an alarm rang off in my mind - endorphins or the whisper of a spirit guide? Yes, here *was* a cheerio, I agreed. But the same one? And if it was—how did it get *here*? Twelve feet through the kitchen, then an abrupt and inexplicable right-angle turn, and fifteen feet more down the corridor leading towards the den? How could you explain that logically? Caught off guard, my father examined the nearby walls and doors. Someone might have kicked it there, he said, at last. *Without noticing*, I demanded. Well, what other explanation could there be? Eyes newly alight, I declared that if this *were* the same cheerio, the only possible means by which it could have relocated itself to the site in which he had found it, and which he had so carefully documented in photographs, would have had to have been paranormal in nature. Example? It would have had to have flown there by itself! Or else to have been transported there by invisible beings—as in angels or fairies. Perhaps lost in time, I added, picked up, examined, and left in a slightly different location by a Native American warrior of the past, or a time-traveler of the future. Of course, my father laughed at my theories, but with a false pretense of heartiness, only, for his own "Pelé theory," as I called it, was not entirely satisfying to him; and no wonder. Upon closer inspection, it was little less fantastic than my theory of transport by fairies.

There we were, two grown and supposedly intellectually developed men, come to another impasse like Little John and Robin Hood on the bridge, when my little sister resolved the debate without saying a word. We observed her walking by with a bowl of Cheerios from the kitchen towards the den, to watch TV, and at once suspected. Upon further questioning, we learned that she was, indeed, in the habit of eating snacks of cereal in the TV room, and, in fact, did so every day at this same hour. A plausible explanation, beating both of us back, and saving both of us, at the same time. The cheerio found in the hallway was not THE cheerio, but only one of *her* cheerios.

And so, we were back to where we had begun. Back, after a moment of flux, a rush of excitement, and the feel of wind on our faces, to square one; back in the motionless trenches, without the means to conquer, and without danger of being conquered, each of us invulnerable, each of us unassailable, each of us master of his own trench, and not one inch more of the No Man's Land between us. Father and son, their lives forever changed by the case of the missing Cheerio—*or were they?*

SNOW WOMAN

She was made out of snow. A woman made of snow. I know there are a lot of stories about people like that, snow people, and usually they all end the same way. The snow people are dearly loved, but from the beginning they are doomed, doomed to melt and leave the ones who loved them heartbroken.

In this story, however, the snow woman does not melt. Not even the fire she ignited in the heart of the first man to understand the *second her*, could melt her, could counteract the frozen beauty that he worshipped by remaining lonely. *The second her.* She'd flourished once before, *the first her*, the innocent, childish one trying to expand, to leave the tight grip of her culture, not knowing it was in her, making her silent until she wasn't heard, because here we don't hear souls until they disgrace themselves.

She was a blossom then, young, underneath balloons and in the middle of parties, singing with the children, and clutching dark edges of society that made her like herself more, borders of nonconformity, aromas of poems, piercings that said, 'I'm not a prisoner', dreams of tattoos that she didn't go through with, traces of revolution like Molotov cocktails filled with mild criticisms. She rebelled in her own way, like a lion roaring from inside a cage. And it was enough while she was young, fresh, beautiful, and the music of a beautiful child enraptured the world.

But one day that 'her' broke. *The first her.* Like Chiyo once said, 'Break them, and they give you their perfume. Blossoms of the plum.' That was the *second her.* The after-the-breaking one, covered with the fragrance of her defeat, wisdom locked away in her heart like money in a safe she wouldn't touch. That's the one I knew, the snow woman, the one who tried to laugh but thought of someone else; the one who used my footsteps to fill the emptiness, like the sound of wind chimes. My love wandered into the crosshairs of her sincere misunderstanding; without wanting to, she pulled the trigger of a love that was too huge for me to eclipse, she gunned down my last chance. But she was so beautiful that I went past my last chance, I tried again and again, continued loving her after I died, accepting the endless assassinations, until, at last, she ran away from hurting me, which hurt me even more than being his shadow.

Flames came out of me in those days, flames of love, fierce efforts, in fire, to pry open the silence, the majesty she wouldn't share, and didn't believe in. But the snow held fast. Once, I thought I saw the tiny track of a tear, a trail of slush resting on her snow cheek, but in the morning it was gone, she was as serene as a field of new snow seen out of a window, filling the earth with a purity you cannot kiss, only bow down to.

This second her, the one I loved, for I have never truly loved anyone who did not have a gash, was cold only on the surface, underneath the sometimes-jolly laughter that was like a thin atmosphere above a frozen mountain range. But below that mountain range was lava; there was a world of fire, red, bubbling, steamy, explosions trained to eat themselves, earthquakes trained to say it was just a headache, cities she wouldn't destroy even as they walked over her with contempt she refused to translate, and pressed down on her soul which never forgave her for losing him.

Maybe it was loyalty, the snow. Or just the castle she built around the child whom she loved with a heart that was bigger than the earth she stood on, a heart that was the equal of all the planets. I was, in the end, a wild dog, unpredictable, I couldn't be allowed through the door.

Snow Woman, Snow Woman, Snow Woman, I couldn't melt you! I couldn't melt you from the outside, just as your own fire couldn't melt you from the inside.

At first, there was hate in my love, I couldn't understand you saying 'No' in your wordless way. I wanted to die and wanted to pull you down with me. But, as time went on, and the power of the tragedies you fought through revealed themselves, I learned to love your snow, and to love your love of snow.

It became the place where we met. Child you and child me, who would have ridden a sled together, rung bells together, dropped backwards with arms spread out like angels, into snowbanks waiting for a painting, been the first to make footprints in a changed world. Vapor coming out of our mouths like holiday wreaths. On snowy days, our nostalgias embraced. For as long as the snow lasted, we were Siamese Twins. And all the 'No's' were buried, like the dirty earth.

Yet, even from behind the cracks of our formidable reversion to childhood, scarred adults looked out at the snow-bound world with deep regret, for what is snow, but the beauty of regret, the plaintive cry of empty trees and vanquished green that have finally found the mantle of enlightenment, snow being the awakening, the transformation of loss into the most exquisite form of triumph, turning the destroyed world into a jewel. Then, you can walk among the pillaged trees to find them cloaked in the beauty of our maturity, covered with the weight of all those sad years, shining now, pristine, the murdered rain that has become more beautiful than it was, looking down on us with love, changed, by the cold, into its highest self, like an anxious merchant who became a Buddha.

And though we are far apart, we can hear our footsteps, on those days, I can hear yours from Brooklyn, and you can hear mine from

Queens, crunching the ice, each stride like a statement of love that couldn't be, as our hands, miles long when it snows, reach through the hole in the fence that keeps us apart, to grasp the other's. To squeeze the other's with the passion of the most ardent lover. To say, 'Thank you. Thank you for reincarnating in this world, in this time. Thank you for standing next to my longing, all these years, with your coldness that isn't cold.'

THE BET

It was all because of a bet. I made it with Samson while the angels watched. He'd been a corrupt official in his country and signed the orders that killed thousands, and yet there he was, quoting Nietzsche on a cloud. "What you call morality is merely cowardice," he said, his body scarred by the tears of the many mothers whose sons he'd killed. "You are not better than me, you are only more afraid. Deep in your heart you want to be like me, you lust like I do, you crave wealth and power like I do, but you lack the balls to go for it and the talent to attain it. You disguise your timidity and your sloth as principles. What a pitiful way to suck up to God!"

"It's not true," I retorted under the inscrutable gaze of the angels. "I could have been like you if I'd wanted to. Even worse." I remembered what Sherlock Holmes had once said to Dr. Watson: that, if he'd been so inclined, he would have made a wonderful criminal. And I believed that of myself. "There's more to morality than simply having duller claws. You flatter yourself, Samson."

But he would have none of it. "Here I am, trapped on a cloud that can barely bear my weight, in constant danger of falling through the fluff that, for me, is like thin ice. And there you are, light as a feather, without a care in the world, one of God's pets. I thought God had better eyes than that! It is you who flatter yourself, Johannes! *He who is last shall be first?* Idiocy! You were not last because you chose to be, but because you were slow!"

The angels gave no clue as to what they thought; I believe that for them, the Bible is merely like the bell that signals school has begun, and that they fear nothing, except the possibility of telling you the answer.

"Prove it! Next time, prove it!" Samson dared me. "Screw the world like I did, use it, devour it! You'll see, it's not so bad. A few years of misery, which cannot be much worse than the neuroses you liberals are constantly suffering on the earth anyhow, tormented by this and tormented by that, and then, it will be time to reincarnate! To try again! You can afford to be bad just once, Johannes! Prove to me that you are brave enough to be bad, that I may believe that goodness is a virtue, and not merely an incapability!"

The faces of the angels looked nowhere, they dwelled in an untouchable inner space, there was grace in their eyes, but no road map to the place they had found; their lips were serene, as though satiated from kissing, with no lover anywhere in sight, nothing clinging to them or running from them.

"Damn you, Samson!" I cursed, as I felt the attraction of a womb somewhere I could not see. "I will show you what I am capable of! I will make your sins seem like the pompous exploits of little boys stepping on ants! I will cast 'right living' to the winds, I will show you how bad I can be, that you may know there is such a thing as goodness, and that men may choose it; that it is not merely the haven of those whose evil has no skill!" And I let my form evaporate and fly like light into the body of a young woman, lying quietly in bed beside a naked, spent man, asleep with a smile on his face.

There is no need to chronicle my life in detail, to explore the nuances of my childhood, the discoveries and mishaps of my adolescence, the charming gaffes and the dark nights alone listening to records; no need to write of the inspiring teachers or the pathetic ones, the thousands of trajectories suggested to me, the opportunities, the conscious decisions and rolls of the dice. I had made a bet, and everything was channeled towards fulfilling it, guided by the power of a formative thought that drew what was needed directly towards it, like a great magnet of intent. This life was not dedicated to Humanity, nor to any beautiful art which lived lightly on the earth; it was dedicated, instead, to overpowering Samson's cynicism, and to cleansing my lifetimes-of-sacrifice of doubt. It was dedicated to mining the world as though it were my private gold mine, and extracting every treasure I could from it for my own benefit, to prove that I *could* be bad, and that if I was good, it was because I aspired to be good, not because my vileness was lame. Other lifetimes would redeem me. Even if it took a hundred, it would be worthwhile to show Samson he was wrong. Samson, who before he had been Samson and crushed Biafra like a flea, had flown a Junker dive bomber over London, made the streets of Paris run red with the blood of the Huguenots, spit at Jesus as he staggered through the streets of Jerusalem bearing the beam of the cross upon his back, and begun his earthly sojourn as Amalek, the king of the treacherous, the jackal who preyed upon the weak. This lifetime, I would make war on him by making war on the rest of mankind.

Nor here is there much need to go into detail. I succeeded. My mind was as fast and sharp as a steel trap that springs shut on the foot of a hungering animal, seeking something to eat in woods that are bare and covered with snow. My heart, overpowered by the fierce prayers I had made in heaven, did not restrain me: appetite replaced compassion, while discipline of iron prevented appetite from corrupting strategy. A fat eagle cannot fly; a serpent satiated by love cannot bite. I reflected every day, but not to let in God; it was to sharpen the blade of the sword I had become. I spewed poison Om's into the dawn, my chanting was like the engine of a submarine prowling beneath the waves. I engineered, with a Third Eye completely harnessed to my vow, a level of enlightenment that did not challenge my motives but only furthered my goals.

I was a businessman, closely linked to the highest political elites. I bought up vast amounts of land in foreign countries and wooed my defenders in Washington to suppress the revolutions that sought to expropriate them once it became clear that the production of the land I had bought was to be directed towards the consumption of those who were already prosperous. But from the prosperous you can extract more; what good is there in selling to those who can only give you pennies? The land I used to raise cattle for the few, and to produce ethanol so that the rich could drive while the poor starved. I formed PR companies to shield myself with lies, and make my greed seem wise; I invested in armaments manufacture to contain the aggrieved, behind great dikes of war. I hired two coups, and lifted glasses of champagne to my lips, as the streets of poor lands filled with tanks: American thorns encircling the rose of foreign wealth. Let the hands of the needy bleed, reaching for what was theirs! The moist lips of my mistress mattered more to me than their empty stomachs!

When anemic protestors from my own country, who refused their share of the loot, came marching outside of my wrought-iron gates, high like a barrier of upraised, sharpened spears, I merely waited them out. Most of them tired of the battle, it did not pay their bills, and they outgrew it. I got rid of the serious ones who remained by blowing up one of my own limos with a bomb—adieu, José, but chauffeurs come a dime a dozen—whereupon the police swarmed in like a cloud of diving eagles, like the kind that clutch arrows in their talons on our money.

The protests ended, I enriched myself by creating poverty with my cattle and my biofuels, then doubled my profits by reaping the enraged multitudes I had planted all across the earth, with bullets I had shares in. How I loved those impassioned hearts which would not yield, which required my bullets to lay them to rest!

For some, there might have been stress in a life like this, but for me, there was too much excitement to suffer. It was like flying through white-water rapids in a kayak. The board meetings, the favorable reports from the stock market, the parties with spider webs laid everywhere to entangle the powerful and turn them into my accomplices, the money transfers, the handshakes in the night, the selling of political snake oil, the helicopters that made no sound in America, as they carved my name into the flesh of millions who had no voice.

And Alexandra and Janet and Marguerite, and Premio and Perk, my beautiful pair of Afghans, who the magazines loved to photograph whenever Marguerite took them for a walk in the park; and they were so kind as to leave out the bodyguards. And the three obligatory kids by Ann, who was hampered by the prenuptial agreement from weakening the clout of my ego. Little treats, this whole bunch, whenever my eyes became blurry from the chessboard, and I needed time off to restore my edge.

And then, at last, it ended, this magnificent run of empire-building, this enormous new landscape of castles made of sand, which I had to leave behind. Of course, it was ephemeral, but so what? So are we all. While I was on Earth, I had a chair to sit on. I ate the best of foods, I drank the finest of wines, I cavorted with the most beautiful of women, with iron faces and hard hearts, it is true, but their bodies were soft in spite of their soullessness and I only lingered with them long enough to hurl all of the world's woes into their moist interiors, never long enough to be bored. While others prayed to God for a loaf of bread, I ate a hundred loaves of bread without a prayer. While others lived alone, reaching in vain for love, I never asked for more than sex, and never lacked a woman who would lie on her back for me. While others dreamt of how the world should be, I made it the way I wanted it to be. 'Should' is for weaklings! I lived a good life, a focused life, I flew past a million inefficiencies without a thought, straight for the target. I did not take the armor off my heart nor the blinders from my eyes.

When I came back, after a gentle death, euphoric like Bismarck who changed the map of Europe with blood and iron, and sped history along by filling its sails with winds of mourning, I knew I had succeeded. Like Caesar, like Tamerlane, like the Iron Chancellor, who melted all the gold of all the minds of his country into a single war club which he passed on to the future, I had triumphed. I had left my mark on the world, and I had enjoyed leaving my mark. I had been a man of distinction, and for the first time in a thousand lifetimes, I had finished first.

"Take that, Samson!" I cried in triumph as I staggered across rolling fields of clouds back to the starting point.

"Take what?" he demanded, as sullen as ever.

"I have proven you wrong!" I boasted. "I have beat you at your own game!"

But he only shook his head, and spit at the earth. "You're crazy, Johannes," he said. "You haven't gone anywhere. You've been here all the time."

"What are you talking about?" I demanded.

And with his head, he motioned off into the distance, where I saw a million mothers whose sons I had not killed, and a million farmers tenderly checking on the corn that was their own, and miles of winding streets that had no soldiers or tanks in them.

"What you think you did was just a dream," he told me. "You chose to be born to a woman who didn't want you. You were aborted. You didn't do anything of what you'd planned to do. See?" he demanded. "You don't have the guts! It's just like I said."

And suddenly I broke down weeping, though I knew he would mistake it for weakness: weeping tears of joy that I had lost my bet, that I had failed to prove I could be as evil as he.

MYSTERIOUS LITTLE MACHINE

The man was odd. Intense, small, trying to pretend that he wasn't there and wasn't paying attention. A rather large box like an old-timey camera, only much larger, dangling in front of his chest, suspended by the strap behind his neck. Curious spectators could see puzzling knobs and dials protruding from it, some kind of meter with a dancing needle, and a viewport the man was able to look down into as though staring into a crystal ball.

"What you got there?" a curious man, tucked into a fashionable raincoat that seemed to be snickering because of the sun, asked the stranger on the sidewalk.

"Nothing much," the man replied.

"Is it a camera?"

"Not quite," the man replied again, in a voice that seemed like a foot that's fallen asleep. Shrugging, the interrogator moved on, as the man with the machine continued doing, or not doing, something.

Moments later, a pretty young woman passing the same way, asked, "Are you taking pictures?"

"Not really," the man said.

"Not really? Does that mean 'sort of'?"

She tried to look into the viewing port the man was riveted to, but he swiped some lever like a magician, and all she could see was a curved glass lens with nothing in it.

"If you are," she said, anyway, "I don't give you permission to use my image. I'm supposed to be at work. Do the pictures have date-time stamps? What's with this guy?" she asked someone else just passing by. "Does he speak English?" Shaking her head, she went on, after firing one more warning behind her. "I don't give you permission to use my photo!"

Attracted by the unanswered questions and unusual behavior, Jerry, an off-duty cop in a t-shirt and jeans, decided to follow the man with the machine to see if he could discern what he was up to. He didn't suspect criminal activity, and this was a public street, so as long as the man didn't unduly impede or harass the flow of pedestrians, he had a right to take the pictures—if that is what he was doing.

"Great!" the man with the machine said suddenly, to himself, as a group of four high-school-aged friends came down the sidewalk together, approaching from the other direction. "Let's see!"

The man seemed as interested as if he were filming a nature show, and he had just spotted a lion, promising great footage.

As the friends came down the sidewalk, a middle-aged woman, who was just in front of the man with the machine, stopped, distressed by the fact that the friends weren't leaving any sidewalk for her.

"So easy for one of them to drop back, or for all of them to go single file," the man was narrating to himself. "But no, they're taking up the entire sidewalk, and not giving her a lane."

Jerry noticed an inert light on the man's device began to flash red. When one of the kids scowled at the lady who had held her ground, because he had to move a foot to the right not to walk into her, another red light began to flash beside the first. The kid didn't say anything to the woman, but the look in his eyes was like spitting.

Just as fast as all this, the man with the machine pushed another set of buttons, then spoke into what seemed to be a small mike linked to the machine by a wire and jack. "Feed it in."

"Maybe he's documenting urban behavior, or something. Sociology," mused Jerry. "Too young to be a student. Continuing Education?" Somehow, he didn't look like a professor. He didn't seem neutral enough, he didn't have footnotes in his blood.

Moments later, Jerry saw a deliveryman with a big box trying to get into a building. Just ahead of the delivery man was a woman, moving along with spirited strides, maybe angry at something. She had a stylish dress, a short skirt and embarrassed legs, high heels which she had surrendered to, and earrings that seemed like stolen land.

The woman seemed to notice the delivery man with his overwhelmed arms, because she stiff-armed him with her a look of annoyance, almost as if she assumed he must be lusting for her. She was one who rode an elevator, he was the one who went down the stairs, into the darkness of mailrooms and loading docks.

In spite of seeing him, and the way the box he was carrying was actually dragging him behind it, she acted as if he were not there, leapt through the building door just ahead of him, and, without holding it, let it close in his face as he lowered his shoulder to try to fight his way in. Spinning around and contorting his body, he finally managed to squeeze through. It was as dramatic as a baby being born.

With great interest, Jerry saw the red lights on the mysterious man's machine blinking on and off again, almost furiously, as though offended, or possibly just frightened.

He was about to approach the man to ask him about his device when, all of a sudden, the man whistled to himself. "Let's see what this does!"

And Jerry pointed his eyes towards the target of the man's eyes, and saw one man, and then another, and then another walking along the other side of the street with heads buried in cell phones, right past a beautiful cherry tree in full bloom. Like a woman in the prime of her beauty, the pink blossoms of the tree were singing a beautiful song that no one was hearing. The branches were reaching out, like lonely arms, also like loving arms, ready to embrace anyone who was dying.

Once again, the red lights were flashing.

When the man with the machine saw a young woman near the tree take a selfie of herself, but without the tree in the picture—just herself, her face, so pleased to be her, that face which all the Universe needed— he couldn't help but blurt out: "That's the icing on the cake!"

"The icing on the cake?" Jerry asked.

"On the cake," the man said, in the same voice with which he talked to himself.

Then, shaking his head, he muttered something which Jerry heard as: "It's every bit as bad as I thought! God help us!"

Jerry watched as the man, disturbed, seem to touch the knobs on his machine as if he were shutting some part of it down, but not all of it; and then as the man began to look around, as if searching for something. At last, he found it. He didn't see it with his eyes, but located it inside of his mind; a memory, but of what?

Jerry followed the man as, filled with renewed purpose, he strode down the city streets like a migrating bird flying towards its home after the bitter winter has lost its war to stay forever. It turns out, the man's 'home' was a bench underneath some trees in something that wasn't quite a park but was more than an ordinary street.

Surreptitiously, Jerry crept behind the man, spying on him like a cloud.

Once more, the man was hitting dials, and now, at last, the large lens on top of the mysterious machine was beginning to light up like a TV, with suddenly vivid streams of images pouring out of it, like a river exceeding its banks and beginning to prey on the towns beside it.

Jerry saw, in the viewing port of the man's machine, dirty, tragic shacks, a giant swarm of them, clinging to hills of despair, looking down on a beautiful city that had turned its back on them. There were hungry children and mothers with eyes like fires put out, moist with tears that had no more strength to come out, cheeks as dry as a desert, but with the fissures of months of crying dug into them. There were fathers destroyed like trees that have been cut down; pools of stagnant water like blood clots; twinkling stars at night that were like the jewels of the rich, locked away in safes.

"You, foolish woman, who did not hold the door!' cursed the man.

And briefly, Jerry saw the image of the woman who had not held the door open for the delivery man, before the imagery shifted.

This time, he saw their city with water in the streets.

"The oceans!" the man was cursing.

And then, there was a vast plain of tree stumps, and in the distance, genie-like clouds of smoke rising from an unseen valley. You could almost hear the sound of chainsaws and bulldozers. And somewhere else, someone was coughing, and saying, "They put something in the water." And in another scene, there was a giant room as large as a city, with thousands of people in cubicles, staring at small blue screens, and where windows had been, there were just walls. And for one moment, Jerry could see inside the chests of some of these workers, as if he were viewing a sonogram, and their hearts were tiny, the size of acorns. And on one desk of one man in a cubicle, he saw a potted plant, and it was drooping and near death.

And Jerry was once more about to speak to the man, when all at once he saw in the viewing port, replays of the throngs who had walked past the cherry tree as if it were not there.

Before he could overcome his surprise, even more disturbing images had begun to erupt from the man's machine. Images of tanks rolling through the streets. Soldiers kicking in doors, charging in with bayonets. Missiles jumping out of hiding, like deadly snakes. Drones shooting up vehicles on a congested road. Blinding flashes of light, the sound of crumbling buildings, breaking glass, a kind of whispering thunder that wouldn't stop, and occasional piercing cries of mothers looking for their children, and screams of humans being vivisected by someone else's pride.

And then Jerry saw the youths from before, walking four abreast on the sidewalk, seeming to think it belonged to them alone; not even malicious about it, with brains that no longer had the map of anyone else. How can you do wrong to people who don't exist?

"Bastards!" exclaimed the mysterious man. "Look at what you have done!"

Unable to endure the puzzle any longer, Jerry finally found a way to break through the mystery man's concentration, and to demand of him: "What is this? What is this machine? What does it do? What is it all about?"

The man slowly turned his head, to watch the off-duty cop as he circled around, and dared to sit down on the bench beside him. Even though he hadn't spoken, just the fact that he was looking at Jerry was a start.

"Is this some kind of movie? You record videos, but then, the other scenes..."

'It is the microcosm machine," the man said, surprisingly clear and forthright.

Jerry just looked at him.

"From the small comes the large. From the minute comes the huge. Out of the inconsequential is born the life and death of men, and worlds. Good heavens," he exclaimed, observing Jerry's bewildered look, "are you truly that clueless?"

"Sorry," Jerry said, "but you mean..."

"Of course," the man replied. "From the microcosm comes the macrocosm. The great sweeping dramas of history, the joys and woes of the world, the storms that rattle the newspapers and change the maps, that gouge out huge chunks of the earth, take the crown off of one head and put it on another; at the same time the kisses of new ideas or renewed love that save millions —it all comes from this. From the stitching, the needlework of daily life; the tiny values that are mighty, that collectively build or tear down empires, that give birth to species and preserve them, or erase them with extinction! These little actions are the foundation, these little commitments and minute acts of awareness, like a billion matches, that can light the sun, but which can also be blown out by a tiny gust of wind."

Jerry looked at the man with horror. "But…"

"That's right," the man said. "It's been a bad day, here, for me and my machine. But…" And now he pointed to a mother walking past them, her baby wrapped up in a blanket and pressed close to her chest, the mother's long black hair flying behind her like a flag, her skin like earth shaped on a potter's wheel into the most beautiful country.

"But," he continued, "there's still hope."

His machine was brilliant at detecting the darkness, of which there was a terrible abundance where we lived; these little bridges to the end of the world made from our personal lives, our little islands of the night holding hands to make the whole world night. But there were also silver linings, and yearnings that could crack open the harshest logic to reveal flowers as strong as bullets.

The microcosm machine is not a perfect invention, but even when it threatens us, it is here to help us. To remind us that when the mire of politics becomes too impassable, too depressing to dip our hands in any longer, impervious to our dreams, prayer-proof, like some armored juggernaut that our votes just bounce of, there is still this with which to fight back: the actions of our daily lives and the way we treat each other on the side of history, which will become history. The sum of our meaningless lives which have the power of God to remake the world in our own image.

THE CLAMOR OF SPIRITS

My wife and I moved into the house two Januarys ago. It was a dark, yet somehow welcoming Tudor, with narrow windows overlooking a garden that, for the first time in our lives, belonged to us. Busy city streets were within walking distance, and yet, our new home seemed to belong to a world apart, nestled in a tiny sanctuary of green lawns and spacious residences, bound together by private roads behind stone walls. We did not feel as though we were against the city in which our favored enclave lay hidden, but rather, as though the city had bestowed some special privilege upon us as a reward for the swiftness of our minds and the economic fertility of our lives.

I was a legal professional who enjoyed dabbling in creative writing on the side. My wife was a CPA with major clients, and a massive inheritance to boot. We had no children to worry about, and were in no way extravagant in our wants. Given the nature of our lives, the house was only logical.

We had already committed ourselves, signed the contracts, parted with the down payment, moved in all our things, and burned the bridges behind us, before the first ghost appeared to us.

My wife is the one who saw it first, shoving me violently as I lay asleep in the bed beside her, whispering: "Nick! Nick!" She was trying to shout, but had no voice; the fear had taken it from her.

"What is it, Adie?"

"Wake up!"

"What is it?" I opened my eyes, none too pleased, for I had important work to do in the morning, when I saw her: a sad-looking Japanese woman in a long, flowing kimono, holding a fan in her hand, and simply staring at us. "What?!" I gasped, shaking my head fiercely, as when a boxer struggles to clear his head after receiving a tremendous punch. As I did so, the woman vanished. Beside me, Adelaide was weeping.

After turning on all the lights and comparing notes, we realized that we had shared the same vision. "Nick," my wife told me, distraught. "It was a ghost! We have a ghost!" It was frightening, and absolutely real, like seeing a cobra or a black widow spider in your house.

"There's no such thing as ghosts," I said, knowing, in my heart, that I was lying, because all my body, shaking and dripping with sweat, filled with emotions that were crackling like electricity, knew the truth.

"We have a ghost!" my wife wept, clinging to me as though I were strong.

We comforted each other and sat up in chairs for the rest of the night, all the lights in our home left on. And the following days, we slept with the blue nightlight on, and with a glass of water constantly beside the bed, for my wife had once heard, from the superstitious maid who helped to raise her, that spirits are appeased by water. "There are no such things as ghosts," I repeated as a mantra, even as we made efforts to satisfy the apparition. We tried to bury the experience with what we knew of science.

But the ghostly visitations were only just beginning.

Sometime in the middle of March, my wife, who was taking photos in the backyard, came running into the house screaming, "I saw her! I saw her again! In the garden!"

"Who?" I demanded, as I sat staring at a blank computer screen, attempting to begin writing a novel, because I felt it would make me a more complete person.

"The ghost! The Japanese woman!"

An awful chill went through my body. "But Adie," I exclaimed, "it's in the middle of the day!"

"I saw her—in broad daylight!" Adie wept. That was not a good sign, for our nightmares ought to limit themselves to the darkness. "What can we do, Nick? What can we do?"

Since Adie had seen it, and not me, this time I was inclined to interpret it as a delusion and to see it as her problem. Maybe the last time, when I saw the ghost, I had only succumbed to the power of suggestion, been swept away by Adie's conviction, fallen prey to her imagination because I loved her.

I told her to be brave, with all the courage of someone who is safe.

But poetic justice pervades the universe like hydrogen, like gravity. Days later, it was my turn to be visited, only this time, it was not by the enormously sad Japanese woman, but by a tall, emaciated man with a sword, who I saw walking behind me as I was looking in the mirror, my face covered with shaving cream. Crying out in pain, for I cut myself as soon as I saw him, I whirled around to see nothing but the wall.

"Careful, I don't want to lose my husband," Adie told me, when she saw me with the Band-Aid on my throat. "What were you thinking about?"

I was embarrassed to tell her, but she, sensing that I was being evasive, gave me that serious look with which she never failed to extract my deepest secrets, just as a dentist pulls a rotten tooth from the mouth of his unwilling victim. "Did he look Japanese?" she asked me. "Was he a samurai?"

"No," I told her, even though it shattered the theory, which you could see her attempting to construct. "He was wearing a long white garment that seemed to be some form of underclothes and carrying a large broadsword, which appeared medieval. He had the look of a knight who has not yet put on his armor, except for his thin build, his pale skin, and the wild brightness in his eyes, which made him seem a madman. He looked like he had not eaten in days, like he was fasting, or merely oblivious to his body, famished by dreams that had no connection to his stomach."

My wife looked at me, and after a moment of extreme puzzlement, seemed to dismiss my vision as I had dismissed the one she had had alone. She did not say as much, since she needed to maintain my goodwill in case she should have another vision of her own and need my sympathy, but you could tell from the way her face relaxed, and from the air-like nature of her reassurances.

Maybe it was only my imagination, I told myself, nearly convinced by her lack of excitement. But two days later, I saw the same gaunt figure once again, this time touching the wall of the den, running his hands along it like a blind man feeling the face of someone he knows but has not seen in a long time, and wants to remember.

"Damn!" I shouted in dismay and terror.

The figure turned to look at me with serious, recriminating eyes, but made no effort to reach for his sword. Instead, he merely vanished, and I staggered out of the den, my face as white as a sheet, telling Adie what I had seen, except that she was not here but was gone to the store to buy something. I determined to keep the experience to myself, but to return to taking the phenomenon seriously.

＊＊＊＊＊

For a time, none of us spoke about the ghosts. It was as if, by merely mentioning them, we might bring them back to haunt us.

But our new defensive mechanism was as useless as trying to shelter oneself from a torrential downpour with a Kleenex. One April night—"April showers bring May flowers" —I was awakened by a terrible pinch, Adie, who, this time, had no shred of a voice at all. I looked up and saw in our bedroom a furious, desperate looking young man, utterly disheveled, as pale as I had been when I saw the ghost in the den, and probably was now; in his hand there was a bloody axe, I saw him dropping a gold watch into the pocket of a ragged but formidable coat that seemed out of place for where we lived, in April. Seeing that we saw him, he seemed to start, almost to panic. Then his desperation turned to rage. He turned towards us as if to strike us dead with the axe. A small sound escaped from Adie's paralyzed vocal cords, halfway between a whimper and the scream of someone far away. Then, she seemed to faint. "She was a bitch!" the young man cursed. "A cheapskate, hoarding money that others need! The brilliant and the useful wither on the vine of people like her. But the other one— poor, stupid girl, at the wrong place at the wrong time! But now that you've seen me, you must die, also, the die is cast! You'll go straight to the police! If you didn't, I could spare you, but you will, no matter how earnestly you insist that you won't. Liars: you, too, deserve to die!" I leapt out of bed, screaming, and suddenly, he was not there.

*****

"We need to get out of here," Adie sobbed, after I had revived her.

We spent the next week in a hotel.

After being resuscitated by the predictability of the establishment, which offered no surprises, and was filled with the comfort of businessmen, tourists, and travelers, whose eyes were firmly fixed on the world we live in, on its pleasures, opportunities, and highly cooperative dangers which follow the laws of physics, we finally decided that fleeing from the beautiful new house we had just moved into was not the thing to do: not yet. But we also decided that the phenomenon that was turning our lives upside down could no longer be dismissed. We could not bury our heads in the sand or cover our eyes with our blankets and wait for it to go away. We must do something. Soon.

Since modern psychology is an appendage of the paradigm that spawned it, and is limited to the vision of that paradigm, we felt that there was no point in seeking counseling or psychoanalysis. "They'll only end up trying to medicate us," Adie warned, "and if any of this gets out, it could damage our reputation. In businesses like ours, you cannot get by without your reputation."

"We live in a haunted house," I said.

She nodded. "We have both seen the ghosts, twice at the same time. People do not have the same delusion, simultaneously," she conjectured.

"There are multiple-witness sightings of UFOs," I said, undermining my previous assertion, because it frightened me. "Thousands of people claimed to see the miracle at Fatimah. I read a book that claimed that a whole ship of sailors saw a sea monster."

"We had no previous expectations," she insisted. "I didn't tell you what I saw before I saw it. How could *both* you and I see a Japanese woman, and that crazy young man with the axe, if it was only in our minds? Minds don't work that way! If I'd told you first... but I didn't!"

"Maybe one of us is telepathic," I said, "and either transmitting to the other, or picking up from the other, what is the delusion of only one of us."

She looked at me with anger, because if that were the case, she knew on whom I intended to pin the delusion. "Telepathy is as crazy as ghosts!" she blurted out, at last. Then, to clarify her position, she added: "Nick, we have ghosts!"

She decided, as discreetly as possible, to bring in a psychic who specialized in hauntings to consult with us, and to go through the house.

"If going to a psychologist about this could discredit us, what could inviting in a psychic do?" I demanded of her.

"Nick," Adie said, with gritted teeth: "the ghost had a f**king bloody axe in his hands!"

*****

James was a very likable but strange young man who seemed as though he might be possessed by the spirit of someone's grandmother. Certainly, he was the kind of man more likely to be found drinking tea and eating biscuits than lowering his spear at Thermopylae. "Keep an open mind," Adie growled, simultaneously trying to defeat my prejudices and skepticism, as I stood off at a distance, arms crossed.

"It's a very nice old house," James said, strolling through the rooms with a sometimes alert, sometimes utterly distracted and conversational demeanor. "Such nice curtains, Mrs. Enloe, did you pick them yourself?"

I thought: "What a bargain: we get a psychic and an interior decorator for the price of one."

"A lot of old energy here, someone was depressed," James was telling Adie. "You've brought in a new energy, but it's still not the predominant energy here. Did you cleanse the house with sage before you moved in? Sage is wonderful—especially if you mix it with sweet grass; the sage itself can appeal to warrior spirits, who might not go. But before that— before the energy became depressed—had the person who owned this house recently passed away? There was a vibrant energy here, very bright and lively, it was as if the narrow windows of this Tudor were twice their size, and a lot more light was coming in. The depression— sickness—no, something about fathers and sons. Generations. They don't always see eye to eye. Who will pass it on to the future? Something that must be saved."

I rolled my eyes; Adie kept me in line with a dirty look.

"Was anybody ever murdered here?" she asked the psychic.

The psychic closed his eyes as if he had a headache and was trying to remember where he had left the car keys. At last, he said: "It's an old house, so of course it has a history. Was it built around 1920?"

"A little earlier," Adie said.

"I think an old lady died in it, but that was some time ago. She has moved on," he said, his eyes still closed. "She is at peace. She was welcomed by the light, over half a century ago. She's no longer here. Besides that, a child. But the child died in a hospital. A little girl was very sick here, but died in the hospital. You can't help but have things like this around, traces of tragedy, in a house so old. It's the nature of history, of life."

"Is she still here?" Adie asked him.

"No. The spirit of the little girl was never deeply attached to this house. She is in a wonderful place, now. She chose the sacrifice to humanize her parents, to teach them a lesson. Thanks to her, they learned to respect the suffering of others."

I began to fidget.

"Don't you feel anything?" Adie demanded. "Anything at all? You don't sense the presence of ghosts? We're sure of what we've seen."

James sat down with us at the kitchen table, and finally won my respect by saying: "I don't feel anything right now. Or, that's not quite right. I feel a sense of disappointment and of loss. And it's like a door. An open door. I feel a father betrayed by his son. That's all. It's created an instability. But I don't feel murder. You know, the really hardcore ghosts are very easy to pick up; my hair stands up on end right away."

"Well, if a ghost with a bloody axe in his hand isn't hardcore, who is?" I demanded.

James's mouth dropped open.

We described to him, in great detail, the three ghosts we'd seen, and James, who had studied a fair amount of history to aid him in his work, said at once: "It sounds like you're talking about a Japanese lady from the Heian period, a knight from the late middle ages, if that, and someone from the late 1800s, and very likely not of this country. Wasn't this house built in 1920?"

"A little earlier," said Adie.

"These ghosts can't be connected with the house," he told us. "They could never have lived here."

"Are you saying, then, that our house isn't haunted after all?" I asked him.

"No," he admitted. "I am saying that it is not haunted by anyone who ever lived in it. Perhaps the objects!" he cried out with glee, for like any detective, he wanted to solve the mystery.

But after a careful search of our possessions, which made me anxious, for privacy is a very important matter to me, he found no objects associated with feudal Japan or the Middle Ages, nor any military artifacts in our house which might have carried with them psychic shreds of their violent history. Once more, he was puzzled. After a while, he left us with a bundle of incense after leading us in a round of prayer. "Call me if anything further happens," he told us, from the window of his car.

We hoped that it would not, but we were soon to be disappointed.

*****

It was May, and the cherry tree out in back was in full bloom, when Adie, who loved to garden in her spare time, ran into the Japanese lady sitting beside the tree, fanning herself. The lady turned towards her, her face streaked with tears, and said to Adie, or perhaps only to the universe which Adie happened to inhabit: "Men are so disingenuous. They are so outwardly brave, but inwardly they are afraid to be swept away by the sentiments of the women who they profess to admire. Beautiful, beautiful flowers!" she mourned, turning once more to the cherry tree. "Perfect blossoms, but soon they'll fall! We have no greater duty on the earth than to admire them while they are in bloom!"

"Who are you?" Adie asked her, and then she was gone.

"Nick! Nick!" Adie cried, rushing into the house, where I was struggling with my first novel, like the soldiers at Normandy, clinging to a beachhead of five pages.

I looked up, and right away, I knew. "The Japanese lady?" I asked.

"How did you know?"

"You came from the garden—that look on your face!"

Adie flung herself into my arms.

"Well, she, at least, doesn't come with an axe!" I said.

But one week later, we were visited yet again. Although it was not by the man with the axe, which was a good thing, this visitation was still considerably disturbing, because it involved yet another apparition, and our abode was already psychically overcrowded. One more ghostly resident was the last thing we needed.

This time, Adie and I were out on the couch, watching a DVD on the television, when a distraught and angry young woman in flowing garments that seemed from another time, crossed our path, the light of the TV flickering momentarily across her rustling gown. Her hair was long and loose, her demeanor wild and defiant. "Kill me then, I don't care! Justice matters more than life! I fear nothing, this crime was holy!"

For a moment, she passed in front of the screen, eclipsing the trivial program we were watching, although she was without physical substance. Adie's hand was in mine, squeezing my flesh with all the might her frozen body possessed.

As the apparition continued on her way, leaving us to the movie we were no longer watching, we heard her say: "Your edict, King, was strong, but all your strength is weakness, itself, against the immortal laws of God. Those laws are not merely now: they were, and shall be, operative forever, beyond man utterly." And she said, again, "Kill me, I don't care!"

Hand shaking, I stopped the DVD with the remote.

"Where is she going?" Adie asked me.

"Into the den," I said, nearly paralyzed myself.

After a while, turning on all the lights I could, so that no shadow had the slightest chance of surviving inside our home, I finally flung open the door to the den, which we used as a lounge (we had converted an unoccupied bedroom into our TV room), and at the same time shouted out in terror at what I might find. But there was nothing there, only silence, an empty room that we had not yet figured out a use for. I wiped the sweat from my face.

*****

This time, James came with Mary, an intense, small woman with a tan complexion and a bandana, as well as two men with boxes of electrical equipment, which housed sensors of some kind and an array of highly reactive meters.

"You haven't seen the man with the axe again?" James asked us.

"No," we told him.

He breathed a sigh of relief. "Thank God! Charles, here, and Dr. Hecht, who works out at Stony Brook with the physics department, but moonlights as a paranormal researcher, are going to take some readings here."

"Abnormal patterns in electric energy fields usually accompany the presence of spirit-activity," Dr. Hecht told us.

"You believe in this stuff?" I asked him.

"I don't teach it in my classes," he smiled. Then, more seriously, he added: "It's the absolute frontier of human knowledge. How could I avoid it? In places where there are frequent reported sightings of ghosts, we almost always note altered energy patterns. The exact implications of the observations are not yet known: whether the energy relates to actual ghost-like entities, or to some kind of 'psychic residue' or footprint left behind by the dead, or to the mental activity of the witnesses interacting with 'imprinted environments.' We just don't know, but the energetic associations are tangible."

Adie and I liked the way he talked, and therefore put great faith in the results of his investigation.

As he and Charles walked around the house, aiming something that looked like a microphone at the places where we claimed to have encountered spirits, at the same time that they put together a more generalized background reading for our entire residence, James and Mary walked about with strange and distant expressions on their faces.

"Have you researched the history of this house with archives and interviews?" Mary asked us.

"The ghosts they've seen didn't live here," James told her. "Adelaide and Nicholas have either brought them here, themselves, or else they're coming in from somewhere else, through a portal. Do you feel the door? There's a wide-open door for spirits."

"I'm picking up something here," said Charles, at the entrance to the den. "Woah, look at that! Very strong!"

"Amazing," Dr. Hecht concurred, stepping back from the meter as though he had discovered a gigantic pearl in an oyster he had just opened.

"The spirit door is somewhere around here," James agreed.

"Is there a ghost in here?" whined Adie, clawing at my shirt. She didn't want to take another step.

"There is an opening," James said. "No ghost here, but an opening. What do you feel Mary?"

"James, you talk too much," she said.

We looked at her as Charles walked inside and aimed the detecting device at the walls and ceiling of the den.

Mary, saying nothing, went slowly up to one of the walls and gently ran her fingers along it, exactly as the mysterious knight I had seen! My throat felt dry. I began to fear her. After a while, she discovered a hole in the wall, expertly filled and painted over, and saw that it was but one of a series of holes that had previously been drilled into the wall. The holes had been plugged as part of the pre-sale renovation of the house. "There used to be shelves here," she said, at last.

"It would make sense," James replied. "I have shelves like that in my own den. I keep my candles and my crystals on them." Inspired by Mary to be more observant, he looked around, then pointed up to the ceiling, and added: "They have also changed the position of the light fixture. See where it used to be? They've taken away some of the solidity of the room, de-materialized it to a certain extent. All that fiddling around..."

Mary frowned and left the room as though she had just been insulted. James watched her go, perplexed and upset, because his need to be loved was a matter of life and death, and he had a way of taking everything personally. He would overhear somebody who was angry with someone else, and think they were talking about him.

"The aberrations in the energy field are strongest right here," said Charles, standing by one of the walls: the same wall I had seen the frightening knight caressing before he vanished! The same wall that Mary had just explored and seemed to hug!

"The door!" James exclaimed. "Yes, I can feel it, now, right here! *Right here!*" Was this an independent verification, or was he only following?

"What do you mean 'door'?" demanded my wife.

"A gap in the dimensions which separate our level of existence from the level of the spirits," James said.

"Does the door have a knob?" I asked him.

"Nick!" Adie chided me.

"It's not physical," James said, "it's not made of matter. It's not like all the spirits are behind that wall or crammed inside of it. It's sort of like a wormhole, an access point into hyperspace. Imagine a funnel, a narrow opening, at the bottom of the ocean, but the whole ocean is able to pour through it. Except the funnel isn't material, it's the way energy interacts. Help me out here, will you, Dr. Hecht?"

Dr. Hecht said, "We're working on the frontier of science. I can't tell you anything, except that there is an energy correlation to reported paranormal activity of this nature, and that right here, we are detecting such a correlation. This is, in fact, a very intense manifestation of the phenomenon."

For a moment, we all just stood there, like those British explorers who first stumbled out of the jungles of Africa, into the clear, to behold the staggering sight of Victoria Falls. Except that we saw nothing but the walls of our den and did not know if we had really discovered something or not.

"So—now what?" asked Adie, at last. "You have an energy reading. How does it change our lives? Can you do anything about the ghosts?"

Dr. Hecht regarded her, astounded, for a moment, that anyone could possibly miss the scientific importance of this work, or even stoop to think of their own peace of mind while in the midst of such a revolution. "Research of this kind can change the way we think about the universe—about life and death, matter and soul," he exclaimed at last.

"Is *your* house haunted?" Adie demanded.

"Let's all come in here and hold hands and pray," James suggested, trying to be practical. And before anyone could evaluate his proposal, he had seized my hand and Adie's, and was saying: "Please, Spirits, go back, go back! Go back to the light! The earth is for those who assume an earthly form, please, go back! Do not come here, you are disturbing Adelaide and Nicholas! They are good people and this is their home, the base from which they wish to do good things in the world." (*How do you know?* I thought. *We're just like everyone else, trying to get ahead and live the good life.*) "Please respect them, please respect the energetic barriers between your world and theirs!" he continued. "Go to the light, stay in the light! GOD, bless them please, these lost and disoriented spirits, and guide them to the light! Bring them back home! Amen!"

"Amen!"

Outside the den, as Charles and Dr. Hecht packed up their equipment like a movie crew closing down a set, and as James wiped great streams of sweat from his face, Mary came up to Adie and told her, decisively: "Talk to the ones you bought the house from. You need more information."

"Did you get anything, Mary?" James asked, coming up to her. "Did you feel anything?" In spite of the way she treated him, he adored her and respected her, which is why he had brought her along to help him.

Mary looked at him, then at us. "They're coming from the den," she agreed, referring to the apparitions. "They are associated with the previous owner."

"The previous owner is dead," Adie told her. "His son inherited the house, and sold it because he wanted to liquefy his assets."

"Go to the son," Mary told us.

*****

It isn't easy to go talk to someone who is normal about a haunted house, but then, stress can drive you to do things that you never thought yourself capable of. When we saw, once more, the young, disturbed man roaming through our house with the bloody axe in his hands, we made the call.

Paul and Ivette met us in their own house in the suburbs, for the house that had once belonged to Paul's father, embedded in the midst of the city as it was, seemed too much to be on the front lines. They imagined thousands of envious and dangerous muggers, only blocks away, waiting to penetrate the fragile sanctuary and to overwhelm it with home invasions. You could tell from the strained smile on Ivette's face that she thought we might be considering a lawsuit, for there was a precedent in a case in Maine, in which owners had sold a house which they were driven from by hauntings, to unsuspecting buyers, without mentioning the real reason why they were leaving it.

"Please don't be offended," Ivette told us, as we enjoyed delicious snacks prepared by a maid from the Caribbean, "but how reliable are these friends of yours? The ones who reported seeing ghosts while they were house-sitting?"

"They're very credible people," Adie told them. "They hold down demanding professional jobs. They are more than competent at what they do, and seem, to us, to possess good judgment."

"Are they into the New Age?" Ivette asked, enjoying the snacks that had been prepared for us even more than we did.

"No, they are pretty much secular," Adie reported. "I remember them hearing something about alien abductions and laughing about it."

"They have their heads on straight," I agreed. "They were very upset. You could tell that something that seemed very real to them had taken place."

"Dad never said anything about hauntings," Paul said, cutting to the chase. "He lived there for thirty years with Mom, and for eight years thereafter, and not one time did he ever see a ghost. I lived there for years, also, I grew up there, and visited frequently thereafter. Nothing. Zero. Zero times zero is zero. We had dinners, watched movies, played chess and Scrabble, celebrated the holidays, and had arguments. We did everything a family does. We *were* a family. Ghosts were not a part of our life."

"Did any of you ever see a ghost somewhere besides your house?" Adie asked.

"No, never," said Ivette. "We're not those kind of people."

"Look, you signed the contract," Paul said, in the gruff voice that served him so well in his profession. "We've moved on. It's too late to reconsider. The legal system doesn't believe in ghosts."

"Paul!" interjected Ivette, wishing to seem as sympathetic as possible while things were still at this stage. Kindness is the best killer of unborn things. Turning to us, she said: "I'm so sorry for what happened to your friends, but luckily, it hasn't happened to you! After all, you are the ones who are living there. They were only house-sitting and didn't have to come back." (My wife flinched.) "I am sure you can find somebody else to house-sit for you in the future; someone less imaginative!"

"Yes, keep your doors barred against artists," Paul said, "they are used to turning the world into something that will look good on their canvas. They turn ordinary people into Gods or homeless people, completely eradicating the middle ground, which is reality. They turn orchards into hurricanes and vomit their nightmares into our world. And instead of cleaning up the mess with a mop and bucket, we put it in a frame and hang it up in the museum. Look at what Van Gogh did to the night sky; he turned it into some kind of feverish visitation by UFOs; look at what he did to the stars! His own times knew better than we did."

For a while, we sat in silence, not knowing where to go with this, until, at last, I asked him: "What was the den like while your father lived there? Before you sold the house?"

"It wasn't much of a den," Paul answered.

Ivette looked at him, which prodded him to go on. (She sensed that this might satisfy us.)

"Dad kind of took it over, and used it as his study," he told me. "He had a large library. A massive collection of books."

"What kind of books?" I asked.

"All kinds of books. Literature, mainly," he said, after a while. "You know, all the classics. Stuff nobody reads anymore. Some of the books were so old they were falling apart."

"The room smelled like mold," complained Ivette. "You should never buy books from second-hand shops, those books have been around so long, in boxes, in attics... He spent more time reading than he did with his kids," Ivette insisted, obviously parroting something which Paul had told her. He seemed guilty as she said it, but did not correct her.

"Where are the books now?" Adie asked, picking up on my line of questioning.

"Who the hell knows?" said Paul.

"We got rid of them," Ivette explained in a tone of utter functionality. "They were old, and we didn't have a place for them. Some of them you wouldn't even want to touch with your hands—who knows where they came from? Second-hand bookshops! I like to read books about travel," she added. "Paul's reading is related to his business."

"Practical," he said. "Time is precious, what's the point in doing things of no use? The kind of books he had were written in such a verbose way. On and on they went, like I have to know what you think about *everything*!? Like *every* one of your feelings has to be recorded!? This is what men of leisure did in the past, while others built the world, made cities, machines, planted, harvested, and constructed. Why would I ever tip my hat to them?"

"His father was very difficult," Ivette explained. "He was an intellectual."

"He made things more complicated than they needed to be. Nothing could just be itself, it was always connected to something else, and you'd have to hear about it! If you accidentally banged your head on the wall, he'd tie it in to some story by Borges. If a neighbor's house burned down, he'd tell you the story of Aeneas escaping from Troy. I still remember this stuff, though I've tried for years to forget it!

Intellectualism is a sickness," he concluded. "It's an excuse for sitting on your ass and letting the world take its own course."

"He put a terrible guilt trip on Paul," Ivette added.

"No need to mention that, honey," Paul told her.

But she felt that it must be fully explained in order to demonstrate her loyalty to her husband. "In his Last Will and Testament, he made the preservation of his library—maintaining the full collection intact and keeping it in the family—a necessary provision for receiving the inheritance."

"Old tyrant!" Paul raged.

"How did you get around it?" Adie asked her, at last.

"The will didn't spell out the time frame," explained Ivette. "So we simply left the collection there for several months, until we had collected the inheritance. Then we got rid of it, since we had, in the strictest legal sense, complied with the terms of the inheritance; and we put the house up for sale. Who was going to be saddled by all those old books? Like wearing a ball and chain!"

"Father loved those books," whispered Paul, with eyes suddenly moist. But he would not let himself be broken by the impractical demands of the dead, especially not while we were there. "Well, but he's dead and gone, and they can be of no use to him, now!" he exclaimed, fighting against a broken promise, which stalked him like a ghost from within; fighting against expectations which he could not live up to, and which he therefore vastly exceeded by a standard of his own. "He enjoyed his books while he was alive, and now, he has no need for them!"

"It's terrible the way the dead impose their agendas upon the living, try to ride them from the grave," Ivette said. "Let every generation live its own life. Let the son be free of the father."

As Adie and I pulled away from their driveway, late that afternoon, agitated, below the surface, by the divisions of strangers, Adie asked me: "Well, now what?"

"You don't see?" I asked her.

She looked at me, drained. "See what?"

"We've found the answer to our haunting!"

*****

This time, the ghostbuster whom we invited to our home was a professor of literature from a local community college, who responded to our ad. Adjuncts are so poorly paid and live such an insecure life that any extra source of income, no matter how bizarre and by how narrow a thread tied to their profession, is more than welcome. Roger was thin, light-boned, with the kind of trim beard literature professors are known for. His eyes were clear and blue, though they seemed to be in some kind of illuminated agony, and his gestures were exaggerated, as though never properly learned. He had been kidnapped by books long ago.

After preparing him with two glasses of brandy and sitting him down on our sofa, we began to work.

"Who, exactly, are we dealing with?" I asked him.

Long before we had him cornered in our house, I had taken Adie back to go over the holes that Mary had spotted in the den, and to envision the shelves that had once been installed there, along the wall, by Paul's father. I had called in a handyman, who had reopened the holes, inserted the appropriate hardware into them, screwed in the supports, and provided us with the strong flat beams to lay across the supports, until we had finally erected a close reproduction of the original bookshelves which Paul's father had lovingly maintained in his cherished den.

Now, as we described to Roger the spirits which had, as of late, afflicted us, his eyes lit up. He knew these spirits well. They were characters from the great works of literature. The Japanese woman was, he thought (though there were at least two other strong possibilities),

Lady Murasaki, the fictionalized persona of the author of *The Tale of Genji*. The crazed knight, whose body seemed to glow with passion that was, to a world reoriented towards profit, only embarrassing, was none other than Cervantes' Don Quixote—the idealistic *caballero* who could not change in spite of the world! The wild, savage man of deep intelligence and tortured soul who had terrified us with his bloody axe was Raskolnikov, the anguished protagonist of Dostoevsky's *Crime and Punishment*. The brave and reckless young woman who exhorted some unseen king, whose power she despised, to destroy her, was Sophocles' Antigone.

Bewildered, my wife regarded me, turned to Roger, then looked back at me. "You mean to say the characters of books are haunting us?" she gasped.

"They are so powerful," I told her, "That they have acquired the force of spirits."

Roger, who was beginning to understand the bizarre nature of his mission, caught fire like a bundle of hay next to a flame; my more ignorant ranting triggered his knowledge, incited the inferiority complex inherent in his field. "A great character in literature," he assured my wife, "is much more than words on a piece of paper which elicit a mental image, much more than a two-dimensional invention, a mere *fiction!* It is a receptacle for the heart and soul of a human being who has lived life and seen others living life; and it is placed into the world from the highest peak of inspiration, where men seek to defeat death by making something that death cannot extinguish. As the creator pours his soul into the character—the receptacle—it becomes alive: alive with him, and with all those whom he carries with him! And it becomes a vehicle for bringing into the world the essence of men and women, which no real person can fully embody, but which is, nonetheless, absolutely real: the well from which all living things drink! This essence, one fragment of which the character brandishes like a flag, is divided into a thousand garments that hang in the wardrobe of our indecision, awaiting our choice. We have given life to the character, and he, or she, as it may be, gives life to us! The character comes from us and gives birth to us! We make it from what we know of ourselves, and it shows us who we can be!"

My wife regarded him. She would have been skeptical except for his passion. When small and nondescript men rave, one does not know whether to be fearful for oneself, or for their fragile body which seems on the verge of exploding.

"As traces of real people leave ghosts behind them in the world," Roger speculated, "so characters so passionately conceived and ardently offered cannot fade away easily. They must have a life of their own! *They must!* They are not to be pushed aside like fantasies, they are practically biological in nature; they are bruised, and they resist!"

My wife turned to me with horror, since Roger no longer seemed reliable. "Nick, what does this mean to us?" she demanded. "The hauntings?"

"Adie," I told her, certain of my instinct, now, "it means that we must bring back the books of Paul's father and place them on the shelves which we have just reinstalled in his den. It was his will that the books should remain, and his love and devotion so raised the energy of the characters of his favorite novels, that they have persisted after his passing, and continue to haunt this house seeking the pages from which they came."

"Nick, this is crazy!" she told me.

"Ghosts are crazy," I reminded her.

"Go to the Light!" she cried out, imitating James, for one moment desperate with the madness of it all, panicking like someone in the movies when the monster appears. "Go to the Light! Leave us alone, please, for God's sakes! Go to the Light!"

"For them," Roger told her, catching on faster than any of us, "we *are* the light! The human heart is their home, and that is where they seek to go!"

"But the books—the old man's books—they got rid of them!" lamented Adie.

"Let us pray that they do not need the same books," I agreed. "We will buy handsome copies, the best we can, the most dignified and worthy, hardbound and well-made. And we shall start with four books: *The Tale of Genji*, *Don Quixote*, *Crime and Punishment*, and *Antigone!*"

* * * * *

Thank God, for all of us, my hunch proved to be right. As we returned to the restless spirits of the characters who haunted our home, the masterpieces from which they came, and gave them prized places on our shelves, they grew quiet and waited for us to meet them on the pages where they dwelled. Their power did not diminish; they merely lost the desperation of the abandoned. What they demanded from us, they gave back a hundred times.

As the months went on, new hauntings emerged, but now we knew what to do. We called our friend Roger, who no longer appeared spiteful like a little dog in the presence of businessmen and scientists, but held his head up high, believing, once again, in the words he spoke, shining like the sun. "All that is deep shall be raised up to my heights!" he exclaimed, paraphrasing Nietzsche. During these days we encountered Oliver Twist, who actually had the strength to take the money out of Adie's purse and to scatter it all around the house before he vanished through a wall; we saw Hamlet wishing for death out loud, yet haunting us that he might live; we saw Caesar perforated with knife wounds, his hands covered with blood he could no longer keep inside his body, staggering through our living room, gasping, "E tu, Brute?" We saw Scheherazade sitting on our sofa, coyly telling the wall, "Too bad I have to die before the story is over," and Gulliver, pants down, urinating on the floor. "Thank God," Adie said, "his piss was only spiritual!"

In each case, we knew precisely what to do. Identify the work of literature. Go to the bookstore, buy it, and put it on the shelf. Whether we actually had to read the tales or not, or whether merely having the book in our possession sufficed, I do not know: for after the hauntings, we could not restrain ourselves from reading the books associated with our ghostly visitors. We could not resist the urge to find out more about them, to know their story.

"It is a terrible thing what sons do to fathers," Adie told me, as we sat down on the sofa, reading together.

"Sometimes," I said, "the transgressions of the sons occur because of the terrible things that fathers do to sons."

She thought about that for a moment, then bulled past it to say: "It is a shame that Paul did not honor the last request of his father, to save and cherish his books."

"He is merely well embedded in our generation," I told her. There was silence, not only because of the things we said between us, but because of the pages in our hands which demanded our attention.

"We cannot afford to lose these characters," Adie said, at last.

"We didn't know that," I said, "until they haunted us!"

www.ingramcontent.com/pod-product-compliance
Lightning Source LLC
Chambersburg PA
CBHW070526310726
48976CB00002BA/548